Moritz Kleine

CSP as a Coordination Language

Moritz Kleine

CSP as a Coordination Language

A CSP-based Approach to the Coordination of Concurrent Systems

Südwestdeutscher Verlag für Hochschulschriften

Impressum/Imprint (nur für Deutschland/only for Germany)
Bibliografische Information der Deutschen Nationalbibliothek: Die Deutsche Nationalbibliothek verzeichnet diese Publikation in der Deutschen Nationalbibliografie; detaillierte bibliografische Daten sind im Internet über http://dnb.d-nb.de abrufbar.
Alle in diesem Buch genannten Marken und Produktnamen unterliegen warenzeichen-, marken- oder patentrechtlichem Schutz bzw. sind Warenzeichen oder eingetragene Warenzeichen der jeweiligen Inhaber. Die Wiedergabe von Marken, Produktnamen, Gebrauchsnamen, Handelsnamen, Warenbezeichnungen u.s.w. in diesem Werk berechtigt auch ohne besondere Kennzeichnung nicht zu der Annahme, dass solche Namen im Sinne der Warenzeichen- und Markenschutzgesetzgebung als frei zu betrachten wären und daher von jedermann benutzt werden dürften.

Verlag: Südwestdeutscher Verlag für Hochschulschriften GmbH & Co. KG
Heinrich-Böcking-Str. 6-8, 66121 Saarbrücken, Deutschland
Telefon +49 681 37 20 271-1, Telefax +49 681 37 20 271-0
Email: info@svh-verlag.de

Approved by: Berlin, TU, Diss., 2011

Herstellung in Deutschland:
Schaltungsdienst Lange o.H.G., Berlin
Books on Demand GmbH, Norderstedt
Reha GmbH, Saarbrücken
Amazon Distribution GmbH, Leipzig
ISBN: 978-3-8381-2271-7

Imprint (only for USA, GB)
Bibliographic information published by the Deutsche Nationalbibliothek: The Deutsche Nationalbibliothek lists this publication in the Deutsche Nationalbibliografie; detailed bibliographic data are available in the Internet at http://dnb.d-nb.de.
Any brand names and product names mentioned in this book are subject to trademark, brand or patent protection and are trademarks or registered trademarks of their respective holders. The use of brand names, product names, common names, trade names, product descriptions etc. even without a particular marking in this works is in no way to be construed to mean that such names may be regarded as unrestricted in respect of trademark and brand protection legislation and could thus be used by anyone.

Publisher: Südwestdeutscher Verlag für Hochschulschriften GmbH & Co. KG
Heinrich-Böcking-Str. 6-8, 66121 Saarbrücken, Germany
Phone +49 681 37 20 271-1, Fax +49 681 37 20 271-0
Email: info@svh-verlag.de

Printed in the U.S.A.
Printed in the U.K. by (see last page)
ISBN: 978-3-8381-2271-7

Copyright © 2011 by the author and Südwestdeutscher Verlag für Hochschulschriften GmbH & Co. KG and licensors
All rights reserved. Saarbrücken 2011

Contents

1. **Introduction**   7
    - 1.1. Problems 8
    - 1.2. Proposed Solution 9
    - 1.3. Motivation 10
    - 1.4. Outline 10

2. **CSP**   13
    - 2.1. Syntax 14
    - 2.2. Operational Semantics 17
    - 2.3. Denotational Semantics 23
    - 2.4. Refinement and Algebraic Semantics 26
    - 2.5. Tools 29
        - 2.5.1. Animators 29
        - 2.5.2. Model Checkers 30
        - 2.5.3. Refinement Checkers 31
    - 2.6. Summary 32

3. **Further Terminology and Notations**   35
    - 3.1. Coordination Languages 35
    - 3.2. Java Concurrency 36
    - 3.3. Infamous Phenomena of Concurrency 38
    - 3.4. Business Processes and Workflows 39
    - 3.5. Summary 40

4. **Simulating Truly Concurrent CSP**   43
    - 4.1. The Transformation T 44
    - 4.2. Assembling the System 46
    - 4.3. Properties 49
    - 4.4. Examples 55
        - 4.4.1. Choice versus Concurrency 55

	4.4.2. One-place Buffer 56
	4.4.3. Dining Philosophers 57
	4.4.4. Van Glabbeek's Owl 57
4.5.	Restricting T 59
	4.5.1. Prohibiting Internal Choice, Hiding and Timeout 61
	4.5.2. Prohibiting External Choice and Timeout 62
4.6.	Discussion 63

5. Conflict, Internal Actions and $\mathcal{FD}$ Preservation 67
- 5.1. Simulation, Monitoring and Interruption 68
- 5.2. Transforming External Choice 70
- 5.3. Transforming Timeout 74
- 5.4. Transforming Interrupt 76
- 5.5. Discussion 78

6. Designing a CSP-based Coordination Environment 81
- 6.1. Unraveling Abstractions 82
  - 6.1.1. Timeout, Hiding and Nondeterminism 83
  - 6.1.2. Duration, Conflict and Concurrency 85
- 6.2. Design Decisions 87
  - 6.2.1. Interpreting T 88
  - 6.2.2. Performing Actions 88
  - 6.2.3. Choosing Events 90
- 6.3. Supported Processes 91
- 6.4. Integrating Specifications of UDFs 93
- 6.5. Categorizing Coordination 95
- 6.6. Discussion 96

7. Coordinating Java Threads 99
- 7.1. General Design Decisions 100
- 7.2. Implementing the CSP Coordination Environment 101
  - 7.2.1. The Environment 101
  - 7.2.2. Assigning UDFs to Events 102
  - 7.2.3. Events and Hidden Transitions 103
  - 7.2.4. Processes and Process Operators 104
  - 7.2.5. Performing Actions 105
  - 7.2.6. Choosing Events 108
- 7.3. Modular Verification 109
- 7.4. Supported Processes 111
  - 7.4.1. Example 112
  - 7.4.2. Turning Bad Processes into Good Ones 113
- 7.5. Discussion 114

8. Using CSP for the Modeling and Coordination of Workflows — 117
- 8.1. A CSP-based Workflow Server 118
- 8.2. Verifying the Server 122
- 8.3. Modeling Business Process in CSP 124
- 8.4. Workflow Definitions 128
- 8.5. Compensation 129
- 8.6. Discussion 131

9. Related Work — 133
- 9.1. Coordination 133
  - 9.1.1. Non-CSP Approaches 134
  - 9.1.2. CSP-based Approaches 135
- 9.2. Truly Concurrent Semantics for CSP 137
- 9.3. CSP-like Concurrency Frameworks 139
- 9.4. Modeling and Managing Business Processes 142
  - 9.4.1. Modeling Techniques 142
  - 9.4.2. Compensation 144
- 9.5. Summary 145

10. Conclusion — 147
- 10.1. Summary 147
- 10.2. Contributions 150
- 10.3. Future Work 151
- 10.4. Related Publications 153
- 10.5. Acknowledgements 153

A. Proofs — 155

B. Examples — 165

Bibliography — 187

1 Introduction

This thesis deals with the problem of developing provably correct concurrent systems, which is still a challenging task and subject to ongoing research. The main problem introduced by concurrency is the increased level of complexity of the system (compared to a purely sequential system). Nondeterminism and state-space explosion are phenomena related to this problem. As a result, concurrent systems are commonly hard to grasp, hard to specify and quickly grow beyond the proof power of nowadays automated verification tools. Even worse, implementations of such systems often exhibit unexpected asynchronous behavior that quite often manifests in subtle bugs.

The use of formal methods to specify concurrent systems helps us to avoid such bugs early in the design phase of a system and to verify desired properties, e. g., deadlock-freedom, of the system. Formal methods tend to describe concurrent systems on a rather abstract level for convenience of modeling and reasoning. For example, CSP is an ideal choice for modeling and reasoning about concurrent systems because of its rather high level of abstraction together with its mature tool support.

Coordination languages offer another approach to taming the complexities of concurrent systems that is more driven by practical needs of programming than by the ultimate goal to support mechanized verification. Their key idea is to separate the interaction behavior from the sequential functional aspects on the implementation level. The interaction behavior is expressed in the coordination language and the sequential functional aspects in its target language. In this sense CSP and coordination languages are quite similar and serve the same purpose. However, while coordination languages were developed to facilitate concurrent and parallel programming (for some target language), CSP targets designs and proofs (completely independent of implementation languages).

In this thesis, we present an approach to combine these two.

1.1. Problems

Several approaches proposed in literature are based on the idea to use CSP to coordinate the operations of components described in some state-based formalism. Examples are Circus [WC02] (combining CSP with Z) and CSP ∥ B [ST04] (combining CSP with B). The common drawback of these approaches is that the CSP part of a system's design must be manually implemented at some point. The problem then is that there is a gap between a formal design of a system and its implementation.

There are two fundamentally different approaches to bridging the gap between a CSP-based design of a system and its implementation. The first approach is to transform one of the implementation level descriptions of the system (e. g., its source code) into CSP and to establish conformance of the result to its design. In [KH09, Kle09], we explore this approach. It is supported by our LLVM2CSP tool [KBG$^+$11] which extracts CSP models from the compiler intermediate representation of concurrent programs. Unfortunately, it does not yet scale up to industrial-size systems.

The second approach is to derive implementations from the designs in a strictly formal way ensuring correctness by construction (as promoted by the B method [Abr96]). Finding methods for deriving implementations from CSP-based models is an active field of research and we establish our solution in this thesis. The main problem is due to the abstractions built into CSP. For example, CSP abstracts simultaneity of actions. Its standard semantics are interleaving ones that identify simultaneity with 'in either order'. This raises the question:

> can we profit from true concurrency?

Furthermore, CSP is equipped with a rich set of process operators supporting the concise modeling of concurrent systems. This raises the question:

> can we use full CSP?

For example, CSP defines deterministic and nondeterministic choice. However, nondeterminism has to be resolved on the implementation level, because the theoretical concept of nondeterminism is not supported by nowadays computing hardware.

CSP has influenced the development of programming languages (e. g., occam [Bar92]) and there are concurrency frameworks extending general purpose programming languages with CSP-like concurrency facilities. Examples are the Java frameworks JCSP [WM00] and CTJ [HBB99], the C++ framework CSP++ [Gar03], and the Python library PyCSP [BVA07]. These frameworks implement channels to facilitate atomic directed communication between threads and free the programmer from dealing with error-prone low-level synchronization primitives. They focus on communication rather than CSP operators and support only a subset of CSP. To complement these frameworks, we do not focus on communication but on supporting the various process operators offered by CSP.

1.2. Proposed Solution

As a solution to the questions raised above, we propose to use CSP itself as a coordination language for truly concurrent systems. True concurrency requires some means to discriminate simultaneous actions from those that may appear in either order but exclusively. To this end, we develop the theoretical background of the coordination, primarily focusing on the CSP part of it. We present a syntactical transformation of processes realizing the simulation of truly concurrent CSP within the framework of its standard interleaving semantics. Different versions of the transformation are discussed that allow us to encode various levels of concurrency while maintaining the interleaving semantics of a process. This transformation can be exploited with standard CSP tools to detect possible concurrency. Furthermore, it is used as the semantical foundation of a coordination environment that we define in a target language independent way.

The coordination environment undoes the abstractions built into CSP in a way suitable for real-life systems. It simulates a coordination process at runtime and performs user-defined functions (the component's operations) when an event is performed. Another key feature of the environment is *noninvasiveness*. This means that the coordinated operations do no have to make use of primitives offered by the coordination environment. Client code remains oblivious to coordination.

The coordination environment is implemented in Java and applied to a case study of implementing a coordinated workflow server. Although we present an implementation of a coordination environment for the target language Java, the approach presented here does not focus on a specific state-based formalism for expressing the functional aspects of the components' operations (the actions) and also claims independence of a specific target language. Formal relationships between concurrent aspects expressed in CSP and properties of actions are presented in a general way. Thereby, we obtain proof obligations that can be expressed in various state-based modeling languages using their specific verification strategies.

1.3. Motivation

This work is motivated by the following famous quotation from Hoare's Turing Award Lecture.

> There are two ways of constructing a software design: One way is to make it so simple that there are obviously no deficiencies, and the other way is to make it so complicated that there are no obvious deficiencies. The first method is far more difficult. [Hoa81]

The process algebra CSP provides a way to express the design of a concurrent system in an elegant and concise manner. It helps us to simplify the design by focusing on the interaction behavior of concurrent components while abstracting from their internal behavior.

Using CSP as a coordination language frees the programmer of the coordinated component's operations from dealing with concurrency primitives at all. Noninvasiveness of our approach ensures that the programmer may implement the operations as if the components were to be used in a purely sequential context.

The main advantages of our approach are twofold: First, it enables us to separate concurrent and sequential concerns of a system, which simplifies the development of concurrent systems helping us to avoid bugs at design time. Second, the use of CSP as a coordination language comes with all the advantages of CSP: concise modeling of interaction behavior, well-defined and well-investigated formal semantics, and, in particular, its mature tool support, which enables the (automated) verification of concurrent systems.

1.4. Outline

This thesis is organized as follows. The theoretical background is presented in Chapter 2. In that chapter, we present the syntax and semantics of CSP and introduce the tools that we use for modeling and verifying processes. We then go on to present more informal background, e.g., the concept of coordination languages and the problems with Java concurrency in Chapter 3. The main

1.4 Outline

part of the thesis is presented in chapters 4 to 8. The formal foundation of our approach is developed in Chapter 4 and extended in Chapter 5. In Chapter 4, we present a syntactical transformation of CSP processes enabling the simulation of truly concurrent processes to be encoded in standard interleaving CSP. Chapter 5 extends the transformation in a way that makes it suitable to serve as semantical foundation of a CSP coordination environment. Both versions of the transformation can be exploited by standard CSP tools to determine possibly simultaneous events in a process. A model of our coordination environment is presented in Chapter 6. There, we explain how the abstractions built into CSP are unraveled to support the implementation of coordinated systems. We also present proof obligations that ensure the safe composition of the implementations of the coordinated actions. For example, possibly concurrent actions must not access shared data. Chapter 7 presents our Java implementation of that environment. The case study presented in Chapter 8 is about implementing a CSP-based workflow server as a coordinated system, and modeling (compensable) workflows in CSP. In Chapter 9, related work is discussed in detail and compared to our approach. The thesis closes with a summary and concluding discussion in Chapter 10.

2 CSP

The process calculus Communicating Sequential Processes (CSP), introduced by Hoare in the late 1970s, was largely stable by the mid 1980s [Hoa85] since when it has been widely applied and developed. Its strength is the specification and verification of reactive and concurrent systems in which synchronization and communication play a key role. CSP provides an algebraic notation based on *events*, process names and process operators tailored for the concise modeling of current systems. Concurrent systems are modeled as *processes* that perform events. If a process offers an event with which its environment agrees to synchronize, the event is performed. Events are both atomic and instantaneous. In [Hoa04], Hoare introduces events as abstractions of atomic actions of a system in the understanding that duration of actions can be modeled by splitting events into start and end events. Events can also be regarded as rendezvous communication between processes. From this viewpoint, processes are anonymous entities communicating synchronously over named channels. Accordingly, an event models the occurrence of a communication identified by the channel name and the message being sent over it. Messages can only be sent if the receiver is willing to accept them.

CSP is equipped with a wide range of formal semantics. Modeling, exploration and verification of processes is supported by a number of industrial-strength tools. The concept of refinement facilitates the step-wise development of processes by gradually restricting their behaviors. In this context, CSP enjoys the property of *compositionality*: given a process that satisfies some specification and another process refining a part of the first process, we may replace that part with the second process and obtain a new process that also satisfies the specification.

A detailed overview of the syntax and its informal description is given in Section 2.1. A process can be thought of as a (possibly infinite) transition system. This view is presented in Section 2.2. From the denotational viewpoint that is introduced in Section 2.3, processes are mapped to mathematical constructs (sequences and sets of events) that describe what a process can do or refuse to do. The algebraic semantics of CSP is introduced in Section 2.4. At the end of this chapter, in Section 2.5, we give a brief overview of CSP tools supporting the analysis of processes.

2.1. Syntax

CSP is equipped with a rich set of process operators that combine events with processes (prefixing) and processes with processes. The syntax presented here is mostly taken from [Ros05] and [GRA05]. We present two flavors of notations: a mathematical one and the machine-readable dialect CSP_M. The mathematical notation is modified in some minor details to fit our needs. Throughout this thesis, we mostly use the mathematical notation. The CSP_M syntax is used to emphasize practical concerns of a process, e. g., automated verification.

There are the following four predefined processes in CSP:

$$SKIP \quad STOP \quad CHAOS \quad div\,.$$

SKIP and *STOP* are 'atomic' processes; the former models successful termination; the latter models deadlock. $CHAOS(A)$ is a process that may nondeterministically perform events from A. It may as well refuse to do anything at all. The phenomenon of infinite internal behavior is known as *divergence* or livelock. It is commonly represented by the process *div*. This process is sometimes used in specifications or arises in proofs.

The set of events that may be communicated by a process P is said to comprise its alphabet Σ_P (or simply Σ if the context is clear). In CSP_M, Σ is written 'Events'. The mathematical notation does not require alphabets to be explicitly defined (Σ can be derived from the syntax of the processes). However, CSP_M requires explicit definition of the alphabets of processes. To facilitate the modeling of communication, alphabets of processes are defined in terms of (parameterized) *channels*. For example,

channel a,b : X

declares channels a and b that communicate values in X. The parameters following the colon are types separated by dots and describe the protocol of the channel. Events are then composed of a channel name followed by the communicated values preceded by dots or the ? and ! decorations to model

2.1 Syntax

input and output respectively. Events have the form

$$channel\_name\ ((\ ?\ |\ !\ |\ .)\ value)^*$$

where *channel_name* stands for the actual channel name and *value* for the values being communicated (or variables of types as defined by the channel protocol). Provided that $3 \in X$, the compound event $a.3$ models communication of 3 over the channel a. Channels that are not parameterized give rise to primitive events being represented only by the channel name. Note that the ? decoration introduces a fresh variable, while ! and . can only be used with fixed values or variables in scope.

Communication is assumed to take place instantly and atomically even if multiple flows of data are encoded in a single event (e.g., $d?x!y?z$ for the channel $d : X.Y.Z$ and $y \in Y$). The communication event is assumed to happen only if all the participants are prepared to perform it.

The $\{|.|\}$ operator can be used to compute the set of events that complete the set of given prefixes (e.g., channels).

Table 2.1 shows the syntax of the CSP (and CSP_M) process operators relevant for this thesis. It uses the following conventions: a and b are channel names, X is a set of values to be communicated, $A \subseteq \Sigma$ a set of events and x a variable representing communication parameters or events. Furthermore, P and Q are processes, g is a Boolean expression, and M is a mapping from events to events.

Prefixing combines events with processes. Table 2.1 shows three different flavors of prefixing. Simple prefixing combines a single event with a process. The (constrained) input decoration offers its environment the possibility to synchronize on any extension on a that matches X. Given the channel $a : C$, the constrained input decoration $a?x : X$ limits the communication over a to $x \in C \cap X$. The actual communication parameter is bound to the variable x. If X is omitted, all values from C are valid. Prefix choice offers its environment all the events in A and binds the chosen event to the variable x. In the context of this thesis, it is important to observe that both compound events and the input/output decorations are merely syntactic sugar. The processes

$$a?x \to P(x) \qquad \text{and} \qquad x : \{|a|\} \to P(x)$$

Table 2.1.: CSP mathematical and machine-readable syntax.

CSP	CSP$_M$	Description
$a \to P$	a −>P	simple prefix
$a?x\!:\!X \to P(x)$	a?x:X −>P(x)	constrained input
$x\!:\!A \to P(x)$	[] x:A@x −>P(x)	prefix choice
$P\,;Q$	P ; Q	sequential composition
$P \mathbin{\Box} Q$	P [] Q	external choice
$P \sqcap Q$	P [~] Q	internal choice
$P \rhd Q$	P [>Q	timeout
$P \mathbin{\triangle} Q$	P /\Q	interrupt
$P \mathbin{\|_A\|} Q$	P [|A|] Q	generalized parallel
$P \parallel Q$	P [|Events|] Q	parallel
$P \mathbin{\|\|\|} Q$	P ||| Q	interleaving
$P \setminus A$	P \ A	hiding
$P \mathbin{\lhd g \rhd} Q$	**if** g **then** P **else** Q	conditional
$g\ \&\ P$	g & P	Boolean guard
$P[a \leftarrow b]$	P [[a <−b]]	renaming
$P[M]$	P [[M]]	renaming

are very similar. Both are willing to synchronize on every event in $\{|\ a\ |\}$ initially. However, the variable x is the parameter communicated over a in the first process while it is the whole compound event in the second.

Sequential composition combines two processes such that the second process only starts after termination of the first.

External and internal choice, timeout and interrupt model four different styles of choices between the combined processes. Combining two processes P and Q using the external choice operator yields a process that offers its environment the choice whether to continue as P or as Q. Internal choice yields a process that internally decides whether to continue as P or as Q. Timeout (sometimes called 'sliding choice') combines the behavior of the external choice operator with the possibility to switch off P if the environment does not agree to perform one of P's events before some timeout occurs. The interrupt operator combines P and Q such that Q is offered until P terminates but Q is discarded if the environment decides to synchronize on an event offered by Q.

The generalized parallel operator synchronizes two processes over the events in A. Parallel and interleaving are its special cases. Parallel requires two processes to synchronize on every event and interleaving does not synchronize at all. Hence, the following two equivalences hold:

$$P \: |\Sigma| \: Q = P \parallel Q$$
$$P \: |\emptyset| \: Q = P \parallel\!\parallel Q \: .$$

In this thesis, we use the term *parallel composition* synonymously to *generalized parallel*.

The Boolean expression g may be used in conditional expressions or as a guard. Guards and conditionals are defined such that the following equivalence holds:

$$g \: \& \: P = P \lhd g \rhd STOP \: .$$

Renaming of event a to b in process P is written $P[a \leftarrow b]$, or more generally $P[M]$ where M is a mapping from source events to target events (e.g., $M = \{(a,b)\}$).

Internal and external choice, interleaving and (generalized) parallel composition support replication

$$\otimes \: x : A \bullet P$$

where $\otimes$ is one of these operators, A a set (which must be nonempty in the case of internal choice) and P the process expression to be replicated.

The mathematical syntax supports the definition of named processes (e.g., $P = a \rightarrow SKIP$) and the definition of anonymous processes (e.g., $a \rightarrow SKIP$). Recursion requires that a process be named. Local processes can be introduced using the μ operator (for defining recursive processes locally). Examples of equivalent recursive processes are

$$P = a \rightarrow P \quad \text{and} \quad \mu \: P \bullet a \rightarrow P \: .$$

The μ operator is not available in CSP_M but can be mimicked by a **let within** clause.

2.2. Operational Semantics

Processes can be regarded as labeled transition systems (LTS). In brief, an LTS is a directed labeled graph representing the states and transitions of a system (refer to [Ros05, Chapter 7.2] for an introduction to LTS). This view gives rise to the operational semantics of CSP. Generally, the operational semantics for a programming language describes how a valid program is interpreted as se-

quences of computational steps where the states of the program are formalized by the nodes of an LTS and the steps are firings of the transitions connecting the nodes. The operational semantics of CSP is given by logical inference rules that define the firing rules of the operators. The general form of an inference rule is
$$\frac{Premise_1, \ldots, Premise_n}{Conclusion} \; Condition \, .$$
Such a rule allows us to draw the specified conclusion if all n premises hold under the side condition *Condition*. An inference rule without any premises is called an *axiom*.

The set of events that a process P offers initially is $initials(P)$. It is often used in specifications and must be effectively computed for purposes of simulation. Examples are
$$initials(STOP) = \emptyset \, ,$$
$$initials(SKIP) = \{\checkmark\} \, , \text{and}$$
$$initials(x : A \to P(x)) = A \, .$$

Inference rules allow us to compute the initial events of a process, and how the process evolves after performing an event. The transition from P to P' due to the occurrence of an event a is represented as $P \xrightarrow{a} P'$. The inference rules enable us to compute the LTS of a given process (such that each labeled transition of the LTS is justified by an inference rule). There is, for example, no inference rule for $STOP$. Accordingly $STOP$ is deadlock: it has no initial events and may not perform any event. This also means that it is guaranteed to be a leaf of any process' LTS.

For (semantic) convenience the alphabet of each process is extended to contain two further events: $\tau \notin \Sigma$ represents an internal transition (an hidden event) and $\checkmark \notin \Sigma$ represents termination. The alphabet extended with $\checkmark$, namely $\Sigma \cup \{\checkmark\}$, is written $\Sigma_{\checkmark}$.

SKIP models successful termination by offering only $\checkmark$. There is a single firing rule (an axiom) dealing with *SKIP*.
$$\overline{SKIP \xrightarrow{\checkmark} \Omega}$$
Hence, Ω represents the state after successful termination of a process. Although it seems to be quite similar to $STOP$ at first glance these processes are very different. First, Ω is a purely semantical process and does not exist on the syntactical level. Second, Ω can only be reached by $\checkmark$ transitions, while

2.2 Operational Semantics

any transition might potentially lead to deadlock. Third, it is also responsible for distributed termination as explained further down.

The process $a \rightarrow P$ offers its environment the opportunity to synchronize on a in which case it then behaves like P. The operational firing rule is

$$\overline{(a \rightarrow P) \xrightarrow{a} P}.$$

Given a set of events $A \subseteq \Sigma$, prefixing is generalized to prefix choice by $x: A \rightarrow P(x)$. This construct reduces to $STOP$ if A is empty:

$$x: \emptyset \rightarrow P(x) = STOP.$$

The inference rule for prefix choice is similar to the one presented above except that any x is substituted with the actual communication event in P. Similarly, in the case of a (constrained) input communication $(a?x: X \rightarrow P)$ any occurrences of x in P are substituted with the actual communication parameter (refer to [Ros05, Chapters 6.1 and 7.3] for a discussion of variable scopes). Throughout the rest of this section, $a \in \Sigma$ and $x \in \Sigma \cup \{\checkmark, \tau\}$.

According to the following two firing rules, the sequential composition $P \,; Q$ behaves like P and, if that terminates, then behaves like Q.

$$\frac{P \xrightarrow{x} P'}{P\,;Q \xrightarrow{x} P'\,;Q}\; x \neq \checkmark \qquad \frac{P \xrightarrow{\checkmark} P'}{P\,;Q \xrightarrow{\tau} Q}$$

$P \,\square\, Q$ offers its environment a choice between P and Q based on synchronization with their initial events. The first two rules show that internal transitions do not resolve the choice. The third and fourth rules specify that the choice is resolved in favor of the operand performing a visible event.

$$\frac{P \xrightarrow{\tau} P'}{P\,\square\,Q \xrightarrow{\tau} P'\,\square\,Q} \qquad \frac{Q \xrightarrow{\tau} Q'}{P\,\square\,Q \xrightarrow{\tau} P\,\square\,Q'}$$

$$\frac{P \xrightarrow{x} P'}{P\,\square\,Q \xrightarrow{x} P'}\; x \neq \tau \qquad \frac{Q \xrightarrow{x} Q'}{P\,\square\,Q \xrightarrow{x} Q'}\; x \neq \tau$$

The process $P \,\sqcap\, Q$ behaves like either P or Q but the choice is made internally, beyond environmental influence. The following two firing rules express this nondeterministic choice.

$$\overline{P\,\sqcap\,Q \xrightarrow{\tau} P} \qquad \overline{P\,\sqcap\,Q \xrightarrow{\tau} Q}$$

A third kind of choice, timeout, combines external and internal influences. Although it can be represented using internal and external choice by

$$P \triangleright Q = (P \square Q) \sqcap Q,$$

it is common to define the following separate firing rules for timeout. The first states that a τ transition on its first operand does not resolve the timeout. The second formalizes resolution of the timeout to the left. The third models resolution to the right by an internal transition.

$$\frac{P \xrightarrow{\tau} P'}{P \triangleright Q \xrightarrow{\tau} P' \triangleright Q} \qquad \frac{P \xrightarrow{x} P'}{P \triangleright Q \xrightarrow{x} P'}\, x \neq \tau \qquad \frac{}{P \triangleright Q \xrightarrow{\tau} Q}$$

These firing rules give rise to an LTS that is different from that of the alternative representation given above. The LTS of the alternative version contains more intermediate states. Their semantic equivalence is given by the fact that both LTS yield the same non-τ events for external synchronization.

The process $P \triangle Q$ behaves like P except that it constantly offers its environment the initial events of Q. If the environment decides to synchronize on one of the initials of Q, P is interrupted and control is passed to Q. As the following firing rules show, interrupt is resolved only if P terminates or Q performs a visible transition.

$$\frac{P \xrightarrow{x} P'}{P \triangle Q \xrightarrow{x} P' \triangle Q}\, x \neq \checkmark \qquad \frac{P \xrightarrow{\checkmark} P'}{P \triangle Q \xrightarrow{\checkmark} \Omega}$$

$$\frac{Q \xrightarrow{\tau} Q'}{P \triangle Q \xrightarrow{\tau} P \triangle Q'} \qquad \frac{Q \xrightarrow{x} Q'}{P \triangle Q \xrightarrow{x} Q'}\, x \neq \tau$$

The parallel composition $P \mid_A \mid Q$ requires P and Q to synchronize on each event $a \in A$, but performs other events of P or Q as determined by those processes. Internal transitions may occur on both sides without synchronization.

$$\frac{P \xrightarrow{\tau} P'}{P \mid_A\mid Q \xrightarrow{\tau} P' \mid_A\mid Q} \qquad \frac{Q \xrightarrow{\tau} Q'}{P \mid_A\mid Q \xrightarrow{\tau} P \mid_A\mid Q'}$$

Events outside A are not synchronized either.

$$\frac{P \xrightarrow{a} P'}{P \mid_A\mid Q \xrightarrow{a} P' \mid_A\mid Q}\, a \in \Sigma \setminus A \qquad \frac{Q \xrightarrow{a} Q'}{P \mid_A\mid Q \xrightarrow{a} P \mid_A\mid Q'}\, a \in \Sigma \setminus A$$

2.2 Operational Semantics

Events from the synchronization set A are to be synchronized.

$$\frac{P \xrightarrow{a} P' \quad Q \xrightarrow{a} Q'}{P \mid_A \mid Q \xrightarrow{a} P' \mid_A \mid Q'} \quad a \in A$$

Termination in parallel compositions requires special care. Either side is allowed to terminate independently if it decides to do so. The whole construction terminates only if both sides have terminated.

$$\frac{P \xrightarrow{\checkmark} P'}{P \mid_A \mid Q \xrightarrow{\tau} \Omega \mid_A \mid Q} \qquad \frac{Q \xrightarrow{\checkmark} Q'}{P \mid_A \mid Q \xrightarrow{\tau} P \mid_A \mid \Omega} \qquad \overline{\Omega \mid_A \mid \Omega \xrightarrow{\checkmark} \Omega}$$

The special cases of synchronization on Σ ($\parallel$) and interleaving ($\parallel\parallel$) are subsumed under these eight firing rules.

The process $P \setminus A$ executes the events in the set A internally, without synchronization by its environment; they can be thought of as being replaced by τ events.

$$\frac{P \xrightarrow{a} P'}{P \setminus A \xrightarrow{\tau} P' \setminus A} \quad a \in A$$

Events outside A (except $\checkmark$) are under environmental control as defined by P.

$$\frac{P \xrightarrow{a} P'}{P \setminus A \xrightarrow{a} P' \setminus A} \quad a \notin A \cup \{\checkmark\}$$

The hiding construction is resolved by the $\checkmark$ event.

$$\frac{P \xrightarrow{\checkmark} P'}{P \setminus A \xrightarrow{\checkmark} \Omega}$$

Conditionals and guards do not need their own firing rules because these two operators merely constrain the set of events that a process offers initially. If an event is performed it is performed as defined by the processes that are within the scope of the conditional or guard operator.

Renaming ($P[M]$) affects only those events that are in the domain of M.

$$\frac{P \xrightarrow{a} P'}{P[M] \xrightarrow{b} P'[M]} \ (a,b) \in M \qquad \frac{P \xrightarrow{a} P'}{P[M] \xrightarrow{a} P'[M]} \ a \in \Sigma \setminus \operatorname{dom} M$$

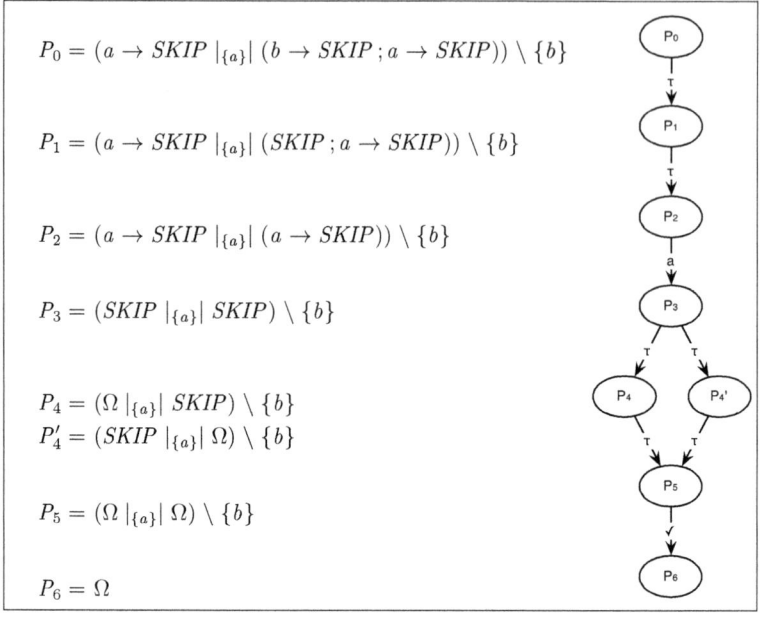

$P_0 = (a \to SKIP \ |\{a\}| \ (b \to SKIP \,; a \to SKIP)) \setminus \{b\}$

$P_1 = (a \to SKIP \ |\{a\}| \ (SKIP \,; a \to SKIP)) \setminus \{b\}$

$P_2 = (a \to SKIP \ |\{a\}| \ (a \to SKIP)) \setminus \{b\}$

$P_3 = (SKIP \ |\{a\}| \ SKIP) \setminus \{b\}$

$P_4 = (\Omega \ |\{a\}| \ SKIP) \setminus \{b\}$
$P_4' = (SKIP \ |\{a\}| \ \Omega) \setminus \{b\}$

$P_5 = (\Omega \ |\{a\}| \ \Omega) \setminus \{b\}$

$P_6 = \Omega$

Figure 2.1.: LTS of process P shown in equation (2.1)

Internal transitions are not affected by renaming. The ✓ event resolves the renaming construct.

$$\frac{P \xrightarrow{\tau} P'}{P[M] \xrightarrow{\tau} P'[M]} \qquad \frac{P \xrightarrow{\checkmark} P'}{P[M] \xrightarrow{\checkmark} \Omega}$$

For example the following process P, defined as an abstraction of components that synchronize on a, simply offers the event a and then terminates successfully.

$$P = (a \to SKIP \ |\{a\}| \ (b \to SKIP \,; a \to SKIP)) \setminus \{b\} \qquad (2.1)$$

The LTS of this process is shown in Figure 2.1. The initial state is labeled P_0, hence $P_0 = P$. Initially, the operands of the parallel composition cannot synchronize. The only transition that can fire is the τ transition introduced by the hiding of b. Before synchronization on a can happen, the right-hand side must resolve the sequential composition by another τ transition. Now both sides may terminate finally resulting in distributed termination of the parallel composition and of the hiding construct.

2.3. Denotational Semantics

The fundamental idea of denotational semantics is to interpret the dynamic notion of reduction by the static notion of equality. The semantics of a compound statement derives from the denotations of its immediate parts.

CSP has a range of denotational semantic models, the most basic of which are: the traces model $\mathcal{T}$; the stable failures model $\mathcal{F}$; and the failures-divergences model $\mathcal{FD}$ [Ros05]. These models express the semantics of processes in increasing levels of detail. For example, internal and external choice are indistinguishable in the traces model but resolved in the stable failures model, whilst divergence is resolved in the failures-divergences model. In the following, we briefly introduce these three models. Throughout this thesis Σ^* denotes the set of finite sequences of events. t, u are sequences, the concatenation of sequences t and u is written $t \frown u$.

A sequence of events that a process may perform is called a *trace* of the process. In the traces semantics of CSP, a process is represented by the set of all its possible traces; the result is useful in specifying safety properties. Traces are always *nonempty*

$$traces(P) \neq \emptyset$$

and *prefix-closed*

$$\forall\, t, u \in \Sigma^* : t \frown u \in traces(P) \Rightarrow t \in traces(P).$$

The former property holds because each process may perform the empty trace $\langle\rangle \in traces(P)$. The latter property must be satisfied to ensure that all subtraces of a trace of a process are also traces of that process.

Examples of how traces are computed are the following:

$$traces(STOP) = \{\langle\rangle\}$$
$$traces(SKIP) = \{\langle\rangle, \langle\checkmark\rangle\}$$
$$traces(a \to P) = \{\langle\rangle\} \cup \{\langle a\rangle \frown t \mid t \in traces(P)\}$$
$$traces(P \triangleleft b \triangleright Q) = \text{if } b \text{ then } traces(P) \text{ else } traces(Q)$$

Internal and external choice are indistinguishable in the traces model.

$$traces(P \sqcap Q) = traces(P) \cup traces(Q)$$
$$traces(P \square Q) = traces(P) \cup traces(Q)$$

As a consequence, the traces model fails to describe liveness properties: while $P \square Q$ cannot refuse to synchronize on any of the initial events of P or Q, $P \sqcap Q$ can do so but this fact cannot be derived from the traces of a process.

The traces of processes synchronizing on their whole alphabets are easily defined as shown below. Interleaving and generalized parallel composition are defined using auxiliary operations on traces which can be found in [Ros05, pages 67 and 70].

$$traces(P \parallel Q) = traces(P) \cap traces(Q)$$
$$traces(P \interleave Q) = \bigcup \{t \interleave u \mid t \in traces(P) \land u \in traces(Q)\}$$
$$traces(P \mid_X \mid Q) = \bigcup \{t \mid_X \mid u \mid t \in traces(P) \land u \in traces(Q)\}$$

The traces of a process can be defined inductively on its syntax (as shown above) or derived from its LTS (as shown in the previous section).

The traces semantics records behaviors that a process can do. In the stable failures semantics this is enriched with sets of events that can be constantly refused by a process after a particular trace. These sets are called *refusals*. A failure is a pair (t, X) where $t \in \Sigma_\checkmark^*$ is a trace and $X \subseteq \Sigma_\checkmark$ a refusal set. The notion of stability is explained best using the operational semantics of CSP: a process is in an unstable state if the state has outgoing τ edges; otherwise it is a stable state. Process P_2 of Figure 2.1, for example, represents a stable state, while P_3 represents an unstable state. Unstable states do not give rise to a failure, but stable states do. The failures of P_2 are

$$\{(\langle\rangle, X) \mid X \subseteq \Sigma_\checkmark \setminus \{a\}\}.$$

The stable failures semantics, by additionally recording the refusals of a process, is useful in specifying a system's safety and liveness properties. Deadlock-freedom of P, for example, is specified as

$$\forall t \in traces(t) : (t, \Sigma_\checkmark) \notin failures(P).$$

Closely related are the failures of $STOP$

$$failures(STOP) = \{(\langle\rangle, X \mid X \subseteq \Sigma_\checkmark)\}.$$

2.3 Denotational Semantics

Internal and external choice are resolved in this model.

$$failures(P \sqcap Q) = failures(P) \cup failures(Q)$$
$$failures(P \square Q) = \{(\langle\rangle, X) \mid (\langle\rangle, X) \in failures(P) \cap failures(Q)\}$$
$$\cup \{(t, X) \mid (t, X) \in failures(P) \cup failures(Q) \wedge t \neq \langle\rangle\}$$
$$\cup \{(\langle\rangle, X) \mid X \subseteq \Sigma \wedge \langle\checkmark\rangle \in traces(P) \cup traces(Q)\}$$

The informal explanation is that $P \sqcap Q$ is in an unstable state initially. After resolving the internal choice, it behaves either as P or as Q resulting in the set union presented above. The external choice, however, may be in a stable state initially removing the initial events of each of the choice's operands from the refusals of the other respectively.

Since the interrupt operator plays an important role in this thesis (especially in Chapter 5), its traces and failures are presented here. The traces of $P \triangle Q$ are the union of P's traces with all nonterminating traces of P continued with Q's traces. The failures are not as easily derived because of possible termination of P. The failures of the whole construct contain the failures of P up to the point just before termination. After each trace $t \in traces(P)$ such that P might terminate after t, $\checkmark$ cannot be refused (even if $\checkmark \in refusals(Q)$). After termination of P, any event can be constantly refused (the whole construct has terminated). Before termination of P, Q may take over any time thus ignoring the refusals of P.

$$traces(P \triangle Q) = traces(P) \cup \{t \frown u \mid t \in traces(P) \cap \Sigma^* \wedge u \in traces(Q)\}$$
$$failures(P \triangle Q) = \{(t, X) \in failures(P) \mid t \in \Sigma^*\}$$
$$\cup \{(t, X) \mid t \frown \langle\checkmark\rangle \in traces(P) \wedge X \subseteq \Sigma\}$$
$$\cup \{(t \frown \langle\checkmark\rangle, X) \mid t \frown \langle\checkmark\rangle \in traces(P) \wedge X \subseteq \Sigma_\checkmark\}$$
$$\cup \{(t \frown u, X) \mid t \in traces(P) \cap \Sigma^* \wedge (u, X) \in failures(Q)\}$$

The traces model is about what a process can do, while the stable failures model enables us to reason about what a process must do or what it can refuse to do. However, the stable failures model fails to resolve infinite internal behavior because each node on an infinite path of τ transitions represents an unstable state. Thus, in addition to traces and refusals, a complete description of the behavior of processes must take divergences into account. The failures-divergences model solves this problem by additionally recording the states in which a process can diverge. Divergence can be introduced by hiding (resulting in loops of τ events), the symbol *div* and by ill-formed recursion like $P = P$.

See [Ros05, Chapter 8.3] for an in-depth presentation of the failures-divergences model.

In the rest of this thesis, we will primarily focus on the stable failures semantics of processes because the stable failures and failures-divergences semantics collapse for livelock-free processes (and we are mostly interested in livelock-free processes). Therefore, we will always discuss if a construction or operation on processes may cause or eliminate divergence.

In Section 2.2, we have introduced the *initials* of a process: the set of events that the process offers initially. The initials of a process are mostly relevant for its operational semantics but can also be given in terms of its denotational semantics:
$$initials(P) = \{x \mid \langle x \rangle \in traces(P)\}.$$

Closely related to the notion of *initials* is the 'after' operator P/t that describes P after performing the trace $t \in traces(P)$. It is defined for traces only and satisfies
$$traces(P/t) = \{u \mid t \frown u \in traces(P)\}.$$

To illustrate its connection to initials this equality can also be stated as
$$P \equiv_\mathcal{T} x : initials(P) \to P/\langle x \rangle.$$

It is important to note that this operator is not a part of the CSP language and cannot be used to model processes. However, it is often used in proofs when it is assumed that a process has already executed a particular trace.

2.4. Refinement and Algebraic Semantics

Conformance in CSP is expressed by *refinement*. Informally, $P \sqsubseteq Q$ (speak 'P is refined by Q') means that Q conforms to P, or that Q's behaviors are contained in those of P. Formally, for any of the three semantic models $\mathcal{M} \in \{\mathcal{T}, \mathcal{F}, \mathcal{FD}\}$,
$$P \sqsubseteq_\mathcal{M} Q \Leftrightarrow \mathcal{M}[\![Q]\!] \subseteq \mathcal{M}[\![P]\!]$$
where $\mathcal{M}[\![P]\!]$ denotes the semantics of process P in semantic model $\mathcal{M}$. Based upon the notion of refinement, CSP provides a refinement calculus supporting process development.

2.4 Refinement and Algebraic Semantics

Refinement in the traces model $\mathcal{T}$ is about restricting the behaviors of a process. The most refined process in this semantics is $STOP$ because for every process P

$$P \sqsubseteq_\mathcal{T} STOP.$$

Refinement in the stable failures and the failures-divergences models is about removing nondeterminism. Deterministic processes (those without unstable nodes) cannot be refined further in these models. This is expressed formally by the basic refinement law 'resolution of nondeterministic choice'

$$P \sqcap Q \sqsubseteq P. \tag{2.2}$$

Containment in the failures-divergences model is defined such that divergence is the greatest element in the refinement relation. Hence,

$$div \sqsubseteq_{\mathcal{FD}} P$$

holds for every process P.

Algebraic reasoning is supported by refinement laws that correspond to containments in the failures-divergences model. However, although the following laws can be derived from the denotational semantics and stated as theorems, they are given as a set of algebraic laws of an algebraic semantics.

Processes are no longer interpreted in terms of sets of events they may perform or refuse but simply by the process terms that they are composed of. Theorems in the algebraic semantics are all those equivalences that can be derived from the basic laws (axioms).

The most fundamental laws are the following *unit*-laws.

$$STOP \,\square\, P \;=\; P \tag{2.3}$$
$$SKIP\,;P \;=\; P \tag{2.4}$$
$$P\,;SKIP \;=\; P \tag{2.5}$$
$$SKIP \,|||\, P \;=\; P \tag{2.6}$$

Law 2.6 can be generalized to

$$SKIP \,|_A|\, P = P \quad \text{if} \quad \Sigma_P \cap A = \emptyset. \tag{2.7}$$

Another group of fundamental laws (the *step*-laws) describe the stepwise behavior of processes.

$$(x:A \to P) \; \square \; (x:B \to Q) \;=\; x:A \cup B \to ((P \sqcap Q) \mathbin{\triangleleft} x \in A \cap B \mathbin{\triangleright} (P \mathbin{\triangleleft} x \in A \mathbin{\triangleright} Q)) \quad (2.8)$$

$$STOP \;=\; x:\emptyset \to P \quad (2.9)$$

$$(a \to P) \setminus X \;=\; \begin{cases} P \setminus X & \text{if } a \in X \\ a \to (P \setminus X) & \text{if } a \notin X \end{cases} \quad (2.10)$$

Law 2.8 states that the external choice operator is resolved nondeterministically if the initial events of its operands overlap and that it is resolved to the side that performed the event otherwise. Law 2.9 justifies the understanding of $STOP$ as a process without initial events.

Let $P = s:A \to P'$ and $Q = x:B \to Q'$. The initials of $P \;|_X|\; Q$ are then $C = (X \cap A \cap B) \cup (A \setminus X) \cup (B \setminus X)$. Using these definitions, we state the step law for generalized parallel composition as follows:

$$\begin{aligned} P \;|_X|\; Q \;=\;\; & x:C \to (P' \;|_X|\; Q') \mathbin{\triangleleft} x \in X \mathbin{\triangleright} \\ & (((P' \;|_X|\; Q) \sqcap (P \;|_X|\; Q')) \mathbin{\triangleleft} x \in A \cap B \mathbin{\triangleright} \\ & ((P' \;|_X|\; Q) \mathbin{\triangleleft} x \in A \mathbin{\triangleright} (P \;|_X|\; Q'))). \end{aligned} \quad (2.11)$$

Accordingly, the event x is synchronized if it is in X. If it is offered by both P and Q, it is performed nondeterministically by either P or Q. Otherwise, it is performed by the process that offered it.

Further important laws are the following *idempotence*, *symmetry*, and *associativity* laws.

$$P \square P = P \tag{2.12}$$
$$P \sqcap P = P \tag{2.13}$$
$$P \triangleleft b \triangleright P = P \tag{2.14}$$
$$P \square Q = Q \square P \tag{2.15}$$
$$P \sqcap Q = Q \sqcap P \tag{2.16}$$
$$P \mid_A \mid Q = Q \mid_A \mid P \tag{2.17}$$
$$(P \setminus A) \setminus B = (P \setminus B) \setminus A \tag{2.18}$$
$$P \square (Q \square R) = (P \square Q) \square R \tag{2.19}$$
$$P \sqcap (Q \sqcap R) = (P \sqcap Q) \sqcap R \tag{2.20}$$
$$P \mid_A \mid (Q \mid_A \mid R) = (P \mid_A \mid Q) \mid_A \mid R \tag{2.21}$$
$$P\,;(Q\,;R) = (P\,;Q)\,;R \tag{2.22}$$

Proofs presented in this thesis are mostly based on the algebraic semantics of CSP but sometimes resort to the denotational or the operational semantics. Further algebraic laws are derived from the denotational semantics when needed.

2.5. Tools

There are many tools available that support the modeling, understanding, or formal analysis of CSP processes. Such tools include animators, automated refinement checkers, model checkers and theorem provers (e.g., for proving refinements of infinite state processes). Of the tools presented in the rest of this section, FDR and ProB are the most important for this thesis.

2.5.1. Animators

Animators offer users the possibility to step through processes and explore their behaviors. For this purpose, animators implement the firing rules given by the operational semantics and unroll (interpret) the process under consideration according to these firing rules. While unrolling the process, an animator (partially) computes the LTS of the process and outputs a trace corresponding to a single branch of the LTS. Animators allow the user to play environment of a process as well as to control its internal transitions to explore its behavior.

This is a great help in developing and understanding processes and in teaching CSP.

Animators that are widely used in the CSP community are ProBE [Ros05], ProB [LF08] and the process analysis toolkit PAT [SLD08]. ProB supports LTL model checking in addition to process animation. PAT is equipped with refinement and LTL model checking capabilities. The CSP_M toolkit [Fon10] offers implementations of the firing rules for reuse in custom CSP tools and also offers its own CSP animator.

Sometimes, animators are also called simulators. For the purpose of this thesis, the notion of simulation is distinguished from animation. *Animation* refers to the act of a human playing with a tool that interactively explores the state space of a system. This technical view relates to the common understanding of animation as 'creating the illusion of movement'. *Simulation*, in contrast, denotes a relation between (labeled) transition systems that is useful in the study of operational semantics. Intuitively, a system simulates another if it can match all of its moves. This matches the common understanding of simulation as 'imitating the appearance or character of somebody or something' in the sense that a system imitates the behavior of another.

2.5.2. Model Checkers

Generally speaking, model checkers check whether a temporal logic specification ϕ holds on a given model M, formally $M \models \phi$. Model checkers are mostly concerned with finite state systems and exhaustively search the state space of the system under consideration. However, some model checkers also support infinite state systems, but then the checking procedure is not guaranteed to terminate in general. Well-known temporal logics used for model checking purposes are Computational Tree Logic (CTL) and Linear Temporal Logic (LTL) which are both subsets of CTL* [CGP99]. Both ProB and PAT support LTL model checking of CSP processes. In the context of this thesis, LTL is considered exclusively. Readers not familiar with LTL may refer to [CGP99] because it is not introduced here.

ProB supports the LTL[e] dialect [PL08]. This dialect is remarkably rich in terms of temporal operators and atomic propositions. The [.] operator, for example, targets traces and checks if an event is performed by the process under consideration. The $e(.)$ operator targets failures and checks if an event is enabled (cannot be refused). For example, the formula

$$\phi = G([a] \Rightarrow e(a))$$

specifies that the event a is available when it is performed. Hence, ϕ is a tautology. However,

$$\psi = G(e(a) \Rightarrow [a])$$

is not a tautology but satisfiable. The following process P, for example, satisfies ψ ($P \models \psi$) while $Q \not\models \psi$:

$$P = a \rightarrow P$$
$$Q = a \rightarrow STOP \,\square\, b \rightarrow STOP$$

The reason is that P must perform a whenever it is enabled but Q may perform b even though a cannot be refused initially. LTL formulas given in the subsequent chapters are set in LTL[e] syntax.

The LTL dialect supported by PAT targets specifications on traces only. It does not offer an operator to specify the availability of events in LTL properties.

The relationship between refinement checking and LTL model checking was investigated by Leuschel et al. in [LMC01] and more recently by Lowe [Low08]. An important result is that there are LTL properties that cannot be expressed as refinement relations and vice versa (in the semantic models considered here). Thus we use both model checking and refinement checking for the purposes of this thesis.

2.5.3. Refinement Checkers

Refinement checking refers to proving if the behaviors of a process are contained in the behaviors of another. Automated refinement checking of finite state processes is supported by FDR [Ros05], PAT [SLD08] and ARC [PY96], for example. Infinite state systems can be interactively checked using the CSP-Prover [IR05] (built atop of Isabelle/HOL [NPW02]).

In this thesis, we focus on the automatic refinement checker FDR (version 2.83). This tool proves or refutes assertions of the form $P \sqsubseteq_\mathcal{M} Q$ (where $\mathcal{M} \in \{\mathcal{T}, \mathcal{F}, \mathcal{FD}\}$ as described in Section 2.4). It also supports predefined assertions for checking if a process is deterministic and if it is deadlock- or livelock-free.

```
channel a,b
P = (a -> SKIP [|{a}|] (b -> SKIP; a -> SKIP)) \ {b}
Q = a -> SKIP
assert P [FD= Q
assert Q [FD= P
```

Figure 2.2.: CSP_M encoding of example process P shown in Equation 2.1 (p. 22).

FDR inputs processes expressed in CSP_M, which is now the *de facto* standard for machine-readable CSP (and also supported by ProB). CSP_M expresses CSP by a small but powerful functional language, offering constructs such as *lambda* and *let* expressions and supporting pattern matching and currying. It also provides a number of predefined data types, including Booleans, integers, sequences and sets, and allows user-defined data types. The alphabet of the processes of a CSP_M script is defined by the script's typed channel definitions.

Figure 2.2 shows the CSP_M encoding of the example process P (equation (2.1) introduced in Section 2.2). The last two lines of the CSP_M script assert $P = Q$ (in the failures-divergences model $\mathcal{FD}$ but also in $\mathcal{T}$ and $\mathcal{F}$). When examining the operational semantics of P, we found that P is able to perform the trace $\langle a, \checkmark \rangle$ and we also found that it cannot avoid doing so. Thus, as expected, both assertions hold. See [GRA05] or [Ros05] for further details on CSP_M.

2.6. Summary

This chapter has presented the process algebra CSP. We have introduced its syntax focusing on the role of events. In the context of this thesis, events are regarded as abstractions of arbitrary actions of a system (possibly involving communication but also describing local data transformations). Then, we have introduced the operational, denotational, and algebraic semantics of CSP. The operational semantics allows us to regard processes as states and events as transitions allowing the system to evolve from one state to another. Hence, it allows us to 'execute' CSP processes. The denotational and algebraic semantics are mostly used in proofs. There is a close connection between these semantic models because the denotational semantics of a process can be computed from its labeled transition system (using its operational semantics) and the laws of the algebraic semantics can be derived as theorems from the denotational semantics. At the end of the chapter, we have described some of its most

2.6 Summary

widely used tools. FDR and ProB are the ones being used in the rest of the thesis. Both tools support CSP_M.

3 Further Terminology and Notations

In this chapter, we introduce further terminology and notations. The concept of coordination languages is introduced in Section 3.1. We then go on to present Java concurrency and its weaknesses in Section 3.2. Infamous phenomena of concurrency (those that the approach presented here aims to avoid) are briefly introduced in Section 3.3. Finally, the most basic terminology used in the context of Business Process Management, relevant for Chapter 8, is introduced in Section 3.4.

We presume basic knowledge of Z, Petri Nets and the Java programming language. The mathematical notation used in this thesis is a subset of the Z mathematical toolkit as presented in [Spi92]. For example, we use # to denote the cardinality of a set as well as the length of a sequence. Petri Nets (see, e.g., [GV03] for an overview) strongly influenced formal approaches to the modeling of business processes. Petri Nets also appear in the context of approaches to coordination. We use the Java programming language to implement the concepts presented in this thesis to explore the applicability of our approach.

3.1. Coordination Languages

In [GC92], Gelernter and Carriero, the inventors of the Linda language, introduce the term *coordination language*.

> We introduced this term [i.e., coordination language] to designate the linguistic embodiment of a coordination model. The issue is not mere nomenclature. Our intention is to identify Linda and systems in its class as complete languages in their own rights, not mere ex-

tensions to some existing base language. Complete language means a complete coordination language of course, the embodiment of a comprehensive coordination model. [GC92, p. 99]

The basic observation underlying the concept of coordination languages is the orthogonality of concurrency and parallelism to sequential aspects of a system. For example, Linda [ACG86] is a coordination language adding parallelism to sequential target languages such as C or Fortran. It allows tasks to be distributed dynamically at runtime. Linda comprises a model of coordination and communication among several parallel processes in a machine- and language-independent way. The communication model of Linda is based upon virtual associative shared memory, the so-called *tuplespace*. It is used for storing and retrieving objects and also for distributing tasks among the participating processing units. Linda defines operations for reading a tuple, writing a tuple, atomically reading and removing a tuple from the tuplespace, and the distribution of tasks. These four operations are implemented for specific target languages and machines and allow sequential programs to be turned into concurrent or parallel ones. The Linda programming model treats process coordination as a separate activity from computation and subsumes various levels of concurrency. For example, it allows multi-threaded programs to be turned into parallel ones without change. However, the Linda programming language does not offer an approach for the specification and verification of concurrent systems. It can be regarded as a proof-of-concept of coordination languages.

In the context of this thesis, coordination refers to the abstract idea of supervising and controlling the behavior of concurrent components. Thus, we understand systems such as Reference Nets [Kum02], CSP $\|$ B [ST04], rCOS [CHL06], and the approach presented in this thesis, as formal approaches to coordination.

3.2. Java Concurrency

Java is a very popular programming language used in the development of desktop applications, servers and mission-critical enterprise applications. It offers built-in concurrency and is often used to develop multi-threaded programs to take advantage of concurrent threads running on symmetric multi-processors or on networks of processors. Java threads are ordinary Java objects residing in shared memory space. Unlike ordinary method calls, the call to *Thread.start* is intercepted by the Java Virtual Machine (JVM) to execute the method in

3.2 Java Concurrency

```java
class Synchronized {
  private final Object o = new Object();
  synchronized void doSynchronized0(){
    while (...) {
      try {
        this.wait();
      }
      catch(InterruptedException e){...}
    }
  }
  void doSynchronized1(){
    synchronized(o) {
      while (...) {
        try {
          o.wait();
        }
        catch(InterruptedException e){...}
      }
      o.notify();
    }
  }
}
```

Figure 3.1.: Example class skeleton illustrating Java concurrency primitives.

its own thread of control. The synchronization facilities of Java are based on monitors on objects. Monitors control the interplay of threads. The primitives are

- *synchronized*
- *Object.wait*
- *Object.notify*, and
- *Object.notifyAll*.

The *synchronized* keyword obtains and frees monitors on objects. The other primitives interact with the scheduler of the JVM. *Object.wait* causes the current thread to wait. *Object.notify* notifies a nondeterministically chosen waiting thread and *Object.notifyAll* notifies all waiting threads. In both cases only one thread may enter the monitor. Figure 3.1 illustrates the use of these primitives. A thread calling the *Synchronized.doSynchronized0* method obtains a monitor on that very instance of *Synchronized*. The second method (*doSynchronized1*) uses another object as monitor ensuring independence of the two methods.

These primitives are considered weak and leave even the skilled programmer vulnerable to error. D. Lea put it this way when posting the Java Specification Request (JSR) 166:

[...] such facilities are notoriously hard to get right and even more difficult to optimize. The concurrency facilities written by application programmers are often incorrect or inefficient. [Lea02]

The fundamental difficulty lies in the use of monitors as the basic synchronization primitive. The problem arises from the fact that a thread passes control from one object to another by calling its methods. Thus, when implementing a method that needs to access some shared data (or more generally needs to synchronize in some respect) it is not always obvious what monitors a potential caller might belong and what monitors callees of the current method may acquire. As a consequence, rules for coordinating access need to be designed and enforced if chaos is to be avoided. A more elaborate – and very illuminating – discussion on Java concurrency is given in [HBB99].

Some research has therefore been done to tame the complexities of concurrent Java programs by developing concurrency frameworks atop Java threads to hide the Java synchronization primitives from the developer, e. g., the frameworks which we present later on in Section 9.3. To overcome the problems of Java concurrency, JSR 166 was finally released in 2004 as part of Java 5 in the *java.util.concurrent* [Sun] package. The new concurrency package offers abstractions that hide the above-mentioned Java concurrency primitives but still lacks the support of automated verification. Furthermore, the Java Modeling Language (JML) [LBR06] does not yet explicitly address concurrency. Extending JML towards concurrency is still an active field of research. The authors of [BCC$^+$05], for example, pose the question

How should concurrency properties be specified (in JML)?

Our answer to this very question is to have concurrency expressed in a specialized formalism, e. g., CSP, and to use additional proof obligations relating the CSP specification with the state-based JML specification.

3.3. Infamous Phenomena of Concurrency

In the previous chapter, we have introduced CSP as a formalism for specifying, modeling and reasoning about concurrent systems. In that context we have presented *deadlock* and *livelock* as two basic pathological phenomena. Both are explicitly modeled in CSP by the processes $STOP$ and div.

Java programs may also suffer from these phenomena. Deadlock arises when a group of threads reaches a state where each one of them is waiting for another to do something that will enable it to proceed. For example, the threads are either blocked on a monitor entry or have put themselves to sleep by calling *Object.wait* and are waiting for another thread to call *Object.notify* or *Object.notifyAll*. In this situation, the system is stuck and has evolved to *STOP*.

Livelock occurs if a group of threads get into an infinite cycle of interaction amongst themselves and refuse to respond to anything outside their group. This corresponds to the CSP notion of divergence.

Two further phenomena are threats to concurrent systems: *starvation* and *data races*. Starvation is observed when a single thread is blocked indefinitely, waiting for a condition that the other threads never set up for it. A system that allows a shared variable to be concurrently accessed without proper locking or synchronization possibly produces a data race. This may result in nondeterministic final values of the shared variable. While starvation can still be checked for on the CSP level, detection of data races needs more information than is available on that level (as discussed in Section 6.4).

Livelock and Starvation are often caused by repeated (local) choices that are always resolved in the same way. Process P in

$$((\mu P \bullet a \to P) \,|||\, (\mu Q \bullet b \to Q) \,|_{\{a,b\}}|\, (\mu R \bullet a \to R \sqcap b \to R)) \setminus \{b\},$$

for example, is subject to starvation if the internal choice in R is always resolved to the right-hand clause. In that situation, the whole process is subject to livelock. Although this situation is theoretically valid, it is often unlikely to arise in reality. This fact is expressed by the notion of *fairness*. The notion of fairness conditions refers to conditions that 'cure' processes that behave badly under the assumption that repeated (local) choices can always be resolved in the same way. The process shown above, for example, is well behaved under the assumption that the internal choice in R is a fair one. Fairness can be specified on different levels of granularities (e.g., local or global) and can be regarded as an abstraction of probabilities. FDR does not support fairness but PAT explicitly deals with fairness, as described in [SLDP09].

3.4. Business Processes and Workflows

The notions of *business process* and *workflow* are often used as synonyms for each other. In this thesis, we follow the definitions as given by the *Workflow Management Coalition* (WfMC) in [Coa99]. A *business process* denotes the abstract concept of processes that are performed by employees of an organization to realize the goals of that organization. The WfMC defines a business process as

> a set of one or more linked procedures or activities which collectively realise a business objective or policy goal, normally within the context of an organisational structure defining functional roles and relationships. [Coa99, p. 10]

The model of a business process defines roles, tasks, activities, conditions and events and the relationship between those. A workflow defines how, by whom and by which means the business process is to be executed. We call such a model of a business process a *workflow*. The WfMC states that a workflow describes

> the automation of a business process, in whole or part, during which documents, information or tasks are passed from one participant to another for action, according to a set of procedural rules. [Coa99, p. 8]

Incarnations of workflows for a specific workflow server are called *workflow definitions*. Workflow servers manage workflow definitions and allow users to create instances of workflows controlling the tasks and activities necessary for dealing with the documents or data being processes to satisfy the modeled business process. If one is solely interested in the control structure of a workflow, e. g., for proving deadlock-freedom, it is often sufficient to disregard aspects such as roles and access control. An example of such an abstract model of a workflow modeled as a Petri Net is shown in Figure 8.2. It represents a workflow composed of the basic tasks a, b, c, d, e, f, g, h.

3.5. Summary

This chapter has presented further notations and terminology used throughout the thesis. The concept of coordination languages is based on the idea to segregate interaction behavior of a concurrent system from its sequential functional aspects. Java concurrency is based on monitors and primitives to synchronize on monitors. The drawback of Java concurrency is that the primitives are error-prone to use and that it is not yet supported by JML. Concurrent Java programs are threatened by deadlock, livelock, starvation and data races. Fairness assumptions may help to rule out bad behavior on the semantical level but then it must also be ensured that implementations adhere to these assumptions. The two most basic unwanted phenomena of concurrency are deadlock

3.5 Summary

and livelock. These can be detected with FDR. Finally, the basic terminology of business processes were briefly introduced. A workflow is a model of a business process and a workflow server is a system controlling workflow definitions and instances of workflows. Workflows are only relevant for chapters 8 and 9.

4 Simulating Truly Concurrent CSP

> Es gibt nichts Praktischeres
> als eine gute Theorie.
>
> *(Immanuel Kant)*

As motivated in the Introduction and presented in Chapter 2, process algebras, like CSP, allow synchronizing processes to be combined in parallel with the result that the system designer need not be concerned about exploiting simultaneity, which may arise naturally in an implementation conforming to the design. But sometimes, for example for purposes of simulation, it is useful to know what potential simultaneity a design embodies, and then the abstraction carefully built in to the process algebra must be revoked.

In this chapter, we study one way to make explicit the simultaneity of events implicit in a CSP process. Events were designed in CSP to be instantaneous, on the understanding that duration can then be modeled by splitting an event into start and end events. Our approach starts by unravelling that assumption, and proceeds by constructing a faithful, controlled simulation of the process.

An important consequence of the approach taken here is that sets of events that may occur concurrently are computed statically. As a result, the approach is suitable for realistic simulation (in the sense that functions attached to events may be executed concurrently and may require positive duration). Indeed any (non-$\checkmark$) event (even synchronization events) can be linked to a terminating user-defined function, and the functions executed concurrently, as we will see in Chapter 6. There, the model of a CSP-based coordination environment simulating a coordination process at runtime is presented. In that environment, a user-defined function is started immediately after its corresponding start event and after its termination the corresponding end event becomes available.

Section 4.1 introduces a syntactical transformation of processes T that splits events into a start and an end event. Then Section 4.2 shows how the transformed process can be used to compose a system that simulates the original process while collecting concurrency information. The construction is shown to be faithful in the sense that the simulated version equals the original process in the traces semantics. Properties used to prove that the construction preserves the semantics of the original process are presented in Section 4.3. The approach is shown at work on four small but typical examples which are presented in Section 4.4. In Section 4.5, we present two subsets of CSP such that Ext preserves the failures-divergences semantics of every process in these subsets. This chapter closes with a discussion in Section 4.6.

4.1. The Transformation T

In this section we present the transformation T that achieves the simulation motivated above. T models duration of events by splitting them (as described in [Hoa85] and discussed in [vGV97]). Internal transitions are exposed by introducing fresh events. The purpose of the transformation is to put the transformed process $T(P)$ into parallel with a control component (being introduced in the next section) that records the start and end events of every transition of the original process P (including hidden events). The control component can then record possible simultaneity in T and thus be used to compute possible concurrency in P.

Throughout this chapter processes are expressed using the syntax

$$SKIP \mid STOP \mid (x:X \to P(x)) \mid P\,;Q \mid P \mathbin{\Box} Q \mid P \mid_A \mid Q \mid$$

$$P \setminus A \mid P \sqcap Q \mid P[M] \mid P \vartriangleright Q\,.$$

for the 'atomic' processes, prefix choice, sequential composition, external choice, parallel composition, hiding, internal choice, renaming and timeout respectively.

Let $I = \{ic\_0, to\_0, \ldots, ic\_n, to\_n\}$ be a set of fresh events relative to Σ_P modeling timeout and resolution of internal choice. Furthermore, let

$$s, sh, e, eh : \Sigma_P \cup I$$

4.1 The Transformation T

be fresh channels relative to Σ_P. The transformation T is defined as follows.

$$\begin{aligned}
T(SKIP) &= SKIP \\
T(x\!:\!X \to P(x)) &= s?x\!:\!X \to e.x \to T(P(x)) \\
T(P\,;Q) &= T(P)\,;T(Q) \\
T(P \,\square\, Q) &= T(P) \,\square\, T(Q) \\
T(P \mathbin{|_A|} Q) &= T(P) \mathbin{|_{\{s.x,e.x|x\in A\}}|} T(Q) \\
T(P \setminus A) &= T(P)[s.x \leftarrow sh.x, e.x \leftarrow eh.x \mid x \in A] \\
T(P \sqcap Q) &= sh.ic\_i \to eh.ic\_i \to (T(P) \sqcap T(Q)) \\
T(P[M]) &= T(P)[s.x \leftarrow s.y, e.x \leftarrow e.y \mid (x,y) \in M] \\
T(P \triangleright Q) &= T(P) \,\square\, (sh.to\_i \to eh.to\_i \to T(Q))
\end{aligned}$$

T does not affect $\checkmark$. For prefix choice, T splits each event x into its start event $s.x$ and end event $e.x$. As special cases,

$$\begin{aligned}
T(STOP) &= STOP \\
T(x \to P) &= s.x \to e.x \to T(P)\,.
\end{aligned}$$

T distributes over sequential composition, external choice and parallel composition, in the latter case by synchronizing on the split events instead of the original events. For hiding, T communicates the split events over the channels sh and eh (standing for 'start hidden' and 'end hidden', respectively). For each internal choice, thought of as resulting from an internal transition, T introduces a fresh hidden event labelled $ic\_i \in I$ for that transition where the i denotes the i-th occurrence of the process operator in the input process. It is then split and communicated over the sh and eh channels responsible for hidden events. T distributes over renaming by lifting the renaming to the split events. Finally T distributes over the operands of a timeout, replaces the timeout by external choice and introduces a fresh timeout event labelled $to\_i \in I$ for each timeout communicated over the channels sh and eh responsible for hidden events (recall the motivation for the timeout operator to express the abstraction of one initial event in an external choice; see, for example, [Ros05]).

The alphabets of P and $T(P)$ are disjoint, since

$$\Sigma_{T(P)} \subseteq \{\!|\, s, e, sh, eh \,|\!\}\,.$$

To illustrate T, Figure 4.1 shows the stepwise transformation of the example process given in equation (2.1) (p. 22). First, the hiding operator is transformed, second, the parallel composition. T distributes over sequential

$$
\begin{aligned}
&T((a \to SKIP \mid_{\{a\}}\mid (b \to SKIP \,;\, a \to SKIP)) \setminus \{b\}) \\
&= \hspace{4cm} T(P \setminus A) \\
&T(a \to SKIP \mid_{\{a\}}\mid (b \to SKIP \,;\, a \to SKIP))[s.b \leftarrow sh.b, e.b \leftarrow eh.b] \\
&= \hspace{4cm} T(P \mid_A\mid Q) \\
&(T(a \to SKIP) \mid_{\{s.a,e.a\}}\mid T(b \to SKIP \,;\, a \to SKIP)) \\
&\hspace{4cm} [s.b \leftarrow sh.b, e.b \leftarrow eh.b] \\
&= \hspace{4cm} T(P \,;\, Q) \\
&(T(a \to SKIP) \mid_{\{s.a,e.a\}}\mid (T(b \to SKIP) \,;\, T(a \to SKIP))) \\
&\hspace{4cm} [s.b \leftarrow sh.b, e.b \leftarrow eh.b] \\
&= \hspace{4cm} T(x \to P) \\
&(s.a \to e.a \to T(SKIP) \mid_{\{s.a,e.a\}}\mid (s.b \to e.b \to T(SKIP) \\
&\hspace{2cm} ;\, s.a \to e.a \to T(SKIP)))[s.b \leftarrow sh.b, e.b \leftarrow eh.b] \\
&= \hspace{4cm} T(SKIP) \\
&(s.a \to e.a \to SKIP \mid_{\{s.a,e.a\}}\mid (s.b \to e.b \to SKIP \,;\, s.a \to e.a \to SKIP)) \\
&\hspace{4cm} [s.b \leftarrow sh.b, e.b \leftarrow eh.b]
\end{aligned}
$$

Figure 4.1.: Example transformation.

composition in the third step. The next step deals with prefixing and perform the splitting of a and b. Finally, $SKIP$ is mapped to $SKIP$. The resulting process can simplified to

$$sh.b \to eh.b \to s.a \to e.a \to SKIP$$

using laws 2.4 and 2.11 and applying the renaming.

While concurrency cannot be distinguished from choice in the interleaved semantic models $\mathcal{T}$, $\mathcal{F}$ and $\mathcal{FD}$, the transformation T allows them to be distinguished because start and end events of two events x and y may interleave only if x and y are concurrent in P. There is, for example, no such interleaving of start and end events in the example process shown above.

4.2. Assembling the System

The 'control process' to be placed in parallel with a transformed process to record possible simultaneity is defined in terms of a parameter X denoting a bag; bag union is denoted $\uplus$, bag difference $\uplus$, and bag comprehension is written $[\![x_0, \ldots, x_n]\!]$. Initially the bag is empty. Let *term* be a fresh event modeling the possibility to synchronize before successful termination. The

4.2 Assembling the System

control process is defined as follows.

$$\begin{aligned}
C(X) = \quad & s?x \to C(X \uplus [\![x]\!]) \\
\Box \ & sh?x \to C(X \uplus [\![x]\!]) \\
\Box \ & e?x \to C(X \uplus [\![x]\!]) \\
\Box \ & eh?x \to C(X \uplus [\![x]\!]) \\
\Box \ & term \to SKIP
\end{aligned} \tag{4.1}$$

As outlined in the previous section, the process $C(X)$ is to be put in parallel with the transformed process. We define $S_{Con} = \{\!|\, s, sh, e, eh, term\, |\!\}$ to be the alphabet on which the transformed process $T(P)$ and the controller synchronize. Now because $term \in S_{Con}$ but $term \notin \Sigma_{T(P)}$, the controller C cannot terminate while $T(P)$ is still active. Since we aim at establishing traces-equality, the parallel composition must be able to terminate if P terminates successfully. Thus, because of the Ω semantics and distributed termination of parallel composition, $T(P)$ is sequentially composed with the process $term \to SKIP$ in the following construction. The construction starts by transforming an input process P to $T(P)$ and combining the result with the control process (4.1) to achieve the result $Con(P)$ (standing for *controlled*).

$$Con(P) = (T(P)\,;\,term \to SKIP) \mid_{S_{Con}} \mid C([\![\,]\!]) \tag{4.2}$$

The events $s.x$ are renamed to x, and the events in

$$H = \{\!|\, sh, e, eh, term\, |\!\}$$

are hidden using Hr (standing for *hidden* and *renamed*)

$$Hr(P) = P \setminus H\ [s.x \leftarrow x \mid x \in \Sigma_P] \tag{4.3}$$

resulting in a process

$$Ext(P) = Hr(Con(P)) \tag{4.4}$$

(the *extension* of P) that we think of as simulating P but enabling it to benefit from true concurrency.

Using the construction Con given above, possible concurrency is captured by the bag X maintained by the controller process $C(X)$. Whenever the size of the bag exceeds one, it holds the names of events that are performed concurrently at that point.

To ensure that a process is not 'corrupted' by Ext we must show that it is a fixed point of Ext in the traces semantics:

Theorem 1 *For each process P of the form given above,*
$$P \equiv_T Ext(P).$$

The intuition is that Ext splits each event in its argument, relabels the start event back to the original and hides the end event and does so whilst faithfully translating the process combinators. A proof by structural induction is given in Appendix A.1, using the results of the next section, which enforce the intuition and enable the proof to proceed uniformly.

Equality (in the traces model) with the original process is established by renaming the start events of the split events back to their original names and hiding the end events and all those events corresponding to internal actions ($\{\!| \, sh, eh \, |\!\}$). The exposition of internal transitions disallows equality in the stable failures (and in the failures-divergences) model, because in general

$$(P \mathrel{\Box} Q) \setminus A \neq P \setminus A \mathrel{\Box} Q \setminus A$$

in these models, but

$$(P \mathrel{\Box} Q) \setminus A \equiv_T P \setminus A \mathrel{\Box} Q \setminus A.$$

For example, Ext preserves the traces but not the failures of

$$P = (a \rightarrow STOP \setminus \{a\}) \mathrel{\Box} b \rightarrow STOP. \tag{4.5}$$

By algebraic reasoning we obtain $P = b \rightarrow STOP$ (using laws 2.10 and 2.3), while

$$Ext(P) = (b \rightarrow STOP) \mathrel{\sqcap} STOP. \tag{4.6}$$

The proof is shown in Appendix A.2. Now

$$traces(P) = \{\langle\rangle, \langle b \rangle\} \quad \text{and} \quad traces(Ext(P)) = \{\langle\rangle, \langle b \rangle\}$$

but

$$(\langle\rangle, \Sigma) \notin failures(P) \quad \text{while} \quad (\langle\rangle, \Sigma) \in failures(Ext(P)).$$

Unfortunately, there is no construction F using parallel composition, hiding and renaming such that $F(T(P \square Q)) = P \square Q$. However, there are constructions using the interrupt operator to transform (and simulate) the external choice operator as we show in Chapter 5.

The information stored in the bag held by C can be exploited in various ways. One obvious way is to introduce guards $g_0, \ldots, g_3$ as follows.

$$\begin{aligned} C_0(X) = \quad & g_0(X) \ \& \ s?x \rightarrow C_0(X \uplus [\![x]\!]) \\ \square \ & g_1(X) \ \& \ sh?x \rightarrow C_0(X \uplus [\![x]\!]) \\ \square \ & g_2(X) \ \& \ e?x \rightarrow C_0(X \uplus [\![x]\!]) \\ \square \ & g_3(X) \ \& \ eh?x \rightarrow C_0(X \uplus [\![x]\!]) \\ \square \ & term \rightarrow SKIP \end{aligned}$$

Since the guards restrict the behavior of C_0 relative to C, we have $C \sqsubseteq_\mathcal{T} C_0$. Modifying the extension Ext of P to use C_0 yields

$$Ext_0(P) = Hr((T(P); term \rightarrow SKIP)\,|_{S_{Con}}|\,C_0([\![\,]\!]))\,.$$

By construction of C_0 and Theorem 1 we have

$$P \sqsubseteq_\mathcal{T} Ext_0(P)\,.$$

In the case that checking with FDR fails to establish the refinement

$$Ext_0(P) \sqsubseteq_\mathcal{T} P\,,$$

it provides a counterexample leading to a state violating g_i. Examples exploiting the controller process to obtain concurrency information of processes are shown in Section 4.4.

4.3. Properties

The Ext construction presented in the previous section splits the events making duration of actions explicit. It uses a control process to record start and end of actions and uses hiding and renaming to reestablish the alphabet of the original process. In this section, we present the basic properties of the construction that allow us to prove that Ext preserves the traces semantics of its argument.

Throughout this thesis, t, u are sequences, the concatenation of sequences t and u is written $t \frown u$, $t \restriction X$ restricts t to the elements that are contained in

X and $\#t$ denotes the length of the sequence t. Containment of an element x in a sequence t is written x in t. In the following, we use the abbreviations $\overline{s} \in \{s, sh\}$ and $\overline{e} \in \{e, eh\}$ to denote visible or hidden start and end events respectively. Furthermore, the functions

$$\overline{s}_{of} : \{e, eh\} \to \{s, sh\} \quad \text{and} \quad \overline{e}_{of} : \{s, sh\} \to \{e, eh\}$$

defined by $\overline{s}_{of}(e) = s$ and $\overline{s}_{of}(eh) = eh$ and $\overline{e}_{of}(s) = e$ and $\overline{e}_{of}(sh) = eh$ are used to obtain the corresponding $\overline{s}$ (or $\overline{e}$) channel for a given $\overline{e}$ (or $\overline{s}$) channel. The results of this section are used in proving Theorem 1. The following propositions hold by construction of T.

First observe the following relations between $\overline{s}$ and $\overline{e}$ events.

Proposition 1 (*s-e-precedence*) *Each instance of an event $\overline{e}.x : \Sigma_{T(P)}$ is preceded by its corresponding instance $\overline{s}.x : \Sigma_{T(P)}$:*

$$\forall t \frown \langle \overline{e}.x \rangle : traces(T(P)) \cdot \#(t \restriction \{\overline{s}_{of}(\overline{e}).x\}) > \#(t \restriction \{\overline{e}.x\}).$$

Proposition 2 (*e-non-refusability*) *After event $\overline{s}.x$ has occurred in $T(P)$, no event $\overline{e}_{of}(\overline{s}).x$ can be refused until $\overline{e}_{of}(\overline{s}).x$ has occurred:*

$$\forall (t \frown \langle \overline{s}.x \rangle \frown u, R) : failures(T(P)) \cdot \overline{e}_{of}(\overline{s}).x \text{ iń } u \Rightarrow \overline{e}_{of}(\overline{s}).x \notin R.$$

Traces are normally used to follow the evolution of a process using the 'after' operator. Here we instead use failures, so that instances of events are identified uniquely; as a result the resolution of nondeterministic choices can be observed directly, without introducing a τ operator. For example, evolution of the process $(a \to STOP \sqcap b \to STOP)$ to $a \to STOP$ is recorded as evolution from

$$\{(\langle\rangle, \{\}), (\langle\rangle, \{a\}), (\langle\rangle, \{b\})\} \quad \text{to} \quad \{(\langle\rangle, \{\}), (\langle\rangle, \{b\})\}.$$

Now instances of two events x and y are said to be possibly *conflicting* in P if they are exclusive at some point (determining the instance) of P's evolution. For example, the events a and b are conflicting in the initial state of

$$a \to STOP \square b \to STOP.$$

4.3 Properties

The opposite is conflict freedom: x and y are said to be *conflict-free* at some point of P's evolution if they are not exclusive. The following weak definition of conflict freedom captures this intuition.

Definition 1 (*Conflict freedom*)   Events x and y of P are conflict-free at the point determined by $(t, R) : failures(P)$ in P if

$$\forall (t \frown \langle x \rangle, R') : failures(P) \cdot y \notin R \Rightarrow y \notin R'.$$

T is constructed such that the set of $\overline{s}$ events that can be refused at some point is guaranteed not to grow if an $\overline{e}$ event is performed. This property is formalized by the following proposition.

Proposition 3 (*s-e-conflict freedom*)   The $\overline{s}$ and $\overline{e}$ events are conflict-free throughout $T(P)$:

$$\forall (t, R), (t \frown \langle \overline{e}.x \rangle, R') : failures(T(P)) \cdot (R' \cap \{\!|\, s, sh \,|\!\}) \subseteq R.$$

The term *conflict* is also used informally throughout this thesis, having the operational semantics of CSP in mind: the transitions $x, y \in \Sigma \cup \{\checkmark, \tau\}$, leading from P to the states P_x, P_y, $P_x \neq P_y$ respectively, are conflicting in P if x cannot fire in P_y or y cannot fire in P_x. This deliberately includes the case $x = y$, because events can be auto-conflicting (if they lead to different states). This also extends to τ transitions, because conflicts between those are also possible (as, e.g., in $(a \rightarrow P \,\square\, b \rightarrow Q) \setminus \{a, b\}$).

If two events can be performed simultaneously at some point in time we say that they are possibly *concurrent*. Note that events may be possibly conflicting and possibly concurrent at the same time (such a process is discussed in Section 4.4.4, for example). Possible concurrency can be detected by exploiting the bag X maintained by the controller process as explained further down.

Definition 2 (*Possible concurrency*)   Let $\Sigma_x = \Sigma \setminus \{e.x, eh.x\}$. The set of all possibly concurrent events of P is defined:

$$conc(P) = \{(x, y) \mid \exists\, t \frown \langle \overline{s}.x \rangle \frown u \frown \langle \overline{e}_{of}(\overline{s}).x \rangle : traces(T(P)), u : (\Sigma_x)^* \cdot$$
$$\overline{s}.y \text{ in } u \,\vee\, \overline{e}.y \text{ in } u \}.$$

Then event $y : \Sigma_P$ is said to be possibly concurrent with event $x : \Sigma_P$ in P if and only if $(x, y) \in conc(P)$.

This definition ensures that a single event is not auto-concurrent. For example,
$$conc(a \rightarrow STOP) = \emptyset,$$
but
$$conc((a \rightarrow STOP) \mathbin{|_\emptyset|} (a \rightarrow STOP)) = \{(a, a)\}.$$

To expose the concurrency information recorded by the controller C we enhance the construction presented so far. We introduce a new channel
$$co : \operatorname{bag} \Sigma_P$$
to communicate the recorded concurrency information and modify the processes C, Con and Ext as follows.

$$\begin{aligned}
C_1(X) = {}& co.X \rightarrow (s?x \rightarrow C_1(X \uplus [\![x]\!]) \\
& \square\ sh?x \rightarrow C_1(X \uplus [\![x]\!]) \\
& \square\ e?x \rightarrow C_1(X \uplus [\![x]\!]) \\
& \square\ eh?x \rightarrow C_1(X \uplus [\![x]\!]) \\
& \square\ term \rightarrow SKIP) \\
Con_1(P) = {}& (T(P); term \rightarrow SKIP) \mathbin{|_{S_{Con}}|} C_1([\![\,]\!]) \\
Ext_1(P) = {}& Hr(Con_1(P))
\end{aligned}$$

We observe that: (a) hiding of co does not cause divergence because there are no adjacent co events in any trace of $Ext_1(P)$; and (b) co is not in conflict with any event in C_1, so hiding of co does not introduce nondeterminism and consequently changes neither the failures of $Ext_1(P)$ nor its traces.

Hence
$$C_1(X) \setminus \{\!|\, co\, |\!\} = C(X)$$
and
$$Ext_1(P) \setminus \{\!|\, co\, |\!\} = Ext(P).$$

The controller process C never refuses any events offered by $T(P)$ thus, again, the following proposition holds by construction of Con.

4.3 Properties

Proposition 4 *The controller process C records the concurrent events of P:*

$$\forall (x,y) : conc(P), \exists t \frown \langle co.b \rangle : traces(Con_1(P)) \cdot x \text{ in } b \wedge y \text{ in } b.$$

The controller C is designed to record concurrency information but not change the behavior of the transformed process $T(P)$. This is captured formally by the following lemma:

Lemma 1   *For any process P as above,*

$$Ext(P) \ = \ Hr(T(P)).$$

Proof 1 *The proof follows by 'reduction of parallel composition'. By definition of parallel composition, $P \mid_{\Sigma_Q} \mid Q = P$ if Q never refuses an event $x : \Sigma_Q$.*

$Ext(P)$

$=$ \hfill *definition of Ext*

$Hr(Con(P))$

$=$ \hfill *definition of Con*

$Hr((T(P); term \to SKIP) \mid_{S_{Con}} \mid C(\llbracket \rrbracket))$

$=$ \hfill *reduction of parallel composition: $C(\llbracket \rrbracket)$ never refuses $x : S_{Con}$*

$Hr(T(P); term \to SKIP)$.

$=$ \hfill *term $\in H$*

$Hr(T(P))$.

$\square$

The exposition of internal transitions is important from a practical point of view because it allows the assignment of user-defined functions to computations that are (although present) not observable from outside the computing system, enabling the determination of events concurrent with those internal transitions. On the theoretical side, this decision restricts equality of the source process P with its extended version $Ext(P)$ to the traces model because hiding does not distribute over external choice if initial events are affected. Neither does hiding distribute over parallel composition if the hidden alphabet intersects with the synchronization set. The following lemma shows that parallel e events can safely be removed from the synchronization sets in T so that the two sets no longer intersect, and distributivity of hiding over parallel composition holds in T.

Lemma 2 *Writing $A' = \{s.x, e.x \mid x \in A\}$ and $A'' = \{s.x \mid x \in A\}$,*

$$Hr(T(P) \mid_{A'} \mid T(Q)) = Hr(T(P) \mid_{A''} \mid T(Q)).$$

Proof 2 *The proof follows by s-e-precedence (1), e-non-refusability (2) and s-e-conflict-freedom (3).*

First, the equality holds trivially if $A = \emptyset$; thus assume $A \neq \emptyset$. By (1), any $e.x$ event is preceded by (a not necessarily adjacent) $s.x$ event; thus we focus on s events. Since the result does not affect $x \notin A$, we can further restrict attention to $s.x, x : A$. Thus assume $s.x, x : A$ have occurred on both sides. By definition of T, neither side can refuse $s.y, (x, y) \in conc(P \mid_A Q)$. So assume both sides have performed $t : \{s.x \mid x \in A\}^*$. By proposition 2, neither side can refuse any of $e.x, s.x \in t$, whilst by proposition 1, any $e.x, s.x$ in t is refused. Furthermore, by proposition 3, no $e.x$ event conflicts with any of the subsequent s events. Thus, synchronizing on $e.x, x : A$ does not affect subsequent s events. □

Finiteness of P is not required in the proof. One might suspect that hiding of e events might introduce divergence, but this could happen only if there were unbounded sequences of $\overline{e}$ events. Such sequences could be introduced by a cycle of $\overline{e}$ events but the construction of T prevents cycles of $\overline{e}$ events. Furthermore, processes such as $\mu P \bullet (x \to SKIP \mid_\emptyset \mid P)$, although infinite state, cannot perform unbounded sequences of $\overline{e}$ events either. The s-e-precedence property asserts that each infinite sequence of $\overline{e}$ events must be preceded by an infinite sequence of $\overline{s}$ events. But unbounded sequences of $\overline{s}$ events would prevent the occurrence of any $\overline{e}$ event; so whenever $\overline{e}$ events are observable there cannot have been unbounded sequences of $\overline{s}$ events in $T(P)$; so divergence cannot occur.

4.4. Examples

In this section, we apply our approach to the following examples: (a) the example used to motivate [KP95], illustrating the difference between concurrency and conflict; (b) a one-place buffer from [GRA05]; (c) a modification of the dining philosophers from [GRA05]; and (d) van Glabbeek's owl taken from [vGV97]. Due to technical limitations of ProB and FDR, the typing and naming scheme used in the accompanying CSP_M scripts differ slightly from the models presented here. For example, the controller maintains a list instead of a bag because CSP_M has no support for bags built-in. The example scripts are shown in Appendix B.

4.4.1. Choice versus Concurrency

Consider the processes

$$P = a \to b \to STOP \square b \to a \to STOP$$
$$Q = a \to STOP \;|_\emptyset|\; b \to STOP.$$

Evidently $P = Q$, although the latter offers concurrency of a and b not allowed by the former. That is revealed using our technique as follows.

By the definition of T,

$$T(P) = s.a \to e.a \to s.b \to e.b \to STOP \square s.b \to e.b \to s.a \to e.a \to STOP$$
$$T(Q) = s.a \to e.a \to STOP \;|_\emptyset|\; s.b \to e.b \to STOP.$$

To use FDR we define

$$SPEC = \square\, x : \{[\![\,]\!], [\![a]\!], [\![b]\!]\} \bullet co.x \to SPEC.$$

Now $Ext(P) = P$ and $Ext(Q) = Q$ but using Ext_1 (see the explanation of definition 2)
$$SPEC \sqsubseteq_T Ext_1(P) \setminus \{a,b\}$$
while
$$SPEC \not\sqsubseteq_T Ext_1(Q) \setminus \{a,b\}.$$

The trace generated by FDR leading to the violation of the second refinement relation, namely
$$\langle co.[\![\,]\!], co.[\![b]\!], co.[\![a,b]\!]\rangle,$$

reveals that the events a and b may occur simultaneously in Q but not in P.

The same result can be obtained using the LTL model checking capabilities of ProB. We introduce the fresh event $conc\_a\_b$ and define

$$F(P) = P[co.[\![a,b]\!] \leftarrow conc\_a\_b]$$

to check if

$$\phi = \text{G not } [conc\_a\_b]$$

holds on $F(\mathit{Ext}_1(P))$ or $F(\mathit{Ext}_1(Q))$. Expectedly ProB shows

$$F(\mathit{Ext}_1(P)) \models \phi$$
$$F(\mathit{Ext}_1(Q)) \not\models \phi.$$

The CSP_M script of this example is presented in Appendix B.1.

4.4.2. One-place Buffer

A specification of a one-place buffer is

$$COPY \;=\; \mathit{left}?x \to \mathit{right}!x \to COPY \,.$$

The implementation ($SYSTEM$) presented in [GRA05] is proved to be equivalent (in the failures-divergences model) to that specification. Since it uses parallel composition, it is of interest to check whether or not there are actually any concurrent events in the implementation; there might be concurrent τ events at least. There are no concurrent events in the implementation if the bag never grows beyond size one. This property can be built into the controller by modifying it as follows.

$$\begin{aligned}
C_2(X) = size(X) < 2 \;\&\; (s?x &\to C_2(X \uplus [\![x]\!]) \\
\square \; sh?x &\to C_2(X \uplus [\![x]\!]) \\
\square \; e?x &\to C_2(X \cup [\![x]\!]) \\
\square \; eh?x &\to C_2(X \cup [\![x]\!]) \\
\square \; term &\to SKIP)
\end{aligned}$$

Here, $size(X)$ denotes the sum of the frequencies of all elements in the bag X

$$\sum_{x \in \text{dom } X} X\#x \,.$$

4.4 Examples

Checking $Hr((T(SYSTEM)\,;\,term \to SKIP) \,|_{S_{Con}}|\, C_2(\llbracket\,\rrbracket)) =_\mathcal{T} COPY$ with FDR proves that there are no concurrent events in the implementation.

The CSP$_M$ script of this example is presented in Appendix B.2.

4.4.3. Dining Philosophers

The well-known example of the dining philosophers reveals a disadvantage of our approach: poor performance within FDR. Indeed the size of the transition system of the controller grows rapidly. In this example, N is the number of philosophers. The number of events available is $3N + 2N^2$. The set of all lists containing event labels and with maximum length n has $\sum_{i=0}^{n}(3N + 2N^2)^i$ elements, which is 20,440 for $N = 3$ and $n = 3$ or 551,881 for $N = 3$ and $n = 4$. Reducing these sets to create specifications like the one presented in the first example does not solve this problem. The set of all lists with maximum length n and at most one renamed *eat* event in it contains 19,756 elements for $N = 3$ and $n = 3$ and 517,420 in the case of $N = 3$ and $n = 4$. So checking the assertion that the *eat* event never occurs concurrently with another *eat* event with $N = 3$ takes about 90 minutes.

The CSP$_M$ script of this example is presented in Appendix B.3.

4.4.4. Van Glabbeek's Owl

In [vGV97], van Glabbeek and Vaandrager give examples of processes that show different behavior when their events are split into n events compared to when their events are split into $n + 1$ events. This might come as a surprise or even sound like a contradiction to the claim made in this chapter that splitting of events does not corrupt the semantics of a process. In fact, it is not a contradiction but just another wording of our claim and relates to the *possibility* of concurrency and conflict at the same time. The splitting of the events gives us more information about the internal structure of a process revealing phenomena such as conflict and concurrency.

The *owl* example presents the two Event Structures E and F shown in Figure 4.2 (see, e.g., [Win86] for an introduction to Event Structures). The dotted lines denote conflict and the solid lines stand for causality. Any other events may be performed concurrently. Thus, both owls model two parallel processes starting with a or b respectively and then evolving as specified by

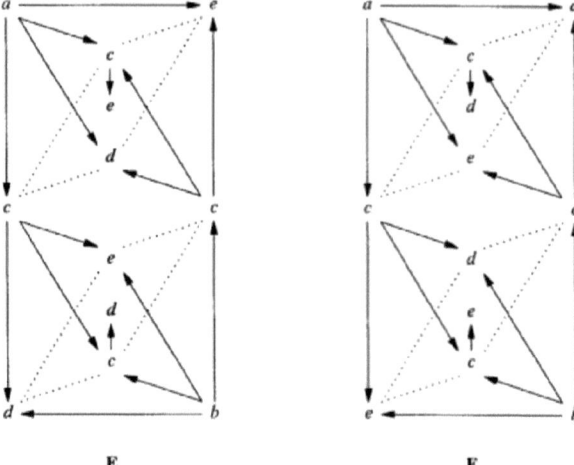

Figure 4.2.: Two indistinguishable Event Structures (taken from [vGV97]).

causality and conflict. The conflicting events in both owls are identical:

$$Conf = \{(c,c),(c,d),(c,e),(d,e)\}.$$

F can be obtained from E by exchanging the event labels d and e. Both Event Structures give rise to the same labeled transition system shown in Figure 4.3. These Event Structures can be translated into CSP by numbering the events from top left to bottom right (zero to eleven) and then assembling processes according to the conflict and causality relation expressed by the Event Structure. Processes equivalent to E and F are then obtained by renaming the events accordingly. The corresponding CSP_M script is shown in Appendix B.4.

The CSP_M encodings OWL_E and OWL_F of the owls are trace equivalent and so are their transformed versions (as observed by Glabbeek and Vaandrager). The use of FDR reveals the following pairs of possibly concurrent events for both owls.

$$Conc = \{(a,b),(a,c),(b,c),(c,c),(c,d),(c,e),(d,e)\}$$

Now, interestingly, $Conf \subseteq Conc$ for both owls.

However, inserting another event between the start and end events in the transformed versions, reveals a difference of the two owls. Analogously to

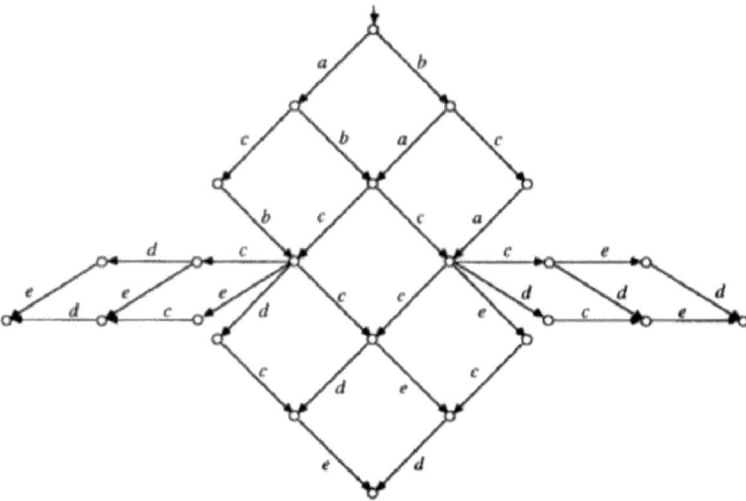

Figure 4.3.: Labeled transition system of owls E and F (taken from [vGV97]).

propositions 2 and 3 this is a safe operation (in the sense that it does not alter the processes' semantics in an irreversible way). Hiding this additional event again reestablishes the behaviors of the split owls. The additional event reveals how conflict is resolved in situations where conflict and concurrency overlap. Verifying the owl example with FDR proves the results presented by Glabbeek and Vaandrager.

The learning of this example is that there is even more information hidden in a process than revealed by T (but which can be extracted by repeated splitting, for example).

4.5. Restricting T

As we have shown in the preceding sections, the transformation T is suitable for simulating truly concurrent processes in the standard interleaving semantics of CSP. T is designed to fulfill two main purposes. First, we are striving for a method to enable static computation of possibly concurrent events. Second, we aim to use CSP for the construction of truly concurrent systems aided by a runtime coordination environment formally based on T.

While T satisfies the first purpose, it fails to satisfy the second. It is suitable for computing sets of possibly concurrent events, but it is not suitable to serve as a semantic model of a CSP-based coordination environment because it preserves only the traces (and divergences) of its input processes but not their failures.

It is, for example, not a satisfying situation proving the process

$$P = (a \rightarrow SKIP) \,\square\, ((b \rightarrow STOP) \setminus \{b\}) \qquad (4.7)$$

deadlock free and then encountering deadlock when simulating $Ext(P)$ (compare with process P, equation 4.5 on page 48) to coordinate a truly concurrent system, for example. Deadlock occurs, if the hidden b event internally resolves the external choice in its favor (because T exposes the start of the internal transition introduced by the hiding of b). This behavior violates law 2.3 and is clearly undesirable. The problem here is that hiding of initial events does not distribute over external choice in the failures-divergences semantics.

As shown in the preceding sections, the construction

$$Ext(P) = Hr(Con(T(P)))$$

places the transformed process ($T(P)$) into parallel with a control process ($C(\llbracket \rrbracket)$) recording all of its events without changing its behavior and uses hiding and renaming ($Hr(P)$) to reestablish equality of alphabets ($\Sigma_P = \Sigma_{Ext(P)}$). We think of $Ext(P)$ as simulating P but enabling it to benefit from true concurrency and also (or maybe even more importantly) to exhibit concurrency information of P. The intuition is that Ext splits each event in its argument, relabels the start event back to the original, hides the end event and does so whilst faithfully translating the process combinators. Lemma 1 allows us to eliminate the controller process without changing the semantics of Ext. Thus, in the following we use $Hr(T(P))$ instead of $Ext(P)$. The construct $Hr(T(P))$ is what we understand as the formal model of a coordination environment: T simulates the truly concurrent version of P but only the starting points of non-hidden events are available on the external interface of the system.

Theorem 1 states $Ext(P) =_\mathcal{T} P$ and hence also $Hr(T(P)) =_\mathcal{T} P$. Its proof (see Appendix A.1) proceeds by induction on the construction of P. Two cases are of special interest: External choice and timeout because these are the cases that do not preserve failures but only traces. Both cases use distributivity of hiding over external choice which is only true in the traces model. As a consequence, we can make T a failures preserving transformation by restricting its domain to processes that do not introduce internal transitions that conflict with visible events.

4.5 Restricting T

The two subsets of CSP being presented in the following satisfy

$$Hr(T(P)) = P$$

for all processes P of these subsets. Interestingly, all processes shown in Section 4.4 fall into one of these subsets.

4.5.1. Prohibiting Internal Choice, Hiding and Timeout

As outlined above, $Hr(T(P))$ preserves the failures of any process P that does not combine external with internal influences. Thus, prohibiting nondeterminism (caused by internal transitions) yields a suitable subset of CSP.

Theorem 2 *Every process P of the syntax*

$$SKIP \mid STOP \mid (x:X \to P(x)) \mid P\,;Q \mid P \,\square\, Q \mid P \mid_A\mid Q \mid P[M]$$

is a fixed point of $Hr \circ T$.

The proof of this theorem is shown in Appendix A.3. Like Theorem 1, it proceeds by induction on P.

Although this subset excludes the operators that are designed to model nondeterminism (internal choice, hiding and timeout), processes in this subset are not necessarily deterministic. For example the process

$$P = a \to STOP \,\square\, a \to SKIP$$

is a nondeterministic process because it offers only a for external synchronization and whether P evolves to $STOP$ or to $SKIP$ after performing a is decided nondeterministically (according to law 2.8). Such processes can also be introduced by renaming, for example. However, this kind of nondeterminism is not a problem because T does not introduce internal transitions in this situation.

We also argue that the timeout operator must be excluded because it combines external and internal influences. By allowing $SKIP$ and external choice in this subset, we also implicitly allow the timeout operator (although in very limited cases). This is due to the law $SKIP$-resolve [Ros05, p.145]

$$P \,\square\, SKIP = P \triangleright SKIP \qquad (4.8)$$

Fortunately, this particular case does not suffer from the problem outlined above because no internal transition is exposed in this case.

$Hr(T(P \square SKIP))$

$= \qquad T(Q \square R)$

$Hr(T(P) \square T(SKIP))$

$= \qquad T(SKIP)$

$Hr(T(P) \square SKIP)$

$=$ neutrality of $SKIP$ w.r.t. hiding and renaming

$Hr(T(P)) \square SKIP$

$=$ induction hypothesis

$P \square SKIP$

The subset presented in this section is of particular practical relevance because it relies on external influences only (besides termination). Subsets like this are frequently found in literature in the contexts of other CSP-based approaches to coordination (as discussed in Section 9.1.2). This subset offers coordination facilities similar to those implemented by the occam language [Bar92].

Note that both processes P and Q of the example presented in Section 4.4.1 fall into this subset of CSP. Neither P nor Q contains τ transitions (whose exposition could destroy failures). Hence, not only

$$Ext(P) \equiv_T P \qquad \text{and} \qquad Ext(Q) \equiv_T Q$$

hold but also

$$Ext(P) = P \qquad \text{and} \qquad Ext(Q) = Q \ .$$

The examples presented in sections 4.4.3 and 4.4.4 fall into this subset as well.

4.5.2. Prohibiting External Choice and Timeout

Like the exclusion of internal choice, hiding and timeout, prohibiting external choice and timeout also yields a subset of CSP that is transformed in a failures-preserving way by T. This is shown by the following theorem.

Theorem 3 *Every process P of the syntax*

$$SKIP \mid STOP \mid (x\colon X \to P(x)) \mid P\,;Q \mid P \mid_A\mid Q \mid P \setminus A \mid P \sqcap Q \mid P[M]$$

is a fixed point of $Hr \circ T$.

Proof 3 *The proof immediately follows from the proof of Theorem 1 by dropping the cases External Choice and Timeout.*

The interesting point here is that prefix choice is included even though it is equivalent to replicated external choice:

$$x : X \to P(x) = \Box\, x : X \bullet x \to P(x)\,.$$

The point is that this subset excludes the pathological case presented in equation 4.7. It is impossible to hide a subset of the initial events (of the replicated external choice) in a manner that would not cause the choice to be resolved. Hence, exposing that transition in T preserves this behavior.

This subset is also of great practical relevance because it still allows us to model systems offering conflicting (alternative) events for external synchronization, while resolving nondeterministic choices internally. It even allows visible and hidden events to be conflicting as, e. g., in

$$(x : \{a, b\} \to SKIP) \setminus \{b\}\,.$$

However, this subset prevents T from generating constructs that illegally resolve choices.

The processes $SYSTEM$ and $COPY$ of the example presented in Section 4.4.2 fall into this subset of CSP. Thus, their transformed versions are failures-divergences equivalent.

4.6. Discussion

In this chapter, we have presented the syntactical transformation T that makes durations of events and internal transitions explicit by splitting events and relabeling them. The construction $Ext(P)$ simulates the behavior of P (in the traces semantics) while allowing us to determine possibly concurrent events. The controller C (used in Ext)) synchronizes with the transformed process. It maintains a bag X whose contents represent the events and internal transitions of the original process that are possibly concurrent after the trace that has lead to the current state. Thus it can be used in various ways to query concurrency information of a process, as shown in Section 4.4. In Section 4.4.1, the controller process C_1 of proposition 4 is used to emit the recorded concurrency information using a fresh channel. That example has also demonstrated application of our approach with ProB. The concurrency information can also be exploited using guards. A very simple application of this is shown in the one-place-buffer example (Section 4.4.2). Finally, we have shown two subsets of CSP which *Ext* simulates in their failures-divergences semantics.

The language considered here overlooks several useful derived operators, like *chaining*, *interleaving*, and *linked parallel* (a generalization of chaining). The reason is simplicity of presentation. Recall that interleaving is the special case of parallel composition without synchronization. Hence it is included by $T(P \mathbin{|_\emptyset|} Q)$. However, interleaving is deliberately excluded to preserve the possibility to handle it as a 'de-parallelizing' operator in future extensions of the work presented here.

Chaining (respectively linked parallel) is excluded because it can be rebuild using the supported operators renaming and parallel composition. The timeout operator, by contrast, is included even if it can be expressed as a combination of internal and external choice because it is also concerned with the abstraction of time (which is an important concern for systems engineering). It is noteworthy, that there are more elaborately defined subsets including the timeout operator. For example, the subset presented in Section 4.5.1 could be extended with the timeout operator given that for every timeout $P \triangleright Q$ the left-hand process P is free of timeouts. Timeouts in P would be exposed by T and illegally resolve the timeout in favor of P.

The *interrupt* operator is also not supported by T. This operator is especially interesting, because the interpretation of an event heavily influences its transformation by T. The issue is whether or not a single event x that is split into two events ($s.x$ and $e.x$) may be aborted. If a single event can be aborted, the event can no longer be interpreted as an action or operation that transforms some state into a well-defined successor state. Furthermore, it would violate the e-non-refusability property (2). If a single event cannot be aborted, the transformed interrupt must take care of unfinished events, which renders the transformation reasonably complicated. A transformation involving the after operator, for example, would violate our ultimate goal to support standard CSP tools such as FDR and ProB (which no dot support the after operator). However, the interrupt operator is included in the extended transformation presented in Chapter 5.

The following two questions were frequently posed after presentations involving the material presented here.

> Why can't concurrent events be deduced by ordering in traces?

> Why hide end and not start of transformed events?

4.6 Discussion

The answer to the first question is that interleaving semantics simply does not distinguish choice from concurrency. The answer to the second question is that only hiding of the end events allows us to observe conflict. Hiding the start events instead introduces nondeterminism as shown by the following example. Let $Hr'(P) = P \setminus \{|s|\}[e.x \leftarrow x]$.

$$Hr'(T(a \to STOP \square b \to STOP))$$
$= \qquad\qquad\qquad\qquad\qquad\qquad\qquad\qquad\qquad\qquad\qquad\qquad T(P \square Q)$
$$Hr'(T(a \to STOP) \square T(b \to STOP))$$
$= \qquad\qquad\qquad\qquad\qquad\qquad\qquad\qquad\qquad\qquad\qquad\qquad T(a \to P)$
$$Hr'(s.a \to e.a \to STOP \square s.b. \to e.b \to STOP)$$
$= \qquad\qquad\qquad\qquad\qquad\qquad\qquad\qquad\qquad\qquad\qquad \text{Definition of } Hr'$
$$(s.a \to e.a \to STOP \square s.b. \to e.b \to STOP) \setminus \{|s|\}[e.x \leftarrow x]$$
$= \qquad\qquad\qquad \text{Introduction of nondeterminism by hiding of initial events}$
$$(e.a \to STOP \sqcap e.b \to STOP)[e.x \leftarrow x]$$
$= \qquad\qquad\qquad\qquad\qquad\qquad\qquad\qquad\qquad\qquad\qquad\qquad \text{Renaming}$
$$a \to STOP \sqcap b \to STOP$$

To put it differently, the transformation T is designed in such a way that it reveals some information inherent to a process. This particular information (which is not captured by the standard interleaving semantics of CSP) is obtained by splitting events and observing their start events.

Perhaps the most important aspect of our approach is that it allows reuse of existing CSP tools such as FDR [Ros94], ProB [LF08] and the CSP-Prover [IR05], because it exploits semantics of CSP already implemented by those tools.

The contents of sections 4.1 to 4.4.3 is published in [KS10a] and also available as a technical report [KS10b].

5 Conflict, Internal Actions and $\mathcal{FD}$ Preservation

In the previous chapter we have shown how concurrency and conflicts inherent to a process can be revealed in the standard interleaving semantics of CSP. To that end, we presented a syntactical transformation of processes named T. For the sake of simplicity, the original transformation T is designed to reveal a rather low level of concurrency. T is embedded in the construction Ext that reestablishes the semantics of T's input processes.

Although Ext in general preserves only the traces of its input processes, two subsets of CSP are identified lifting Ext from preserving the traces of its input processes to their failures and divergences. Unfortunately, none of the two subsets of CSP includes the timeout operator because the transformation of combined internal and external influences destroys the failures of a process. Moreover, T does not yet support the interrupt operator.

As presented in Section 4.3, s-e-precedence (proposition 1), e-non-refusability (proposition 2), and s-e-conflict freedom (proposition 3) are basic properties of T. These properties enable us to regard a pair $(s.x, e.x)$ or $(sh.x, eh.x)$ as an action (an operation that is required to terminate eventually). This notion of an action motivates us to extend the transformation T such that it can serve as formal foundation of a truly concurrent CSP coordination environment simulating a coordination process at runtime and associating events with actions. Any extension of T serving this purpose must maintain the three properties mentioned above, of course.

In this chapter, T is extended to support the interrupt operator. The main challenge of transforming interrupt under event splitting is that a process may be interrupted in between of a pair of start and end events. If this happens, the end event may be refused after the start event, violating e-non-refusability.

The intuition of our solution to this problem is that these operators are transformed such that the interrupted process performs remaining end events before the interrupting process takes over control. More elaborate transformations of external choice and timeout are presented such that *Ext* preserves also their failures. The transformations of these three operators proceed in a unique way. Due to the lifting from traces to failures-divergences, the extended transformation presented in this chapter is suitable as a formal model of CSP as a coordination language for concurrent systems. Like the transformations presented earlier it can also be used with standard CSP tools such as FDR or ProB.

In Section 5.1 we present the general structure underlying the transformation of external choice (Section 5.2), timeout (Section 5.3) and interrupt (Section 5.4). This chapter closes with a discussion in Section 5.5 after presenting the transformations of these operators.

5.1. Simulation, Monitoring and Interruption

As motivated formally in Section 4.5, the trouble with the transformation of external choice and timeout presented in Section 4.1 is that internal transitions resolve these process operators in their transformed versions because of the exposition of hidden events. Exposing hidden events is an important fact of our simulation because hidden events still model actions (although not under external influence) and consequently have to be taken into account when computing simultaneity of actions or when coordinating actions. In the following, transformations of the operators external choice, timeout, and interrupt are presented. The transformations are based on a construction that transforms the operands of the process operator under consideration, separates their alphabets, puts the results into parallel, and uses the interrupt operator to transfer control from one transformed operand to the other if an event is performed that would have resolved the original process operator. Note that it is well-known that the interrupt operator cannot be simulated by any construct that does not use the interrupt operator itself. However, there are constructions using the interrupt operator to simulate timeout, external choice and interrupt itself as we show in this section.

To simulate the behavior of the transformed operators in a manner that makes observable the internal simultaneity of the resulting construct, we proceed as with the *Ext* construction (see page 47)). First, the operands of the original operator are transformed separately. The results are then combined

5.1 Simulation, Monitoring and Interruption

and monitored by a control process (as C in Ext, see page 47). To distinguish the events performed on either side of the transformed operator we define Σ' such that $\Sigma \cap \Sigma' = \emptyset$ and $\#(\Sigma) = \#(\Sigma')$. For syntactical compactness we write $\overline{\Sigma} = \Sigma \cup \Sigma'$ and $x \in \Sigma$, $x' \in \Sigma'$ and $\overline{x} \in \overline{\Sigma}$ in the following. We extend the channels

$$s, sh, e, eh : \Sigma_P \cup I \cup \Sigma'_P \cup I'$$

to support the primed events as parameters. Furthermore, we define

$$\Sigma_T = \{s.x, sh.x, e.x, eh.x \mid x \in \Sigma_P \cup I\},$$
$$\Sigma'_T = \{s.x', sh.x', e.x', eh.x' \mid x' \in \Sigma'_P \cup I'\}, \text{ and}$$
$$\overline{\Sigma}_T = \{\!\mid s, sh, e, eh \mid\!\}$$

such that $\Sigma_T \cap \Sigma'_T = \emptyset$ and $\Sigma_T \cup \Sigma'_T = \overline{\Sigma}_T$. As defined in Section 4.2, $H = \{\!\mid sh, e, eh, term \mid\!\}$. The renaming part of Hr is also extended to deal with primed events:

$$Hr(P) = P \setminus H \left[s.\overline{x} \leftarrow \overline{x} \mid \overline{x} \in \overline{\Sigma}_P \right].$$

The actual renaming is performed by the bijective renaming functions

$$prime : \Sigma \cup \Sigma_T \rightarrow \Sigma' \cup \Sigma'_T, \text{ and}$$
$$unprime : \Sigma' \cup \Sigma'_T \rightarrow \Sigma \cup \Sigma_T$$

to map each member $x \in \Sigma$ to $x' \in \Sigma'$ and vice versa. These functions require $\Sigma \cap \Sigma' = \emptyset$ and $\#(\Sigma) = \#(\Sigma')$ and ensure

$$unprime \circ prime = id\,.$$

A similar approach is used by Roscoe for proving Lemma 3 and Theorem 6 presented in [Ros08b], for example.

The three operator transformations presented in the sequel make use of the fresh channels t_0, t_1, i_0, i_1 to monitor successful termination and to enforce interruption. The hiding set

$$H_u = \{t_0, t_1, i_0, i_1\}$$

is then used to hide these events in the final composition.

The transformations of external choice, timeout and interrupt are quite similar. To stress this, we define the following two auxiliary process operators.

$$P_0 \wr\wr\wr P_1 = (((P_0\,; t_0 \to SKIP) \vartriangle i_0 \to SKIP)$$
$$|||$$
$$((P_1\,; t_1 \to SKIP) \vartriangle i_1 \to SKIP)[prime])$$
$$P_0 \wr_A\wr P_1 = (P_0\,|A|\,P_1)[unprime] \setminus H_\wr$$

The $\wr\wr\wr$ operator composes its two operands sequentially with $t_i \to SKIP$ to signal successful termination of $P_i, i \in \{0,1\}$. These processes are combined with $i_i \to SKIP$ for interruption. The two results are then interleaved. This auxiliary operator is designed to be nested within the $\wr_A\wr$ construct such that the other operand of $\wr_A\wr$ can act as a 'controller' process enforcing any desired interleaving of P_i while maintaining the possibility of graceful termination using the subprocesses

$$t_0 \to i_1 \to SKIP, \text{ and}$$
$$t_1 \to i_0 \to SKIP\,.$$

Accordingly, the $\wr_A\wr$ operator synchronizes its operands over A, unprimes the result (to reunite the alphabets) and hides the control events from the set $H_\wr$. The transformations shown in the following subsections use this nesting. Each operator $\otimes \in \{\Box, \triangleright, \vartriangle\}$ is transformed using the construction

$$T(P \otimes Q) = (T(P) \wr\wr\wr T(Q)) \wr_{\overline{\Sigma}_T \cup H_\wr} \wr C_\otimes\,.$$

This construction is based on control processes $C_\otimes$ designed to simulate the original operators while maintaining the properties s-e-precedence (1), e-non-refusability (2) and s-e-conflict-freedom (3) presented in Section 4.3.

5.2. Transforming External Choice

The following transformation of external choice transforms each of the choice's operands and embeds the result in a construction using $\wr\wr\wr$ and $\wr_A\wr$ as outlined above.

$$T(P \,\Box\, Q) = (T(P) \wr\wr\wr T(Q)) \wr_{\overline{\Sigma}_T \cup H_\wr} \wr C_\Box$$

5.2 Transforming External Choice

The control process $C_\Box$ initially records any event performed by the transformed operands of the external choice. Only after occurrence of the first visible event it restricts the behavior in such a way that the other operand cannot perform any event apart from remaining hidden end events. After termination of one of the transformed operands the control process enforces interruption of the other transformed operand thus allowing the whole construction to terminate successfully. It is defined as $C_\Box = C_{\Box,0}(\llbracket\,\rrbracket)$, where

$$\begin{aligned}
C_{\Box,0}(X) = {} & s?x \to C_{\Box,1}(X \uplus \llbracket x \rrbracket) \\
& \Box\; s?x' \to C_{\Box,2}(X \uplus \llbracket x' \rrbracket) \\
& \Box\; t_0 \to C_{\Box,t}(X, i_1) \\
& \Box\; t_1 \to C_{\Box,t}(X, i_0) \\
& \Box\; sh?\overline{x} \to C_{\Box,0}(X \uplus \llbracket \overline{x} \rrbracket) \\
& \Box\; eh?\overline{x} \to C_{\Box,0}(X \cup \llbracket \overline{x} \rrbracket) \\
C_{\Box,1}(X) = {} & \overline{s}?x \to C_{\Box,1}(X \uplus \llbracket x \rrbracket) \\
& \Box\; t_0 \to C_{\Box,t}(X, i_1) \\
& \Box\; e?x \to C_{\Box,1}(X \cup \llbracket x \rrbracket) \\
& \Box\; eh?\overline{x} \to C_{\Box,1}(X \cup \llbracket \overline{x} \rrbracket) \\
C_{\Box,2}(X) = {} & \overline{s}?x' \to C_{\Box,2}(X \uplus \llbracket x' \rrbracket) \\
& \Box\; t_1 \to C_{\Box,t}(X, i_0) \\
& \Box\; e?x' \to C_{\Box,2}(X \cup \llbracket x' \rrbracket) \\
& \Box\; eh?\overline{x} \to C_{\Box,2}(X \cup \llbracket \overline{x} \rrbracket) \\
C_{\Box,t}(X, ev) = {} & eh?\overline{x} \to C_{\Box,t}(X \cup \llbracket \overline{x} \rrbracket, ev) \\
& \Box\; X = \llbracket\,\rrbracket\; \&\; ev \to SKIP\,.
\end{aligned}$$

The subprocess $C_{\Box,t}(X, ev)$ takes the interrupt event as an argument. Due to synchronizing on $\overline{\Sigma}_T \cup H_\varrho$, it allows remaining hidden end events to be performed and enforces the interrupting event after termination of the last pending action.

The proof for the transformation of external choice uses a construct similar to the one introduced by Roscoe in [Ros08a] for proving Lemma 1 of that paper. There, a construction is presented that simulates the external choice operator by discriminating the alphabets of its operands and uses the interrupt operator to turn one of the operands off after the other has performed an event. Roscoe's construction does not deal with termination because he considers a subset of CSP that excludes SKIP in that paper. So we cannot directly reuse Roscoe's construction. However, the fresh control events from H_ϱ and the use of an additional parallel composition (as by the definitions of $\wr\wr$ and $\wr_A\wr$) allow the following construction to terminate successfully if one of the operands of the simulated external choice terminates successfully. The process $T(P \square Q)$ is then reduced to this construction by steps that maintain the critical properties of T (those presented in Section 4.3).

$$C_0 = (x : \Sigma_P \rightarrow C_0) \square (t_0 \rightarrow i_1 \rightarrow SKIP)$$
$$C_1 = (x' : \Sigma'_Q \rightarrow C_1) \square (t_1 \rightarrow i_0 \rightarrow SKIP)$$
$$P \square' Q = (P \; ||| \; Q) \;{}_{\overline{\Sigma} \cup H_n}\!\|\; (C_0 \square C_1)$$

The following lemma states that $\square'$ simulates the external choice operator.

Lemma 3 *Using the definitions above, the $\square'$ operator faithfully simulates the external choice operator:*
$$P \square' Q = P \square Q \;.$$

Proof 4 $\square'$ *does not introduce divergence, neither does it prevent divergence. prime separates the alphabets of P and Q from each other. Thus, there is no nondeterminism introduced by $\square'$ in monitoring P and Q. $C_0 \square C_1$ initially does not refuse any of the events offered by P or $Q[prime]$. After synchronizing on any event $x : initials(P)$, Σ'_Q is constantly refused and after synchronizing on $x : initials(Q[prime])$, Σ_P is constantly refused. Furthermore, termination of $\square'$ is possible only after termination of either P or Q by synchronizing on t_0 or t_1 respectively. Since these events are hidden (as well as the subsequent i_0, i_1 events) and termination is the only possibility afterwards, $\square'$ simulates the behavior of the external choice operator.*

The proof is based on the observations that $\square'$ neither introduces nor prevents divergence, yields the same initials and refusals as external choice, and behaves like P if an event $x : initials(P)$ is chosen while it behaves like Q if an event $x : initials(Q)$ is chosen. More formally

$$\forall x : initials(P) \cdot (P \square' Q)/\langle x \rangle = P/\langle x \rangle$$
$$\forall x : initials(Q) \cdot (P \square' Q)/\langle x \rangle = Q/\langle x \rangle \;.$$

Synchronization on $\overline{\Sigma} \cup H_n$ enforces that the controller process must perform the same events as the interleaved operands of $\square'$ do. To see that successful termination of P (or Q) is simulated faithfully, consider the case $P = SKIP$. In this case t_0 is immediately available on the left and also offered by the controller process. Hiding of t_0 and the subsequent i_1 event allows interruption

5.2 Transforming External Choice

of Q and termination of $\wr\wr$. Hence,

$$SKIP \,\square'\, Q = Q \triangleright SKIP$$

as required by law 4.8 (*SKIP*-resolve). $C_\square$ is designed such that the following lemma holds:

Lemma 4 $C_\square$ *enforces traces and failures as required by* $C_0 \,\square\, C_1$:

$$Hr((T(P) \,\wr\wr\, T(Q)) \,|_{\overline{\Sigma}_T \cup H_\wr}| \, C_\square)$$
$$=$$
$$Hr(T(P) \,\wr\wr\, T(Q)) \,|_{\overline{\Sigma} \cup H_\wr}| \, (C_0 \,\square\, C_1)$$

Proof 5 *By definition of T and Hr, the left-hand process diverges if and only if either P or Q diverges. Furthermore, the order of s and sh events is independent of synchronization on e and eh because of properties 1, 2 and 3 (compare with lemma 2). Thus, we may apply Hr to the first operand of the parallel composition exclusively, eliminate the e events from the synchronization set and the right hand operand, and rename the s events from the synchronization set and the right hand operator back to their original names. This yields synchronization with $C_0 \,\square\, C_1$ over $\overline{\Sigma} \cup H_\wr$. The events from $H_\wr$ are not touched by this step, so termination is not affected.*

The lemmas above are finally used in proving the following theorem.

Theorem 4 T *faithfully transforms the external choice operator:*

$$Hr(T(P \,\square\, Q)) = P \,\square\, Q \,.$$

First observe that the transformation maintains the properties s-e-precedence (1), e-non-refusability (2) and s-e-conflict-freedom (3). Property 1 is maintained by the interleaving of the transformed operands and synchronization on $\overline{\Sigma}_T \cup H_\wr$. This construction prevents any e event prior to its corresponding s event. Property 2 is maintained by synchronization on $\overline{\Sigma}_T \cup H_\wr$ and construction of $C_\square$. The controller process freely allows exposed τ transitions to be performed. After the first s event is performed it evolves to either $C_{\square,1}$ or $C_{\square,2}$. These processes, again, allow internal actions to be performed but restrict visible events to those belonging to the process originally performing the first visible event. This is the only process that can perform e events. The transformed process can only terminate after every pending e

event was performed. Thus, e-non-refusability is preserved. Although s and e events are conflicting within $C_\square$ it is easy to see that synchronization on $\overline{\Sigma}_T \cup H_{\wr\wr}$ preserves s-e-conflict-freedom. The proof of Theorem 4 is shown in Appendix A.4.

5.3. Transforming Timeout

Timeout is transformed in a way very similar to the transformation of external choice. The only difference is that the hidden timeout transition guarding the transformed right hand operand resolves the timeout to the right. In the following construction, we use to_i as introduced in the previous chapter: the i-th timeout operator introduces the fresh hidden event to_i.

$$T(P \rhd Q) = (T(P) \;|||\; sh.to\_i \to eh.to\_i \to T(Q)) \;|[\overline{\Sigma}_T \cup H_{\wr\wr}]|\; C_\rhd$$

The following control process $C_\rhd$ reuses the $C_{\square,t}$ subprocess that we have used to build the control process presented in the previous section. We define $C_\rhd = C_{\rhd,0}(\llbracket\,\rrbracket)$, where

$$C_{\rhd,0}(X) = s?x \to C_{\rhd,1}(X \uplus \llbracket x \rrbracket)$$
$$\square \; sh?to\_i' \to C_{\rhd,2}(X)$$
$$\square \; t_0 \to C_{\square,t}(X, i_1)$$
$$\square \; sh?x \to C_{\rhd,0}(X \uplus \llbracket x \rrbracket)$$
$$\square \; eh?x \to C_{\rhd,0}(X \cup \llbracket x \rrbracket)$$
$$C_{\rhd,1}(X) = \overline{s}?x \to C_{\rhd,1}(X \uplus \llbracket x \rrbracket)$$
$$\square \; t_0 \to C_{\square,t}(X, i_1)$$
$$\square \; \overline{e}?x \to C_{\rhd,1}(X \cup \llbracket x \rrbracket)$$
$$C_{\rhd,2}(X) = eh?x \to C_{\rhd,2}(X \cup \llbracket x \rrbracket)$$
$$\square \; X = \llbracket\,\rrbracket \; \& \; eh?to\_i' \to C_{\rhd,3}(X)$$
$$C_{\rhd,3}(X) = \overline{s}?x' \to C_{\rhd,3}(X \uplus \llbracket x' \rrbracket)$$
$$\square \; t_1 \to C_{\square,t}(X, i_0)$$
$$\square \; \overline{e}?x' \to C_{\rhd,3}(X \cup \llbracket x' \rrbracket) \,.$$

$C_\rhd$ initially accepts the hidden timeout transition $(sh.to\_i)$ and any event offered by the transformed left hand operand of the timeout. After occurrence of the hidden timeout transition it restricts the behavior in such a way that the left hand operand cannot perform any event apart from remaining hidden end events and after occurrence of the first originally visible event the timeout

5.3 Transforming Timeout

transition is constantly refused. Like the external choice control process, after termination of one of the transformed operands, the timeout control process enforces interruption of the other one thus allowing the whole construction to terminate successfully.

The proof follows the same principle as the proof of $T(P \square Q)$. We first present a construction using $\mathcal{III}$ and $\mathcal{l}_A\mathcal{l}$ simulating the timeout operator and then we reduce $Hr(T(P \triangleright Q))$ to this construction. The construct uses the definitions that were introduced in Section 5.2 to prove the correctness of the transformation of external choice. The only difference is that C_0 and C_1 are not composed by external choice but using timeout.

$$P \triangleright' Q = (P \mathrel{\mathcal{III}} Q) \mathrel{\mathcal{l}_{\overline{\Sigma} \cup H_{\mathit{R}}} \mathcal{l}} (C_0 \triangleright C_1)$$

The following lemma also follows the principles used in proving the transformation of external choice correct. First we need the lemma that $\triangleright'$ simulates timeout.

Lemma 5 *Using the definitions above, the $\triangleright'$ operator faithfully simulates the timeout operator:*
$$P \triangleright' Q = P \triangleright Q \ .$$

The proof proceeds exactly as the proof of Lemma 3 except that the controller process may timeout and subsequently accept events performed by Q while refusing the events of P.

A lemma similar to Lemma 4 is needed to establish the correctness of $T(P \triangleright Q)$. $C_\triangleright$ is designed to enforce behavior conforming to the timeout operator.

Lemma 6 $C_\triangleright$ *enforces traces and failures as required by $C_0 \triangleright C_1$:*

$$Hr((T(P) \mathrel{\mathcal{III}} sh.to\_i \to eh.to\_i \to T(Q)) \mathbin{|_{\overline{\Sigma}_T \cup H_{\mathit{R}}}|} C_\triangleright)$$
$$=$$
$$Hr(T(P) \mathrel{\mathcal{III}} sh.to\_i \to eh.to\_i \to T(Q)) \mathbin{|_{\overline{\Sigma} \cup H_{\mathit{R}}}|} (C_0 \triangleright C_1)$$

Proving this lemma is done analogously to proving Lemma 4. The important difference is that the timeout controller process $C_\triangleright$ enforces behaviors conforming to the timeout operator. To see that this holds we remove the sh, e and eh events from $C_{\triangleright,0}$ except those modeling the timeout transition ($sh.to\_i$ and $eh.to\_i$), inline $C_{\square,t}$, and apply the renaming performed by Hr.

The resulting process is

$$C'_{\triangleright,0} = (x:\Sigma \to C'_{\triangleright,1}) \,\square\, (to\_i \to C'_{\triangleright,3}) \,\square\, (t_0 \to i_1 \to SKIP), \text{ where}$$
$$C'_{\triangleright,1} = (x:\Sigma \to C'_{\triangleright,1}) \,\square\, (t_0 \to i_1 \to SKIP) \text{ and}$$
$$C'_{\triangleright,3} = (x':\Sigma' \to C'_{\triangleright,3}) \,\square\, (t_1 \to i_0 \to SKIP)$$

This process accepts events from Σ, the t_0 event signaling successful termination and the timeout event to_i. The timeout transition is disabled after performing the first event from Σ and performing the timeout transition disables the events from Σ and enables the events from Σ'. Hiding the timeout transition by applying Hr turns this construct into $C_0 \triangleright C_1$.

We can now state the following theorem:

Theorem 5 *T faithfully transforms the timeout operator:*

$$Hr(T(P \triangleright Q)) = P \triangleright Q \;.$$

The proof of this theorem is shown in Appendix A.5. It uses the lemmas above and proceeds very much as the proof of Theorem 4.

5.4. Transforming Interrupt

The principle used to construct the transformations for external choice and timeout also applies to the transformation of the interrupt operator. First, its operands are transformed, embedded into processes that signal successful termination and enable interruption of the operands using the internal control events from the set $H_{\triangle}$. Finally, there is a control process synchronized with the two transformed processes monitoring their evolutions and enforcing the simulation.

$$T(P \triangle Q) = (T(P) \,\|\|\, T(Q)) \,\upharpoonright_{\overline{\Sigma}_T \cup H_{\triangle}} \, C_{\triangle}$$

$C_{\triangle}$ is the interrupt control process that records any events performed by $T(P)$ and $T(Q)$ (and also records the members of $H_{\triangle}$). It recurses as long as the recorded events either originate from P or belong to internal actions of Q. It is defined as $C_{\triangle} = C_{\triangle,0}(\llbracket\;\rrbracket)$ The first occurrence of a visible primed event causes this process to continue with $C_{\triangle,1}$. In case of successful termination of P it records t_0 and then behaves as $C_{\triangle,2}$ to enable graceful termination of the

5.4 Transforming Interrupt

whole construct.

$$
\begin{aligned}
C_{\triangle,0}(X) = \; & s?x \to C_{\triangle,0}(X \uplus [\![x]\!]) \\
& \square \; sh?\overline{x} \to C_{\triangle,0}(X \uplus [\![\overline{x}]\!]) \\
& \square \; e?x \to C_{\triangle,0}(X \cup [\![x]\!]) \\
& \square \; eh?\overline{x} \to C_{\triangle,0}(X \cup [\![\overline{x}]\!]) \\
& \square \; s?x' \to C_{\triangle,1}(X \uplus [\![x']\!]) \\
& \square \; t_0 \to C_{\triangle,2}(X) \\
C_{\triangle,1}(X) = \; & \overline{e}?\overline{x} \to C_{\triangle,1}(X \cup [\![\overline{x}]\!]) \\
& \square \; \overline{s}?x' \to C_{\triangle,1}(X \uplus [\![x']\!]) \\
& \square \; X = [\![\,]\!] \; \& \; t_1 \to i_0 \to SKIP \\
C_{\triangle,2}(X) = \; & eh?x' \to C_{\triangle,2}(X \cup [\![x']\!]) \\
& \square \; X = [\![\,]\!] \; \& \; i_1 \to SKIP
\end{aligned}
$$

$C_{\triangle,1}$ refuses any s and sh events but allows any currently running action of P to finish. P is blocked while Q progresses. Interruption of P (using the event i_0) is performed only after finishing of any of P's actions and termination of Q. $C_{\triangle,2}$ refuses any s', e' and sh' events but allows any currently running action of Q to finish. Only then Q is interrupted. Note that it is safe to refuse the e' events, because no s' was performed so far.

To prove the correctness of $T(P \triangle Q)$ we need to remove the e, eh and sh events from $C_{\triangle,0}$ and apply the renaming of Hr to obtain the controller process of a construction simulating the interrupt operator without splitting the events in its arguments. The resulting process is

$$C'_{\triangle,0} = (x:\Sigma \to C'_{\triangle,0}) \;\square\; (x':\Sigma' \to C'_{\triangle,1}) \;\square\; (t_0 \to i_1 \to SKIP), \text{ where}$$
$$C'_{\triangle,1} = (x':\Sigma' \to C_{\triangle,1}) \;\square\; (t_1 \to i_0 \to SKIP).$$

Using this process, the auxiliary operator

$$P \triangle' Q = (P \;|||\; Q) \restriction_{\overline{\Sigma} \cup H_{i}} \wr C'_{\triangle,0}$$

faithfully simulates the interrupt operator:

Lemma 7 $\triangle'$ *faithfully simulates the interrupt operator:*

$$P \triangle' Q = P \triangle Q.$$

Again, the proof of this lemma is similar to the proof of Lemma 3 and exploits the structure of $C'_{\triangle,0}$. Furthermore, a lemma similar to Lemma 4 is needed to establish the correctness of $T(P \triangle Q)$.

Lemma 8 $C_\triangle$ enforces traces and failures as required by $C'_{\triangle,0}$:

$$Hr((T(P) \; ||| \; T(Q))|_{\overline{\Sigma}_T \cup H_{||}} |\; C_\triangle)$$
$$=$$
$$Hr(T(P) \; ||| \; T(Q))|_{\overline{\Sigma} \cup H_{||}} |\; C'_{\triangle,0}$$

These lemmas allow us to establish correctness of the transformation of the interrupt operator.

Theorem 6 T faithfully transforms the interrupt operator:

$$Hr(T(P \triangle Q)) = P \triangle Q \;.$$

In [Ros08b], Roscoe motivates (in the context of proving Lemma 3 of that paper) that the interrupt operator cannot be simulated in a similar way to external choice (i.e., by using a construction of parallel composition and renaming). The reason is that the interrupt operator turns its left-hand operand off after the first occurrence of an event of its right-hand operand, while constructs using parallel composition and renaming will still allow internal actions of the left-hand operand to be performed. However, our solution presented above prevents internal actions from being started after the interrupting event but ensures that pending hidden end events (of currently running actions) may still be performed before the right-hand operand proceeds.

5.5. Discussion

The constructions presented in this chapter extend our approach to simulating truly concurrent CSP presented in Chapter 4. The transformations of external choice, timeout and interrupt lift T from traces preserving to failures-divergences preserving. This is of great interest from a practical point of view because it allows us to take T as formal semantics of a CSP-based coordination environment mapping events to actions (pairs of s and e events enclosing terminating user-defined operations). This lifting is necessary as soon as deadlock is a possible threat (which is not revealed in the traces model) and the

5.5 Discussion

coordination process is not within one of the failures-divergences preserving subsets presented in Section 4.5.

Interestingly, the transformations exhibit an unexpectedly high degree of concurrency. In particular, the enhanced version of T exhibits a higher degree of concurrency than its earlier version.

The timeout transition to_i, for example, is possibly concurrent to every internal action of the first operand of the transformed timeout operator that may occur initially. Consider the following processes P and Q.

$$P = (a \to SKIP \ ||| \ b \to SKIP) \triangleright c \to SKIP$$
$$Q = (a \to SKIP \ ||| \ b \to SKIP) \setminus \{a, b\} \triangleright c \to SKIP$$

Using the transformation presented in Chapter 4, Ext preserves the failures-divergences semantics of P but only the traces semantics of Q. The events a and b are possibly concurrent in both processes. The extended version of T presented in this chapter, finds a and b to be possibly concurrent in P but determines $\{a, b, to\_0\}$ to be possibly concurrent in Q (because a and b are hidden and do not resolve the timeout). The example script shown in Appendix B.5.

This high degree of concurrency is caused by our modeling of independent internal progress (by performing exposed and split τ events) of operands of the transformed operators. This choice of modeling is justified by the observation that these operators combine processes allowing them to await some external trigger (constantly offering an event) and to perform internal actions at the same time. The standard interleaving CSP semantics do not impose any restrictions here. Hence, the transformations of external choice, timeout and interupt separate visible events of the operands of the transformed operator (according to the notion of conflict) while allowing a very high degree of concurrency on hidden events. For example, the visible events of the right-hand operand of a timeout are separated from all (visible or hidden) events of its left-hand operand. While it seems very natural to separate c from a and b in the example processes P and Q shown above, it is not obvious, whether c should still be separated if it were hidden. The solutions presented here are the ones that we believe to fit best to the implementation of a CSP-based coordination environment.

Semantically, T supports the CSP that is described by Roscoe in [Ros05] and implemented by FDR 2.83 [GRA05] (except the functional parts of CSP_M and derived operators such as *linked parallel*, for example).

6 Designing a CSP-based Coordination Environment

The purpose of the transformation T is to serve not only as a static means to compute possibly concurrent events but also as formal foundation of a coordination environment. In Chapter 4 and Chapter 5 we have focused on properties and static applications of T. In this chapter, we present the idea of a coordination system based on T.

Our approach to using CSP as a formal coordination language is motivated by the need to reduce the complexities caused by the growing parallelism of today's computing systems. Unfortunately, concurrent software is generally much more complex than sequential software, inherently hard to specify and verify and leaves even the skilled programmer vulnerable to error. These complexities can be avoided to a certain degree by using CSP for modeling and reasoning about such a system. The benefit of CSP is that it provides a convenient intermediate-level formalism for the design of concurrent systems by allowing processes to be combined in parallel in such a way that the designer abstracts synchronization mechanisms and implementation details of actions.

The trouble is that unlike, say, the B-method [Abr96], derivation of executable code from CSP processes is not very well developed. Although CSP is equipped with a refinement calculus that allows us to refine systems down to implementation models by eliminating nondeterminism, the resulting models are still on a relatively high level of abstraction and not yet ready to have executable code derived from it. They still lack mechanisms that assign locks (or some other synchronization primitive) to the competing processes. Neither do they provide hints about how to implement such mechanisms. Since every implementation of a concurrent program must deal with these low-level details, it is desirable to bridge this gap by implementing software libraries that deal with the issues that are abstracted away on the higher level of a CSP design.

In this chapter, we present the concept of a coordination environment that allows us to use (even nondeterministic) processes for the coordination of truly concurrent systems and to systematically undo the abstractions built into CSP. Events, for example, are regarded as abstractions of actions being performed by the system. In particular, internal transitions introduced by the hiding of events are understood as internal actions of the system. To emphasize the distinction between visible and hidden events, we use the term *event* for visible events and *internal transition* for hidden events. Actions relate to both of them if not stated otherwise. Whenever the coordination environment performs an event, it performs the terminating action associated with that particular event. When it performs an internal transition, it performs the action associated with the event whose hiding has introduced that internal transition. Actions can implement arbitrary computations, even communication, including shared-memory communication and message-passing. The coordination environment presented in this chapter simulates a process by interpreting its truly concurrent semantics within the standard interleaving operational semantics of CSP. It performs (non-atomic) actions between the (atomic) start and end events of a split event.

Our approach allows us to use CSP for the design and implementation of concurrent systems by adding a coordination environment to a (sequential) host language. The use of CSP enables us to profit from the mature verification support of CSP for verifying coordination processes at design time. By simulating the coordination process at runtime, it is ensured that the properties proved on the CSP level also hold on the implementation level.

The rest of this chapter is structured as follows. Abstractions built into CSP and their relevance for coordination are discussed in Section 6.1. The model of a coordination environment is presented in Section 6.2. Important properties of coordination processes are investigated in Section 6.3. Section 6.4 presents proof obligations relating the coordination process with UDFs, e.g., a proof obligation to ensure data independence of concurrent actions. A categorization of CSP operators into coordination concerns is presented in Section 6.5 This chapter closes with a discussion in Section 6.6.

6.1. Unraveling Abstractions

This section explains, how the abstractions built into CSP can be unraveled to coordinate concurrent systems. The arguments presented here are based on the following assumptions:

6.1 Unraveling Abstractions

1. CSP offers a rich set of operators to facilitate the concise modeling of concurrent systems. This set is intendedly non-minimal and offers different operators to describe semantically equivalent processes. The idea is that the operators model abstractions of different implementations. The coordination environment must be able to unravel these abstractions accordingly.

2. Once a process is proved to satisfy the interaction behavior of the components of a system, the process should be directly usable as a coordination process without being refined further (even if the process is a nondeterministic one).

3. Coordination processes still abstract from data being used in the implementation.

4. Although the standard CSP semantics are interleaving ones, a coordination environment must be able to profit from true concurrency if that is offered by the underlying computing hardware.

5. Coordination processes define the external and internal interactions of a system.

The first assumption is based on the discussion of the purpose of the various CSP operators given by Hoare in [Hoa06]. The second and third assumption stem from our ultimate goal to support mechanized verification of the coordination processes. The last two assumptions are those underlying T: implementations of concurrent systems must deal with simultaneity of actions, even with respect to internal actions.

In the following, we explain how a coordination environment can deal with the CSP operators that are commonly used to model nondeterminism. Then, we discuss issues related to the 'deterministic' process operators of CSP.

6.1.1. Timeout, Hiding and Nondeterminism

The operators timeout, hiding, and internal choice offer abstractions that allow us to develop concise models of concurrent systems. Yet, these abstractions have to be undone for the implementation of a conforming system. For example, although

$$P \triangleright Q = (P \square Q) \sqcap Q$$

holds, the timeout operator offers a convenient abstraction of a process that switches automatically to Q if P fails to perform a visible event within a certain

time interval. Note that T discriminates these two representations by introducing the exposed hidden to_i for a timeout only. A timed implementation allows the construct
$$STOP \triangleright P$$
to delay P for some time because $STOP$ cannot do anything. This is a useful idiom for implementing timers that perform some action after a specified delay. From an implementation point of view this is fundamentally different from $(P \square Q) \sqcap Q$ which can be understood as a process deciding to offer either the initials of P and Q for synchronization or just the initials of Q. Thus, our approach unravels the abstractions built into the timeout operator differently than that built into its semantically equivalent versions. On the implementation level, $P \triangleright Q$ is implemented as a timeout (e.g., using a timer), while $(P \square Q) \sqcap Q$ models a combination of internal and external influences (independent of time).

In the semantic framework of CSP, timeout is introduced by hiding of initial events over external choice as, for example, in
$$(a \rightarrow P \square b \rightarrow Q) \setminus \{b\}.$$
This process is commonly understood as offering its environment the possibility to synchronize on a. If that does not happen within a certain amount of time, it internally performs b and continues as Q. As explained above, our understanding of a timeout is somewhat different. Analogously, we deal with hiding different from its treatment on the semantic level of CSP. There, hiding abstracts events such that the following equality holds:
$$(a \rightarrow STOP) \setminus \{a\} = STOP.$$
Nevertheless, in the operational semantics $(a \rightarrow STOP) \setminus \{a\}$ performs an internal action before evolving to STOP. Our approach adopts this understanding and takes internal actions into account. A coordination process like $P \setminus A$ removes A from the externally visible events and specifies that the system cannot synchronize with its environment on any event from A. However, within P, the events in A are available for synchronization, of course.

A similar argument applies to
$$a \rightarrow P \square a \rightarrow Q = a \rightarrow (P \sqcap Q).$$
The left-hand side models a system that offers two similar actions for synchronization but its future depends on the external decision which one of the two

6.1 Unraveling Abstractions

exclusive actions is chosen. The right-hand side models a system offering a single action to its environment and which then decides internally if it continues as P or as Q. Accordingly, $P \sqcap Q$ is understood as a system performing an internal action to make the decision between P and Q. Thus, when used in a coordination process, the internal (nondeterministic) choice gives rise to a single internal action whose outcome determines which one of the processes is chosen. There are more reasons for allowing the internal choice to be used in a coordination process. For example, it is quite often the case that nondeterministic models of a system are sufficient to express certain properties (e. g., deadlock-freedom). Once a process is proved to express the interaction requirements of a system it is clearly desirable to take it as the coordination process and to implement the missing details on the level of some programming language instead of further refining the CSP model.

Our approach takes CSP as specification and modeling language, consequently allowing nondeterminism on these levels. This nondeterminism is to be resolved by the implementation, of course. This is done by internal actions. It is important to note that resolving nondeterminism at runtime solely produces implementations that conform to their specification. This is due to the law 'resolution of nondeterminism':

$$P \sqcap Q \sqsubseteq P \quad \text{and} \quad P \sqcap Q \sqsubseteq Q.$$

Hence, the implementation satisfies all those properties of the coordination process that are expressible via refinement (because of transitivity of refinement). It also satisfies those expressed in LTL, because LTL properties are universally quantified over the possible behaviors of the coordination process, thus including the runtime behavior of the system no matter how nondeterminism is resolved on the implementation level.

6.1.2. Duration, Conflict and Concurrency

In CSP, events are assumed to be instantaneous and atomic. However, in [Hoa85], Hoare proposes to unravel this abstraction by splitting an event into start and end events to model duration of the original event. We adopt this idea: events are split into start and end events (as defined by T) and the action that realizes the original event is performed between these two. It is important to note that actions can be of arbitrary granularity (i. e., just a few basic operations of a processing unit or a long running service) and may even be internally concurrent. The only requirement is that they are guaranteed to terminate eventually.

Furthermore, we believe that concurrency must be distinguished from choice for the purposes of a coordination language. Designers of concurrent systems should be able to specify which parts of a system may be executed simultaneously (truly concurrent) and which are mutual exclusive. For example, the processes

$$P = a \to b \to STOP \,\square\, b \to a \to STOP$$
$$Q = a \to STOP \,|_\emptyset|\, b \to STOP$$

are equivalent in the standard CSP models (e.g., traces, stable failures and failures-divergences) but we think of them as describing different systems. P describes a system that must perform a and b exclusively while Q may perform a and b at the same time. This observation is of theoretical and practical importance for a CSP-based approach to coordination. The theoretical issue is that the standard semantics for CSP are interleaving ones and thus do not distinguish choice from concurrency. The practical issue is that a concurrent program should be able to profit from the gains promised by concurrency instead of being limited to purely sequential runs (due to interleaving).

As discussed in Chapter 2, there are two ways of understanding a CSP event. Either as synchronous communication between parallel processes (or components) or as an abstraction of some sequential action (not necessarily related to communication). The former understanding gives rise to implementations of channels that can be used by software developers to build their programs using CSP-style communication. Operators like hiding or internal choice are not supported by these approaches. As explained above, our approach interprets events as arbitrary actions that are performed between the start and end events of a split event in the coordination process. As we have shown in the preceding sections, T realizes this by splitting an event into start and end event. It also allows us to determine pairs of possibly concurrent events taking hidden events into account and to distinguish choice from concurrency. On the implementation level, an action is represented by an atomic operation performing the start event, then the execution of the code implementing the action, and another atomic operation performing the end event.

Each of our solutions to the unraveling of the abstractions built into CSP presented in this section, is justified by the standard semantics of (untimed) CSP. An important feature is that nondeterminism is supported on the design level but resolved on the implementation level. The advantage is simplicity of reasoning about the design (e.g., deadlock-freedom is often provable on a quite abstract design level).

6.2. Design Decisions

The ideas presented in the previous section are supported by the transformation T presented in chapters 4 and 5. The transformation splits events into start and end events, and introduces fresh events modeling internal transitions for resolving internal choices and timeouts. The rationale behind these internal transitions is to detect simultaneity even of visible and hidden events (and their actions). T gives rise to a coordination environment that simulates the truly concurrent version of a CSP coordination process at runtime and starts a user-defined function (UDF) after performing the start event of a split event and performs the respective end event after termination of the UDF. A UDF is the implementation of a terminating action provided by the user.

The intent of the coordination environment is to enable coordination of a concurrent system in a *noninvasive* way separating *interaction* and *data* independently from a specific target language.

The notion of noninvasiveness means that existing implementations of components do not need to be modified to be coordinated. The coordination is done on top of the component implementations provided by the user encapsulating the coordinated components, taking their operations as UDFs implementing the actions of the final system.

The separation of interaction and data is important with respect to the modeling of the coordination process (which may involve data but which does not necessarily relate to data being communicated or computed by the actions of the system) and with respect to the final combination of the coordination process with the UDFs of the system. The first aspect means that the variables used in a coordination process may be independent of the actual values being communicated and processed by the system (unlike in CSP $\parallel$ B [ST04], for example). The second aspect means that the UDFs being mapped to possibly concurrent events may not modify data being shared amongst themselves. It is assumed that the coordination does not invoke UDFs outside their preconditions. On the CSP level we completely abstract from the data being processed by the system.

The design-flow associated with our approach allows the concurrency structure and the UDFs to be developed and verified independently up to the point when the system is assembled to a concrete executable concurrent system (by combining the coordination process with the UDFs implementing the actions). Only then, sets of possibly concurrent events must be identified and it must be proved that the UDFs associated with these events do not introduce data races. Furthermore, it must be proved that the UDFs are coordinated such that they are only invoked in states satisfying their precondition. This issue is discussed in Section 6.4. The following subsections present our understanding of how a coordination environment should perform actions and enable actions to be chosen internally or by the environment.

6.2.1. Interpreting T

The coordination environment simulates a coordination process P by interpreting $T(P)$ and presenting $Hr(T(P))$ to the outside environment (recall that Hr hides the events in $\{|\,sh, e, eh\,|\}$ and relabels the s events back to their original names). Table 6.1 presents the initial events of the processes as visible to the coordination environment. For example, $T(SKIP)$ offers ✓ exclusively and $T(P \sqcap Q)$ offers the start event of the internal action resolving the choice. $T(P \setminus A)$ illustrates the renaming of s events to sh events. None of the sets contains $\bar{e}$ events. In these equations $\sqcap_i$ and $\triangleright_i$ denote the i-th operators of their kind in the coordination process.

An implementation of a coordination environment supporting our approach (as the one presented in Chapter 7) must ensure that the processes offer the initial events as shown in Table 6.1. From these initial states the processes evolve according to the operational semantics as presented in Section 2.2. Furthermore, it must deal with ✓ events and also internal transitions due to the hiding of ✓. Such internal transitions are introduced by processes like

$$SKIP \,;Q\,.$$

In the operational semantics, sequential composition turns the ✓ event offered by $SKIP$ into a τ transition leading to Q.

6.2.2. Performing Actions

The purpose of the coordination environment is not only to coordinate concurrent parts of a system but also to execute UDFs when performing actions and to assign the execution of UDFs to threads. This is done while performing an event or a τ transition made visible by T.

The simulation of the original process P is defined by the operational firing rules of CSP unrolling $T(P)$ while hiding the end events of all actions and also the start events of internal actions. The important point is that the events

6.2 Design Decisions

Table 6.1.: Initials of transformed processes.

$$initials_T(STOP) = \emptyset$$
$$initials_T(SKIP) = \{\checkmark\}$$
$$initials_T(x\!:\!A \to P(x)) = \{s.x \mid x \in A\}$$
$$initials_T(P \, ; Q) = initials_T(P) \setminus \{\checkmark\}$$
$$initials_T(P \,\square\, Q) = initials_T(P) \cup initials_T(Q)$$
$$initials_T(P \sqcap_i Q) = \{sh.ic\_i\}$$
$$initials_T(P \triangleright_i Q) = initials_T(P) \cup \{sh.to\_i\}$$
$$initials_T(P \,\triangle\, Q) = initials_T(P) \cup initials_T(Q)$$
$$initials_T(P \mid_A\mid Q) = ((initials_T(P) \cap initials_T(Q)) \cap A)$$
$$\cup \,(initials_T(P) \setminus A) \cup (initials_T(Q) \setminus A)$$
$$initials_T(P \setminus A) = (initials_T(P) \setminus \{s.x \mid x \in A\})$$
$$\cup \,\{sh.x \mid x \in initials(Q) \cap A\}$$
$$initials_T(P[M]) = initials_T(P) \setminus \{x \mid x \in \mathrm{dom}\, M\}$$
$$\cup \,\{M(x) \mid x \in initials_T(Q) \wedge x \in \mathrm{dom}\, M\}$$

(except $\checkmark$) are regarded as actions which are associated with UDFs and that these UDFs are executed between the atomic steps of the actions start and its end.

The following cases are to be considered when performing an action. The action either corresponds to a (a) synchronized event, (b) to a hidden event, (c) to a renamed event, or (d) to any other event.

The first case (a) is commonly considered to be a problem when matching actions with events. The argument against performing actions for synchronized events is the following question:

'which of the synchronized components should perform the action?'

Our answer to this question is that synchronization primarily affects the order of events and not the ownership of actions. Thus, a single action is performed after the start event in an arbitrarily chosen context (either one of the threads that performed the preceding actions, possibly another).

In the second case (b) the original event (being subject to hiding) defines the action to be performed. In the third case (c) the renamed event (not the original one) defines the action to be performed. Although this decision seems to be at odds with case (b), because both renaming and hiding can be regarded as a substitution of the original event's name (in a user-defined way or by τ respectively), the different treatments are necessary for uniquely identifying the UDFs to be executed. The reason is that hidden events cannot be synchronized on but renamed events are available for synchronization.

In the last case, the event directly identifies the UDF to be performed. It is noteworthy, however, that ✓ is not associated with a UDF. It solely models termination of a process, is commonly considered to be outside the alphabet of a process, and it is the only event not being split by T.

As an example, the single UDF to be performed by the following coordination process P (being algebraically equivalent to $SKIP$) is the one identified by event a.

$$P = ((b \rightarrow SKIP)[b \leftarrow a] \mid_{\{a\}} \mid a \rightarrow SKIP) \setminus \{a\}$$

This design decisions described above allow us to relinquish the idea that a sequential process models a single thread of control. A sequential process defines the order of its actions but these can be performed by different threads. This gives us great freedom in distributing the actions amongst processing units of the final system. Load balancing could, for example, be realized by statically creating a task queue and distributing the actions dynamically at runtime. Any of these informal descriptions above conforms to the formal definition of T.

6.2.3. Choosing Events

There must be some additional component added to the coordination environment dealing with the execution of hidden events. Visible events are available for external synchronization and chosen externally. But how to resolve conflicts of internal actions?

As a solution, we propose to use *event listeners* that are called when the internal representation of the initial events of the coordination process (as shown in Table 6.1) changes. These event listeners are UDFs that may choose amongst the visible and hidden events ($s, sh \in initials_T(P)$) and perform a selected event. They enable the user of our coordination environment to inject a strategy for dealing with conflicts between s and sh events. These event listeners reside above the component performing $T(P)$ but they solely deal with $\overline{s}$ events.

$\overline{e}$ events are not visible to the user of our coordination environment. They are performed immediately so that $T(P)$ can proceed and offer any causally dependent $\overline{s}$ events.

This leaves it open to the programmer to decide if hidden events have priority over visible ones as, e.g., in the tau-priority model [Ros05] and how conflicts of internal actions are resolved. Although it seems reasonable in many cases to give hidden events priority over visible events, it is obviously unsatisfying in the presence of timeouts because the timeouts would always be resolved to the right-hand side due to the hidden event introduced by T.

It is important to notice that this does not contradict the noninvasiveness of our approach. By making hidden events on the outermost process available for event listeners internal to the coordination environment, we provide a general way for resolving nondeterminism.

6.3. Supported Processes

The approach presented here supports all finite alphabet CSP processes except the ill-formed recursive process $P = P$ (which is sometimes understood as div). This includes divergent and infinite state processes. The limitation to processes whose alphabet is finite matches the assumption that there are only finitely many UDFs assigned to the events of a process.

The divergent process

$$P = \mu P' \bullet (e \to P') \setminus \{e\},$$

for example, models a process that runs forever without any interaction with its environment. This is not a problem in its own right, because, as we will see in Chapter 8, such situations may naturally arise when modeling active processes that do not depend on external stimuli. In such a situation one would use hiding to express urgency (again, as in the tau-priority model) and implement internal actions that perform the system's business logic. The internal action could, for example, scan log files and generate reports.

The process

$$Q = \mu Q' \bullet (e \to Q' \sqcap SKIP) \setminus \{e\}$$

is also a divergent one, although Q may eventually decide to terminate gracefully. The reason for accepting such processes is that the internal actions resolving the choices can be used to implement local fairness conditions (as introduced in Section 3.3). Consequently, the process Q shown above does not necessarily diverge and might be guaranteed to terminate eventually under certain fairness assumptions. The same applies to other processes containing process control constructs such as internal or external choice, timeout or interrupt allowing the process to eventually exit from cycles of internal actions.

Both tools FDR and ProB can be used to verify that P unavoidably diverges while Q may eventually terminate. FDR proves this in the traces model because
$$\mathcal{T}[\![P]\!] = \{\langle\rangle\} \quad \text{and} \quad \mathcal{T}[\![Q]\!] = \{\langle\rangle, \langle\checkmark\rangle\}\,.$$
In the failures-divergences model $P = Q$ because both processes may diverge initially. The same result can be obtained using the LTL model checking capabilities of ProB. In ProB's LTL syntax, the formula
$$\phi = F\ G\ [tau]$$
states that a process unavoidably diverges (all of its executions eventually end up in an endless cycle of τ events). Now
$$P \models \phi \quad \text{but} \quad Q \not\models \phi\,.$$
The counterexample found by ProB expectedly shows that Q may eventually perform $\checkmark$.

Another interesting example is the infinite state process
$$R = \mu\ R'\bullet (a \to R'\ |||\ b \to SKIP)\,.$$
Infinite state processes such as R are likely to eventually run out of memory, crashing the whole system. It is obviously questionable if any reasonable program conforming to such a design exists. However, infinite state processes can be simulated and there is good reason for supporting them: there are environments that turn these systems into finite state systems. For example, R is clearly well-behaved in an environment that ensures that all of its traces t satisfy
$$t \upharpoonright \{a\} < t \upharpoonright \{b\} + N\,.$$

In this context, it is important to observe that CSP_M scripts modeling infinite state systems cannot in general be checked by FDR because compilation of the script to the internal LTS will not terminate. The ProB LTL model checker, however, performs on-the-fly model checking and quite often succeeds in model checking infinite-state systems [PL08].

6.4. Integrating Specifications of UDFs

CSP can be used as a coordination language independent of the target language. Compared to approaches that integrate CSP with state-based formalisms (e.g., CSP∥B, CSP-OZ or Circus, see Section 9.1.2), our approach is a rather abstract one in the sense that it does not lift the implementation level data types to the CSP level. However, although our coordination environment abstracts from data and state-based properties, UDFs will deal with data. Hence, assigning UDFs to events undoes this abstraction. This gives rise to proof obligations for the final system that are discussed in this section.

We do not consider a particular implementation language for the UDFs (realizing the coordinated components' operations) here. Neither do we dictate the use of a particular specification language. Hence, we present the proof obligations in a purely mathematical way. The proof obligations ensure that UDFs do not introduce data races and that they are not called outside their preconditions.

The proof obligations presented in the following allow us to turn a verified sequential system into a concurrent one by identifying parts of the program that make up the UDFs, adding a suitable CSP script and mapping events to UDFs. Provided that the additional proof obligations can be discharged successfully, modular verification remains valid on that program. This implies that the sequential parts do not have to be modified at all. The coordination environment is the entry point to the final program and solely requires implementation of the mapping from events to UDFs.

The mapping of events to UDFs is formally defined as a partial injective function such that its inverse is a total injection. It is

$$udf : \Sigma \rightarrowtail F, \quad \text{and its inverse is} \quad udf^{-1} : F \rightarrowtail \Sigma.$$

Hence, a UDF uniquely identifies an event but events do not necessarily identify a UDF.

Expressing causality is straightforward. It is, for example, obvious that prefixing should relate to the sequential rule of Floyd/Hoare-style calculi. More specifically, we need to ensure that the postcondition ($Post$) of every UDF implies the preconditions (Pre) of subsequent UDFs. More formally,

$$\forall\, a, b : \Sigma_P \cup I, t : \Sigma^*_{T(P)}\, \cdot$$
$$t \frown \langle \overline{e}.a \rangle \frown \langle \overline{s}.b \rangle \in \mathit{traces}(T(P)) \Rightarrow (Post_{udf(a)} \Rightarrow Pre_{udf(b)}).$$

In contrast to other formalisms, this also takes pre- and postconditions of UDFs related to hidden events (which are exposed by our transformation T) into account.

The proof obligation for proving absence of data races is based on our definition of possible concurrency presented in Chapter 4 and a so-called *frame property* describing the modification behavior of a UDF with respect to another UDF. Refer to [Mül02] for a more in-depth presentation of framing.

Let F be the type of all UDFs and *Var* the type of all modifiable entities (references to objects and primitive types). Then a *data race* is formally expressed using the following functions:

$$shared : F \times F \to \mathbb{P}\ Var$$

$$shared(f, g) \;\hat{=}\; (writes(f) \cap rw(g)) \cup (writes(g) \cap rw(f))$$

$$writes, reads, rw : F \to \mathbb{P}\ Var$$

$$rw(f) \;\hat{=}\; writes(f) \cup reads(f)$$

Definition 3 (*Data Race*) Two UDFs f and g suffer from a data race *if their frames overlap and one modifies data also read or written by the other.*

$$race(f, g) \;\hat{=}\; shared(f, g) \neq \emptyset$$

Let $conc : \Sigma \times \Sigma \to Bool$ be the predicate telling us whether or not two events are possibly concurrent in a given process P (i.e., $conc(x, y) \leftrightarrow (x, y) \in conc(P)$). This predicate is combined with udf^{-1} to the following predicate telling us whether or not two UDFs are possibly concurrent:

$$conc^F : F \times F \to Bool\,, \quad \text{where} \quad conc^F(f, g) \;\hat{=}\; conc(udf^{-1}(f), udf^{-1}(g))\,.$$

The proof obligation ensuring freedom of data races is

$$\forall f, g \in F : conc^F(f, g) \Rightarrow \neg\ race(f, g)\,.$$

A system violating this condition can be corrected by either adjusting the coordination process (by removing possible simultaneity) or modifying the UDFs (by making the frames distinct).

In general, determining the sets *reads* and *writes* of arbitrary UDFs is a hard problem (due to aliasing). Dealing with this issue is beyond the scope of the work presented here. However, it is noteworthy that specialized logics such as separation logic [Rey02] offer a prospective alternative for specifying (and verifying) properties such as the data independence of UDFs.

Besides these data related proof obligations, termination of the UDFs has to be proved to obtain total correctness. Furthermore, it must be proved that the UDFs resolving nondeterministic choices always return a valid process name.

6.5. Categorizing Coordination

Aiming to support 'full' CSP implies that coordination processes do not only define concurrency concerns but also timing, conflict and causality. The process operators supported by T (except hiding and renaming) fall into these categories.

Table 6.2 shows our categorization of the CSP operators according to the aspects that they coordinate. It is important to note that the categories conflict and concurrency denote *possible* conflict and *possible* concurrency as defined in Section 4.3.

Interestingly, the interrupt operator falls into the two categories of conflict and concurrency. This is due to the design decision of the model presented in this chapter that the interrupt operator is by no means an operator that eliminates concurrency from its operands. Thus, the interruption event may occur concurrently with each event of the first operator but is also possibly conflicting with those events. The reason is that the conflict expressed by the interrupt operator is only resolved when the right-hand process of the composition performs an event.

Table **6.2.**: Coordination categories of CSP operators.

timing	$P \triangleright Q$			
conflict	$P \square Q$	$P \triangle Q$		
causality	$a \to P$	$P ; Q$	$P \sqcap Q$	
concurrency	$P \;\vert\vert\vert\; Q$	$P \;\Vert\; Q$	$P \;\vert_A\vert\; Q$	$P \triangle Q$

Prefix and sequential composition express causality but, perhaps surprisingly, internal choice as well. Our understanding of internal choice is that a user-defined operation (modeled as an hidden event ic_i) resolves the choice. This internal action is likely to depend on the current state of the system and hence on the state changes made by preceding actions (if any). In this sense, it clearly expresses causality. The benefit of a coordination environment supporting this understanding of an internal choice is that it allows us to keep the coordination processes reasonably abstract and simple (by law 2.2 'resolution of nondeterministic choice' $P \sqcap Q \sqsubseteq P$).

Other approaches to using CSP as coordination facility (e. g., CSP $\|$ B [ST04], CSP+B [LB05]) tend to focus on communication. The occurrence of an event $a.x$ is interpreted as an operation that inputs or outputs the data value x. By contrast, we treat these communication decorations as mere syntactic sugar. Given a channel $a : X$, the input decoration

$$a?x \rightarrow P(x)$$

is interpreted as replicated external choice (which is semantically equivalent)

$$\Box\, x : X \bullet a.x \rightarrow P(x).$$

T does not restrict the interpretation of the atomic events $a.x, a.x'$ where $x, x' \in X$ and $x \neq x'$ in any way. They may abstract actions communicating some value but they may as well represent independent actions.

6.6. Discussion

The coordination environment presented in this chapter unravels the abstractions built into CSP to support a wide range of coordination constructs. The coordination itself is defined by T. Actions are performed (by executing a UDF) between the split start and end events created by T. T allows us to simulate truly concurrent CSP within the framework of standard interleaving CSP. This is beneficial because these semantics are well-developed, well-documented and supported by a number of industrial-strength tools such as FDR and ProB.

Nondeterminism introduced by the internal choice operator is resolved by implementing a UDF that returns the name of the chosen succeeding process. Nondeterminism introduced by hiding is resolved by attaching listeners to the coordination environment that may deal with hidden events. CSP animators (e. g., ProB [LF08], Probe [Ros05] and PAT [SLD08]) commonly implement a similar approach. They offer the user the choice to perform internal (τ) events

6.6 Discussion

to unroll a process. The only semantic difference between visible events (those from Σ) and hidden ones is that the latter cannot be used for synchronization, neither with other processes nor with the environment (which can also be regarded as a process although an unspecified one). Our coordination environment also realizes this understanding of hidden events. Hidden events are propagated to the outermost process (regarding the process hierarchy imposed by the nesting of process operators) but not available for synchronization.

Our approach does not necessarily map the UDFs implementing two causally dependent actions to the same thread. It merely maintains the order of UDFs as defined by the events of the CSP script coordinating the system. This is comparable to Linda's feature of distributing tasks at runtime and can be exploited for load-balancing purposes.

The coordination environment could even be constructed without explicitly dealing with the initial events of processes and the operational firing rules by implementing the transformation T and reusing a CSP animator such as ProB to simulate the coordination process. Yet, this approach would yield the initials as defined by $initials_T$, shown in Table 6.1.

7 Coordinating Java Threads

The general concepts of a CSP coordination environment are presented in Chapter 6 in a target language independent way. In this chapter we present a Java implementation of a CSP coordination environment targeting the development of provably correct concurrent software. It is based on the understanding that an event models a (non-atomic) action as justified by the theory developed in the previous chapters. The implementation internally realizes the transformation T (as presented in Chapter 5).

The coordination environment contains a simulation kernel that interprets a coordination process as defined by $Hr \circ T$ and a mapping from events to terminating user-defined functions (UDFs). The UDFs are executed between the start and end events of an action which is modeled by an event of the coordination process. Although T makes internal actions visible (to support reasoning about internal concurrency), the internal actions are not available for external synchronization (because they are hidden again by Hr). The implementation presented here coordinates Java objects and allows us to derive verified concurrent Java programs from a coordination process and the implementation of a single Java interface realizing the UDFs.

Even though concurrency was available right from the first public release of Java in 1996 it is still hard to master and lagging in verification support [BCC+05]. Specifying and verifying concurrency related properties in Java is still an active field of research, as put out in [dB07, Loc08, WPM+09], for example. As motivated in the preceding chapters, our approach is based on the observation that problems in concurrent programming are due to complexities that arise whenever concurrency primitives are coupled with complex sequential dependencies. Whenever threads have to access shared resources, for example, deadlock is a possible threat to the programmer. The purpose of a coordination language is thus to hide the Java concurrency primitives from the programmer and to make even complex concurrent Java programs amenable to (automated) formal verification. Even though our simulation kernel is implemented in Java 5, it does not use the new concurrency facilities from the *java.util.concurrent* package (compare with Section 3.2) but rather threads, and the primitives *Object.wait*, *Object.notify* and *Object.notifyAll*. The objective of this decision is to provide an alternative to the existing concurrency abstraction and not just an extension.

One of the very basic properties of the coordination environment presented here is *noninvasiveness*. It does not require the use of some predefined classes in the code of the user's components. This means that our approach does not require the modification of verified sequential parts of a program by using some predefined classes, for example. Instead, our coordination environment provides two interfaces for linking the coordination with the operations of the system. The mapping of events to operations of the components is provided by the user by implementing an interface provided by our implementation.

The rest of this chapter is organized as follows. First, we present the general design decisions underlying our implementation. Selected implementation details of the coordination environment are presented in Section 7.2. In Section 7.3 we relate our approach to coordination to modular verification of the UDFs. We then go on to discuss classes of processes that are supported by the Java coordination environment in Section 7.4. This chapter closes with a discussion in Section 7.5.

7.1. General Design Decisions

The following very basic questions have to be answered when realizing a coordination environment conforming to the model presented in the previous chapter.

- How are coordination processes defined?
- How is T realized?
- How are the firing rules realized?

Our coordination environment supports a subset of CSP_M. To that end, we implement a simple CSP_M parser and generators to either output Java code representing the coordination process or to launch the simulation immediately (without generating code).

Our implementation offers classes realizing the process operators, their transformation and their firing rules. Thus, T is not applied statically but dynamically at runtime. Note that it is also perfectly valid to transform a coordination process statically and to reuse an external simulator to unroll the transformed process. Unfortunately, at the time of writing, there are no suitable frameworks (or tools) available for such an integration.

Another very basic design decision is the following: our coordination environment implements events as objects that are aware of their origin (the process operators that created it). Performing an event is only possible through the object representing it. This allows us to discriminate instances of equally named events. When being performed, the event object delegates to the relevant implementations of firing rules.

7.2. Implementing the CSP Coordination Environment

In this section, we present the implementation of the CSP coordination environment as modeled in Chapter 6. The coordination environment simulates a coordination process at runtime and executes user-defined Java code when performing an event. It implements the operational semantics of the process operators as defined by the simulation transformation presented in Chapter 5. This transformation in turn builds on the operational semantics given in Section 2.2. This way, the simulation kernel limits the set of possible executions to those specified by the simulated coordination process.

In the following, we present the most important Java classes of the coordination environment and explain how UDFs are assigned to actions. We also discuss how the implementation deals with events, internal transitions, and processes.

7.2.1. The Environment

The coordination environment provides the final class *CspEnvironment* encapsulating the coordination process. This class manages the events offered by the coordination process, listeners that deal with changes of offered events, and the mapping of events to UDFs. The mapping of events to UDFs is defined by an implementation of the *CspEventExecutor* interface. The environment immutably references a single instance of a *CspProcessStore* holding the process configurations that describes the coordination process to be simulated.

The *CspEnvironment* provides a start method taking a process name that determines the coordination process instance. When started, the environment retrieves the coordination process from its store and adds the events offered by the process to its set of offered events. Then it informs the event listeners about that change. From that point on, interaction with the coordination environment is done by choosing events from the set of offered events and performing them.

To create an executable system one has to instantiate a *CspEnvironment* with a *CspProcessStore* and a *CspEventExecutor*. One can then create a coordinated system as shown in Figure 7.1. A *CspSimulator* may be used to connect a *CspEnvironment* to the outside world. One useful example is the *SwingCspSimulator* that provides a simple Swing GUI to chose and perform events.

The example code shown in Figure 7.1 assumes the existence of suitable *CspEventExecutor* and *Filter* classes (filters are convenience objects helping event listeners to find the events that they act upon). The instances may be configured to fit the needs of the final system. Then a process store is created and must be filled with process configurations. A *CspEnvironment* is created using the *CspEventExecutor* and *CspProcessStore* instances. To deal with possibly hidden events, a *CspEventConsumer* takes the *Filter* instance as argument and is registered as a listener for event changes at the environment. Finally, the environment is run using a Swing GUI.

```
CspEventExecutor cee = ... ;
Filter filter = ... ;
// setup cee and filter
CspProcessStore store = new CspProcessStore();
// register process configurations
CspEnvironment env = new CspEnvironment(store, cee);
env.registerListener(new CspEventConsumer(filter));
CspSimulator s = new SwingCspSimulator("my_example", env);
s.run();
```

Figure 7.1.: Code stub of a coordinated Java program.

7.2.2. Assigning UDFs to Events

The *CspEventExecutor* interface realizes the mapping from events to UDFs. Thus it must be implemented to enrich the system with the required functionality. It is this interface that allows UDFs to be injected into the CSP model, decoupling functional aspects from concurrency. The interface is shown in Figure 7.2.

7.2 Implementing the CSP Coordination Environment

```
public interface CspEventExecutor {
  void execute(CspProcess process, String event);
  /*@ ensures \old(internalChoice).isValid(\result) @*/
  String resolve(ProcessInternalChoice internalChoice);
  void timedOut(ProcessTimeout timeout);
}
```

Figure 7.2.: The *CspEventExecutor* interface maps events to UDFs.

The first method provided by the *CspEventExecutor* interface deals with executing the UDF for arbitrary (visible or hidden) user-defined events. The second method is solely called by the hidden events introduced by internal choice. This method is naturally required to return a valid process name known by the environment. This is expressed as a postcondition stating that the returned value is the name of one of the allowed successors of the internal choice. The third method is called exclusively when performing a hidden action introduced by a timeout process. The parameters are assumed to be non-null and final (immutable). The implementations of the methods must be guaranteed to terminate (which is the default in JML).

Note that it is perfectly valid for an instance of *CspEventExecutor* to do nothing at all when an action is performed or some process times out. This equals the *nop* operation (no operation performed).

As shown in Figure 7.3 the code responsible for performing an action is

```
environment.getCspEventExecutor().execute(first(), name);
```

7.2.3. Events and Hidden Transitions

Externally, the simulation kernel offers the events as specified by the control process P. Internally, it transforms the processes on-the-fly and performs $T(P)$. The operational firing rule for prefix $(a \to P)$, for example, is

$$\overline{(a \to P) \xrightarrow{a} P}.$$

Since the simulation also realizes T, this firing rule is implemented for the process $T(P) = s.a \to e.a \to T(P)$. Only $s.a$ is offered for external synchronization. After $s.a$ is performed, the UDF related to a is performed, then $e.a$ is performed immediately (recall that the e events are always conflict-free to every other event in T). Then, the process evolves to $T(P)$. Again, from the outside this process appears to be P, because the $\{|\ sh\ |\}$ events are hidden. This principle applies to all events because every event in Σ_P is split by T.

This behavior is implemented by the class *UserCspEvent* which deals with the events from $\{|\overline{s}|\}$. Recall that this set contains the start events of *P*'s events as well as the start events of the exposed internal transitions (introduced by internal choice, timeout and hiding). The relevant firing rules are those dealing with $\Sigma \cup \tau$.

Note that ✓ has to be treated differently from other events because of its very special role in CSP. It deals with termination exclusively. Thus, the transformation *T* deals with ✓ differently from other events and so does its Java implementation. ✓ is handled by the class *TickEvent*.

The common superclass is *CspEvent*. This class defines that events are named and can be hidden. Recall that even ✓ is sometimes hidden (by sequential and parallel composition, for example). *CspEvent* also provides the abstract method *perform*. According to *T*, this method is implemented differently in the subclasses: ✓ is performed atomically while other events perform two atomic transitions.

7.2.4. Processes and Process Operators

The abstract class *CspProcess* defines that processes have a name and offer events to their environment. It provides the following abstract methods.

```
abstract void doStart(CspEvent cspEvent);
abstract void doEnd(CspEvent cspEvent);
abstract void doTick(TickEvent tickEvent);
```

Implementations of these methods discriminate visible from hidden events and realize the firing rules that are triggered when an event (as specified by the argument) is performed.

Subclasses of *CspProcess* are available for the process operators supported by *T*, namely prefixing, sequential and generalized parallel composition, internal and external choice, renaming, hiding, timeout and interrupt.

The environment must also care for multiple instances of a process because instantiation occurs naturally in CSP. Process names can be reused to form different processes, however, their instances evolve independently. There are, for example, two copies of *P* evolving independently in $P \;|||\; P$.

CSP processes are represented in Java as *CspProcessConfig* objects. These objects are stored in a *CspProcessStore* and used to create instances of *CspProcess*. Process configurations reference other process configurations by name. This

7.2 Implementing the CSP Coordination Environment

indirection allows us to reuse process configurations and to have stateful processes. Fresh copies of processes are obtained by looking up the process configuration for a given process name and trigger it to create a fresh process instance. Processes must not discard instances of stateful processes, of course.

STOP and *SKIP* are the only predefined processes that can be referenced by a coordination process. Process stores can be obtained from the CSP_M parser. They can also be created programmatically (e.g., by implementing a *CspProcessStoreFactory*). Generation of *CspProcessStoreFactory* implementations from CSP_M scripts is also supported. Limitations of the CSP_M parser are discussed in Section 7.4.

7.2.5. Performing Actions

The purpose of the simulation kernel is not only to coordinate concurrent parts of the system but also to execute UDFs when performing actions and to assign the execution of UDFs to threads. This is done while performing a visible non-✓ event or an internal action. Those are represented as instances of *UserCspEvent*. A simplified implementation skeleton of *UserCspEvent* is shown in Figure 7.3.

Events have in common that they may result from synchronization or hiding of other events. Thus, the base class provides a member

$$\text{delegates} :: \text{List<CspEvent>}.$$

Note that this also applies to ✓, although ✓ can neither be hidden nor synchronized on. If, for example, P in $P \mid_A \mid Q$ may terminate, it offers the ✓ event which is then hidden by the parallel composition because it may only terminate after P and Q have terminated. This example also motivates our way of dealing with the offering of events. Events 'bubble' from their origin to the outermost process (with respect to the process hierarchy implied by the nesting of process operators). This hierarchy is made available at runtime by the member

$$\text{delegates} :: \text{List<CspEvent>}.$$

For example the construct $P \square Q$ is represented by three processes P, Q and $P \square Q$. Since

$$initials(P \square Q) = initials(P) \cup initials(Q)$$

```
class UserCspEvent extends CspEvent {
  // ... constructors

  void doStart(){
    for (CspEvent e : delegates) {
      ((UserCspEvent)e).doStart();
    }
    for(CspProcess p : offeredBy){
      p.doStart(this);
    }
  }
  // ... doEnd() analogous to doStart()

  void performUserDefinedFunction() {
    // hidden events delegate to the events they are hiding
    environment.getCspEventExecutor().execute(first(), name);
  }

  public final void perform() {
    synchronized(environment){
      doStart();
    }
    environment.assignToThread(
      new Runnable() {
        public void run() {
          performUserDefinedFunction();

          synchronized(environment){
            doEnd();
            environment.offerEvents(last().events());
          }
        }
      });
  }
}
```

Figure 7.3.: Implementation skeleton of the *UserCspEvent* class.

we regard P and Q as subprocesses of $P \square Q$ offering their initial events to the surrounding process. Thus, given an event $a \in initials(P \square Q)$, the *offeredBy* list ends with $P \square Q$ and the previous entry is either P or Q. This applies analogously to all process operators.

Our implementation handles the nesting of process operators and the offered (initial) events of processes in an explicit way. This causes a considerable runtime overhead but allows us to resolve conflicts of actions when an action is started and to leave concurrent actions on offer while an action is performing. The semantic foundation of this functioning is provided by the transformation T and the operational semantics of CSP as explained in Chapter 6. The initial events of the *CspProcess* subclasses are computed according to the equalities listed in Table 6.1.

7.2 Implementing the CSP Coordination Environment

Our implementation of the external choice operator, for example, clears its initial events after performing the start event originating from a visible event and offers its environment the initials of whatever process takes over after termination of the corresponding action. This is due to the conflict expressed by the firing rule for visible events on external choice

$$\frac{P \xrightarrow{x} P'}{P \square Q \xrightarrow{x} P'} \; x \neq \tau \qquad \frac{Q \xrightarrow{x} Q'}{P \square Q \xrightarrow{x} Q'} \; x \neq \tau.$$

By contrast, performing an action offered by the implementation of the parallel composition operator removes it from the set of initial events (in *doStart*) and then adds the initial events of the subsequent process (after *doEnd*). This is due to the firing rules for visible events on parallel composition

$$\frac{P \xrightarrow{a} P'}{P \mid_A Q \xrightarrow{a} P' \mid_A Q} \; a \in \Sigma \setminus A \qquad \frac{Q \xrightarrow{a} Q'}{P \mid_A Q \xrightarrow{a} P \mid_A Q'} \; a \in \Sigma \setminus A$$

$$\frac{P \xrightarrow{a} P' \quad Q \xrightarrow{a} Q'}{P \mid_A Q \xrightarrow{a} P' \mid_A Q'} \; a \in A$$

The first two firing rules allow non-synchronized events to be performed independently from the events offered by the other operand of the parallel composition. Note that this firing rule applies to the s and e events. After any $s.a \in \Sigma_{T(P)}$, the subsequent $e.a$ becomes available either on the side performing $s.a$ independently or on both sides in the side of a synchronized event.

As shown in Figure 7.3, both the *doStart* and *doEnd* methods of the *UserCspEvent* class first inform the delegate events to perform their *doStart* or *doEnd* code respectively. This finally ends up in calls to the *doStart* and *doEnd* methods of the *CspProcess* class from which the events originate. Thus, these methods implement the firing rules of the atomic start and end events as defined by T.

Atomicity of start and end events must be ensured. This can be achieved using a single semaphore (or monitor) in the coordination environment. The *CspEvent* implementations synchronize on the *CspEnvironment* instance itself to ensure atomicity of start and end events of actions as explained below.

The public final *perform* method implements execution of the whole action. This includes the start and end events as well as the execution of the UDF realizing the action. The calls of *doStart* and *doEnd* are performed exclusively in blocks synchronizing on the *CspEnvironment* instance they belong to. The former call is executed within the thread performing the selected event. Then the environment assigns the execution of the event's UDF and the subsequent *doEnd*-call to a thread. Note that different strategies are valid here offering a large potential for optimizations. Load balancing could, for example, be realized by statically creating as many threads as CPUs available and putting the UDFs into working queues of the threads. Also note that the *doEnd*-calls are never performed by the thread which has decided to perform the event.

According to the model presented in Section 6.2.2, the following special cases have to be considered when performing an action: the action corresponds (a) to a synchronized event, (b) to a hidden event, (c) to a renamed event, or (d) to any other event. In the last case, the event has no delegates and simply walks the hierarchy of processes offering that very event when performing its start and end events. This is the base case described above. In case (a), the event has at least two delegate events. These perform the start and end events as required by the firing rules of their offering processes but do not execute the UDF. This is done by the synchronized event to ensure that the UDF is executed a single time per synchronized event. Cases (b) and (c) deal with events that have a single delegate (the hidden or renamed source event). The difference is that in case (b) the UDF is performed by the delegate event while in (c) the UDF is performed by the outermost event and not its delegate. These are the special cases formally defined by T.

7.2.6. Choosing Events

Besides the implementation classes of events and processes, the *CspEnvironment* class is the most important one amongst the classes realizing the simulation kernel. There is a single instance of *CspEnvironment* per system encapsulating access to events and hiding processes from the user. Before starting the CSP simulation kernel, event listeners (implementing the *Listener* interface) must be attached to the *CspEnvironment* instance. This is the only way to interact with the external world (e.g., a user or network connections). Thus when starting the environment, the outermost process offers its initial events (which depends on the initial events of its child-processes) to the environment which then informs the listeners in turn. Subsequently the listeners are informed after every change of the set of events offered by the outermost process. This set changes only when an event is performed. If a client holds a reference to an event that is no longer available, it cannot be performed, of course. It is on this level that a program may decide about performing internal actions (τ events).

Visible events can be chosen arbitrarily from the set of offered events as defined by the standard CSP semantics. For this purpose, our simulation kernel

7.3 Modular Verification

```
public class RaceExample {
    private int x;
    public void increment(){ x++;}
    public void decrement(){ x--;}
}
```

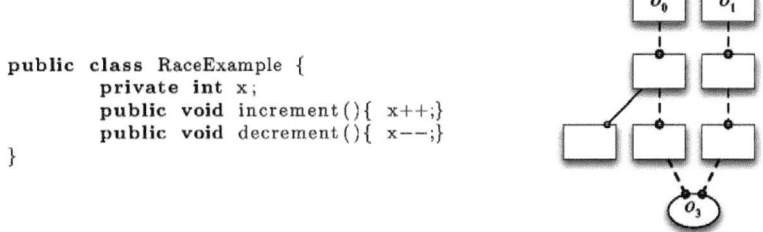

Figure 7.4.: Left: simplistic example of a class possibly introducing a data race on x. Right: an object reference graph giving rise to a data race on O_3.

offers the abstract class *CspSimulator* which is itself an event *Listener* that encapsulates the *CspEnvironment* and defines ways to deal with event changes. For example, its subclass *ConsoleCspSimulator* interacts synchronously with a user, while the *SwingCspSimulator* provides asynchronous access to the events offered by the *CspEnvironment*. However, simulation can be realized by custom listeners attached to the environment without using a *CspSimulator* at all.

7.3. Modular Verification

Noninvasiveness is a feature that enables the components (which are subject to coordination) to be oblivious to coordination. However, obliviousness to coordination gives rise to proof obligations as discussed in Section 6.4. The very simple class *RaceExample* shown in Figure 7.4 shows a class that offers two methods modifying a class member variable. Its methods *increment* and *decrement* modify the same variable x and must not be executed concurrently to prevent data races.

A more complicate situation arises, if the shared data is only reachable via a chain of references. Figure 7.4 shows an object reference graph such that O_3 is transitively reachable by O_0 and O_1. Now given two methods f_0 and f_1 operating on O_0 and O_1, these methods give rise to a data race (according to definition 3) if both read sets follow the dashed bold lines and at least one of them modifies O_3 (or one of O_3's members also read by the other method).

The issue of possibly conflicting memory accesses of concurrent actions requires to also take the implementations of the basic actions of the system into account. Since verification of sequential Java programs is a hard problem in its own right, we touch this topic only superficially.

Although it might come as a surprise to the reader that we do not require the program to work in a message-passing style which is the commonly understanding of CSP-like communication, we leave the style of communication to the programmer without restricting ourselves. Besides using shared memory communication it is, for example, perfectly valid to have a UDF access a remote bean or to use JCSP [WM00] internally to communicate with other UDFs. Using other concurrency facilities such as JCSP would of course introduce new proof obligations. Using JCSP, for example, would require the two UDFs to always occur concurrently because otherwise the communication cannot happen and would block the UDF forever. This way, the assumption of UDFs to be terminating would be violated. In consequence, the respective event will run indefinitely, preventing progress of any behavior dependent on that event.

Modular Verification targets the problem of specifying and verifying components independently such that their specifications and proofs remain valid under composition. In an object-oriented context, modular verification requires specification languages to be capable of expressing features such as subtyping and inheritance. One important problem supporting modular verification is the so-called *frame problem* concerning the modification behavior of methods [Mül02].

The Java Modeling Language (JML) [LBR06] enriches Java with a specification language for specifying invariants on objects as well as pre and postconditions and loop invariants of methods. It is supported by a number of verification tools (see e. g., [BCC+05]). JML is based on Java logical operators enriched with a set of operators to express quantification, normal and abrupt termination of methods, modifies-clauses and abstract (i. e., specification) variables. It supports modular verification to a great extent. Unfortunately, its support for concurrency-related specifications is still lagging [BCC+05]. The problem with concurrency-related properties is that they often cross-cut software modules and tend to introduce dependencies in the program that are hard to grasp and hard to specify. Thus, concurrency complicates the problem of modular verification. The Hoare-Triple

$$\{x = 0\}\ x := x + 1\ \{x = 1\},$$

for example, is valid in a sequential context but invalid if x is a shared variable modified concurrently by another thread.

Modular verification is still a subject of ongoing research in a purely sequential context but it is even harder in a concurrent context.

As pointed out by Welch in [WM00] it is important to make Java concurrency amenable to formal verification and hide the monitor-based primitives from the programmer. However, unlike the other CSP-based frameworks, we do not focus on communication but regard events as abstractions of arbitrary actions. The proof obligations presented in Section 6.4 integrate verification of the system's concurrency structure with the modular verification of the system's UDFs.

Determining *reads* and *writes* of arbitrary Java methods is a hard problem in general (due to polymorphism, dynamic binding and aliasing) but this issue is beyond the scope of this thesis.

7.4. Supported Processes

Our simulation kernel is equipped with a simple CSP_M parser. The parser does not yet support full CSP_M but supports a limited although semantically complete subset of CSP_M. Its input syntax restrict models to be made up of single-operator processes only, excluding input/output decorations (!,?) on events and being free of any functional constructs. Thus, the simulation environment supports the CSP part of CSP_M but omits any syntactical sugar offered by CSP_M.

It is easy to see that these requirements regarding the form of the current input language supported by our simulation kernel do not impose a limit on the processes it supports. The reason is that any CSP_M specification that can be verified by FDR or ProB is internally transformed into this form during the compilation phase (in the case of FDR) or while animating the process (in the case of ProB). Transforming arbitrary CSP_M processes into the required form is done by performing the following steps involving computation of Σ and unfolding the functional parts of the model.

1. Externalize local definitions (**let ... within**) and lambda expressions.

2. Replace productions and extensions by their explicit values.

3. Create a copy for each possible instantiation of a parameterized process definition.

4. Replace usages of parameterized processes with the newly introduced copies.

5. Replace input decorations on events with replicated external choice.

```
ID = {0 .. 1}
channel  lock, release, read, write : ID

SPEC   = |~| x : ID @ read.x -> write.x -> SPEC
LOCK   = |~| x : ID @ lock.x -> release.x -> LOCK
P(id)  = lock.id -> read.id -> write.id -> release.id ->
         P(id)
IMPL   = (( ||| x : ID @ P(x)) [| {|lock, release|} |]
         LOCK) \ {|lock, release|}
assert SPEC [FD= IMPL
```

Figure 7.5.: Simple CSP$_M$ example of a specification SPEC and refinement IMPL.

6. Create copies of processes using variables for each possible instantiation of the variables.

7. Replace processes using variables by replication on the process operator determining the value of the variable in the original process (using the newly introduced copies).

8. Split each process into single operator processes.

This transformation can be implemented using the Haskell CSP$_M$ toolkit [Fon10], for example. The first four steps are simple ones as long as the sets and datatypes used in the script are finite. The fifth one conforms to the semantics of CSP because of the equivalency of input and replicated external choice, as discussed in Section 6.5. However, it is important to note that events do not necessarily relate to data-flow between processes in our approach. Step 6 is similar to the steps 2 and 3 and the last one concerned with computing Σ. The last two steps are simple syntactical transformations.

7.4.1. Example

As an example, consider the CSP$_M$ script shown in Figure 7.5. It contains a specification SPEC and an implementation model IMPL which is proved to be a refinement of SPEC in the failures-divergences semantics. Now assuming, that only IMPL is to be used as coordination model, we demonstrate the transformation of IMPL into a process accepted by our coordination environment. The script does not contain any local or anonymous definitions, so we begin with replacing the production $\{|lock, release|\}$ by its explicit representation

$$A = \{lock.0, lock.1, release.0, release.1\}.$$

7.4 Supported Processes

In a second step copies of P are created for each possible value of id. We obtain the following two processes P0 and P1.

P0 = lock.0 -> read.0 -> write.0 -> release.0 -> P0
P1 = lock.1 -> read.1 -> write.1 -> release.1 -> P1

In the next step replicated interleaved instantiation of P is replaced by the new copies P0 and P1.

IMPL = ((||| x : {P0,P1} @ x) [| A |] LOCK) \ A

Now the variable x used in LOCK is eliminated by introducing the fresh processes LOCK0 and LOCK1 and modifying the replication index set of LOCK accordingly.

LOCK = |~| x : {LOCK0,LOCK1} @ x
LOCK0 = lock.0 -> release.0 -> LOCK0
LOCK1 = lock.1 -> release.1 -> LOCK1

Splitting the processes into single operator processes strictly follows the operator precedence and introduces a fresh process for each process operator. The IMPL process, for example is split into IMPL, IMPL' and IMPL''.

IMPL = IMPL' \ A
IMPL' = IMPL'' [|A|] LOCK
IMPL'' = ||| x : {P0,P1} @ x)

The resulting CSP_M script is shown in Appendix B.6. It is ready for use with our implementation of the coordination environment. The Java code shown in Appendix B.7 turns the coordination process into an executable Java program (assuming that a suitable *CspEventExecutor* implementation exists). The excerpt shows that the CSP process is transformed into Java code creating the process configuration objects in a process store. The process store and a suitable event executor are then passed to the constructor of this system's CSP environment, which is then run by a Java Swing based simulator.

7.4.2. Turning Bad Processes into Good Ones

In Section 6.3 we discussed that even infinite state or possibly divergent processes may be used as coordination processes if they are well-behaved under certain fairness assumptions. Representations of the divergent processes P and Q and the infinite state process R presented in Section 6.3 that are suitable for coordinating a program are shown in Figure 7.6, for example. Both processes may diverge, but only Q terminates if fairness is assumed.

$$P = P' \setminus \{e\} \qquad Q = Q' \setminus \{e\} \qquad R = R' \;|||\; R''$$
$$P' = e \to P' \qquad Q' = e \to Q'' \qquad R' = a \to R$$
$$\qquad\qquad\qquad\quad Q'' = Q' \sqcap SKIP \qquad R'' = b \to SKIP$$

Figure 7.6.: Unfolded versions of the divergent processes P and Q and the infinite state process R.

Fairness can be realized by appropriate *CspEventExecutor* implementations in many cases. The *CspEventExecutor* resolving the internal choice in Q may resolve the internal choice to *SKIP* eventually. This way, it can prevent divergence and allow the program to terminate eventually. The same applies to other processes containing process control constructs such as internal or external choice, timeout or interrupt allowing the process to eventually exit from cycles of internal actions.

Infinite state processes such as R are likely to eventually run out of memory, crashing the whole system. Although R represents an infinite state process, it depends on the environment of R how many states within the process are actually reachable. Thus, there are environments (fair ones) such that infinite state processes such as R are reasonable coordination processes (compare with Section 6.3). Furthermore, if the choice about how many states are actually reachable is under internal control (e. g., consider $R \setminus \{a\}$), suitable fairness conditions can be realized by implementing the *CspEventExecutor* or *Listener* accordingly.

7.5. Discussion

In this chapter, the implementation of a CSP-based coordination environment for Java is presented. It hides Java concurrency from the user and is intended to be used for prototyping and developing safety-critical concurrent software. The coordination environment is realized by a concurrent CSP simulation kernel implemented in Java based on the transformation T (as described in Chapter 5). It offers abstractions to implement the mapping of events ($x \in \Sigma_P$) to actions, to resolve internal choices, to act upon hidden events, and to define time intervals for timeouts. Its most important properties are summarized below.

- The implementation is noninvasive.
- It interprets a coordination process P at runtime.

7.5 Discussion

- It applies T on-the-fly.

To develop a coordinated Java program, it suffices to model a CSP_M coordination process, implement a suitable *CspEventExecutor* and to setup the code combining these two. This can be done by obtaining the *CspProcessStore* either from the CSP_M parser or from a generated *CspProcessStoreFactory* and instantiating a *CspEnvironment*. The environment is connected to the outside world by a *CspSimulator*. This development process is entirely noninvasive.

Our approach allows us to separate concurrency issues from sequential ones, and to reuse the concurrent design of the system at runtime. It also enables us to use state-of-the-art CSP tools such as FDR [Ros05] and ProB [LF08] for the automated verification of concurrency aspects of the software, while enabling verification of sequential aspects using state-of-the-art software verification systems such as Krakatoa [FM07] or KeY [ABB+05].

The use of CSP makes it especially well suited for systems with highly communicative concurrent components. Conformance of the implementation with its CSP model is ensured by the proof obligations mentioned above and the CSP law 'resolution of internal choice'.

Our approach imposes no restrictions on which events can trigger user code, as other frameworks sometimes do. Any event can be mapped to a UDF, regardless of its use within the CSP model. Other approaches either do not use symbolic events but rather channels as the inter-process communication primitive (see Section 9.3 for a presentation of such approaches) or they impose restrictions on which events may trigger UDFs. For example, PAT [SLD08] allows events to trigger user-defined functions but restricts this to non-synchronized events.

The architecture of the implementation of our coordination environment allows us to benefit from load balancing because the actions are not statically assigned to threads but may be dynamically distributed among threads to improve the performance of the system. The most serious drawback of our coordination environment is its runtime overhead due to the explicit interpretation of the coordination processes.

An early version of the coordination environment named *CSP4J* is described in [KB10]. In that paper, the coordination approach is compared to the extraction of CSP models from a compiler intermediate representation of a concurrent program (as described in [KH09] and applied in [KBGG09, GBGK10]). Our approach to coordinated Java programs is applied to the development of a workflow server which is presented in the next chapter. In [BK11] we report on an approach to the modeling of adaptive systems in CSP which builds on the coordination environment presented here.

8 Using CSP for the Modeling and Coordination of Workflows

> Don't fear mistakes, there are none!
>
> *(Miles Davis)*

The modeling and management of workflows often plays a mission-critical role in today's industries. Consequently, there are a wide range of modeling techniques for workflows and systems supporting the management of workflows. Such systems are often based on semiformal modeling techniques such as the Business Process Modeling Notation (BPMN), the Business Process Modeling Language (BPML), or the Unified Modeling Language (UML). Theoreticians claim, however, that more rigorous languages such as Petri Nets or process algebras should be used instead. Unlike semiformal modeling techniques, the process calculus CSP comes with mature tool support enabling the verification of processes at design time. Surprisingly little work has been done on using CSP for modeling business processes.

This chapter provides a case study of using CSP for the specification, verification and implementation of business processes. It is based on the observation that CSP is well suited not only for specifying business processes and verifying workflows but also for executing workflows using the coordination environment presented in Chapter 7. As part of the case study, we model and implement a workflow server, which is specified in CSP and realized using the coordination environment presented in the previous chapter. The server accepts workflows that are modeled in CSP and defined as coordinated Java programs. This allows us to verify the implementation of the workflow server, and to verify business process models at design time. Hence, we present a comprehensive approach to using CSP for specifying, verifying and implementing workflows enabling the use of FDR and ProB for verifying workflow definitions.

The coordinated Java implementation of our workflow server is presented in Section 8.1. Its verification is presented in Section 8.2. Section 8.3 presents our approach to the modeling of workflows in CSP and defines soundness of workflows in CSP. Our workflow server supports workflow definitions that are themselves implemented in Java using our CSP-based coordination approach. These are described in Section 8.4. A model for building compensable workflows is developed in Section 8.5. The chapter closes with a discussion of our approach to the modeling and management of workflows in Section 8.6.

8.1. A CSP-based Workflow Server

In this section, we present a CSP-based workflow server. The server is realized as a coordinated Java program using the coordination environment presented in Chapter 7. We present its CSP coordination process and sketch its most important Java classes and the UDFs that they implement. We first give an overview of the server's architecture and then go on to describe its control processes.

To simplify the architecture and the implementation of the workflow server presented here, we focus on its coordination with respect to the management of workflow definitions. We disregard other important aspects such as user management, access control and persistency for now. The workflow server presented here manages a set of workflow definitions, i.e., it loads, activates and deactivates definitions and allows us to create new instances of workflows. To this end, the server loads workflow definitions from a filesystem directory and polls for new definitions regularly. Before activation, workflow definitions are verified with respect to soundness (definition 4) and user-defined properties. This behavior is realized by concurrent processes modeled in CSP.

The most important components of the workflow server are its CSP_M coordination script and its *CspEventExecutor* implementation class. The coordination script defines the server's main control process (its control interface) and utility processes (dealing with the server's internals). It is shown in Appendix B.9. The coordination process specifies the possible execution traces of the system and divides its sequential parts into events. It is simulated at runtime by our coordination environment. The workflow server's *CspEventExecutor* implementation realizes the mapping of events to UDFs and executes the server's internal logic. The workflow server's main routine starts the coor-

8.1 A CSP-based Workflow Server

dination environment simulating the server's coordination process. The main routine is implemented analogously to the code shown in Figure 7.1.

When started, the workflow server first initializes its environment. If that fails, it prints out an error report and deadlocks. A simplified version of the workflow server's control process looks as follows

$$WfServer = (init \rightarrow (Run \sqcap reportError \rightarrow STOP)) \setminus \{init\}.$$

This process starts with performing the hidden *init* event. The associated internal action performs the initialization of the server's environment. It creates the process definitions directory if it does not yet exist and checks whether FDR is executable, for example. The subsequent internal choice is resolved to the *Run* process only if initialization succeeded. If that process is started, the workflow server starts its internal control processes.

To enable graceful shutdown of the workflow server when it is running, we use the interrupt operator in its coordination process as shown below.

$$Run = Running \triangle shutdown \rightarrow cleanup \rightarrow SKIP$$

The effect is that whatever events the *Running* process offers, the *shutdown* event is alway offered as well. When it is chosen, the *Running* process is aborted. House keeping code (e. g., cleaning up temporary files) is then executed by the *CspEventExecutor* when performing the *cleanup* event before termination of the workflow server.

Furthermore, these excerpts show that the server's startup does not involve concurrent actions. The *init* event models a single action preparing the server's runtime environment. However, we expect the server's *Running* process to involve concurrency. Hence, the *shutdown* event is potentially concurrent to every other action of ther workflow server. The *shutdown* event is a mere control event and is not associated with a UDF. As explained in Section 5.4, the transformation T ensures that *cleanup* is not concurrent with any of the (hidden or visible) events in *Running*.

The *Running* process of the workflow server is defined as follows.

$$Running = (DefLock \mid_L \mid (ServerControl \mid\mid\mid LoaderEntrly)) \setminus L$$

where

$$DefLock = lockDefs \to unlockDefs \to DefLock \quad \text{and}$$
$$L = \{lockDefs, unlockDefs\}.$$

Running encloses the server's main utility processes, *ServerControl* and *LoaderEntry*. The parallel composition of these processes is synchronized with the *DefLock* process on the events *lockDefs* and *unlockDefs*. The *DefLock* process models a lock protecting the active workflow definitions of the server. These events are hidden in the *Running* process because they are not of any interest outside this process.

The process *ServerControl* implements the administrative interface of the workflow server, allowing us to print internal statistics and to start and deactivate workflows. The control process is specified as a replicated external choice over the respective utility processes *PrintStats*, *DeactivateDef* and *StartWf*. Note that these processes are static and do not include dynamically generated events. One might expect that the processes that deal with workflow definitions offer an event for each definition that is known to the server. Since the set of possible workflow definitions is unknown in advance and – even worse – is infinite, modeling these in the server's specification would render the model intractable by FDR. Thus, the code executed for event *selectDef* offers the workflow definitions and has to deal with exceptions. The chosen workflow definition is stored and made available to the subsequent events. The *PrintStats* process simply prints out some general statistics of the server, e. g., the loaded and running workflow definitions.

The most interesting utility process is the *LoaderEntry* process which checks for new workflow definitions to load them. Except for the *lockDefs* and the *unlockDefs* events, all of its events are hidden. Thus, outside the *Running* process that hides the visible events of *DefLock*, the *LoaderEntry* is invisible. This decouples most of the internals of the *Loader* process from the main control process of the workflow server but still allows us to protect the loaded definitions by synchronization on *lockDefs* and *unlockDefs*. The *Running* process shown above combines the processes *DefLock*, *ServerControl* and *LoaderEntry* accordingly. The *Loader* process polls on a directory to automatically load process definition jars into the workflow server in a constant interval. This is realized using the idiom

$$STOP \triangleright P$$

as introduced in Section 6.1.

8.1 A CSP-based Workflow Server

As discussed above, the internal choice operator allows us to check the results of the previous events. The UDF associated with the *poll* event, for example, stores a result value which is then used to decide how to resolve the internal choice in *NewDefs*. If a new process definition is detected by *poll*, the internal choice resolves to *NewDef*, otherwise the process continues as *Loader*. The same principle is used whenever an error occurs. The error is not handled by the current event but is checked later on when the internal choice is resolved. For example, the *loadCSP* event might cause an error. In this case, the subsequent process, *NewDef'*, will resolve to *ReportError* and not to *CheckDef*. The idiom

$$ReportError \sqcap P$$

is used several times in the coordination process shown in Appendix B.9.

The UDF associated with the *startCheck* event launches FDR in a separate operating system process but does not produce an immediate verification result. Subsequent events are associated with UDFs that check if FDR ever comes up with a verification result. The status of the external verification performed by FDR is checked later on in the *checkResult* event. If FDR is still running, the result is not yet available. In this case, the process waits for a specified interval and then checks again if the result is available. If FDR does not produce a result within a given time interval, it is aborted. This case is treated as an ordinary verification error.

Since methods that are attached to events are limited to parameterless methods, temporary values must be stored in objects that are visible to all of the relevant methods. Consequently, we structured the code related to events executed by the workflow server in classes that are to be used by the events that occur in sequential contexts and model a logic entity. Values produced by the UDFs are stored in member variables of fresh objects. These fields are read by subsequent UDFs. The last UDF using the values sets the reference pointing to the parameter objects to *null* (thus discarding the temporary values processed by the preceding UDFs).

The workflow server's implementation of the *CspEventExecutor* interface holds a map of from (visible and hidden) events to instances of the *EventHandler* interface. An *EventHandler* is a parameterized object that is used to perform the code related to a single event. This is especially suitable for modeling and implementing wizard-like control flows, e.g., the *DeactivateDef* process. The code concerned with this utility is encapsulated in a single class and the event handlers call the methods implementing the business logic. Inter-

```
LockEvents = diff(Events,{lockDefs,unlockDefs})

assert DefLock [F= Running'\LockEvents
assert Running'\LockEvents [F= DefLock

assert Running :[deadlock free [F]]

assert WfSPEC [F= WfServer
```

Figure 8.1.: Assertions for the untimed server processes.

mediate data, e. g., the selected process definition, is held in member variables (the references to the parameter objects relevant for the UDFs).

8.2. Verifying the Server

Our approach allows us not only to reason about workflow definitions but also to verify the coordination process of the workflow server itself. One critical issue is the locking of loaded workflow definitions. To ensure that the lock is released after use, we checked the first two assertions shown in Figure 8.1. These assertions state that the two processes are equal in the stable failures model:
$$DefLock \equiv_\mathcal{F} Running' \setminus (\Sigma \setminus \{lockDefs, unlockDefs\}) \,.$$

Since both assertions hold, one possible reason for deadlock of the workflow server is ruled out. Furthermore, we checked the stronger assertion of deadlock-freedom of the *Running* process. This one holds as well. Due to synchronization with the *DefLock* process, the events *lockDefs* and *unlockDefs* are suitable for enclosing a critical region for accessing the server's workflow definitions.

We also check if the server's behavior is a refinement of the following specification

$$WfSPEC = CannotRun \sqcap ((\mu P \bullet \sqcap x\colon WfEvents \bullet x \to P) \vartriangle Shutdown)\,,$$

where $WfEvents = \Sigma \setminus \{init, shutdown, cleanup\}$. The last assertions encodes this in CSP_M and is successfully verified with FDR. Hence, the workflow servereither does not start at all or performs events different from those in *WfEvents* while running and terminates only if the *shutdown* event is eventually performed.

Unfortunately, the *WfServer* is not livelock-free. Divergence is considered to be catastrophic, so the question is whether there is something wrong here.

8.2 Verifying the Server

The answer is that divergence arises because of the high level of abstraction of CSP. In this case, the abstraction of time leads to the theoretically catastrophic behavior, which does not occur in the implementation of the workflow server. As described by Roscoe in [Ros05], the *tock* event is commonly used to model the passage of time in CSP. A modified version of the workflow server's coordination process extended with the *tock* event to model passage of time, is shown in Appendix B.10. The process *Timed* synchronizes with the *Poll* process on the events *poll* and *checkResult*. These two events are at the beginning of a possible recursion. Thus, the *Timed* process enforces a *tock* event before each occurrence of either of these events. The resulting process is combined with the other components of the workflow server to form the final *TimedWf-Server* process. This model is divergence-free, showing that the abstraction of time actually caused the divergence. The last two assertions show that even without any visible behavior except the passage of time, the workflow server can always terminate successfully. As previously shown, this is due to the *shutdown* event.

Note that imposing a fairness condition on the interrupt operator in *Run* yields a similar result.

To verify absence of race conditions in the UDFs implementing the workflow server, we apply the transformation T to the server's coordination process and identify possibly concurrent actions. The transformed process is shown in Appendix B.11. The transformed version does not contain the parts modeling startup and shutdown of the server, because these parts do not contain any concurrent events (as discussed in Section 8.1). However, the event *shudown* is not mapped to an UDF to prevent data races when the server shuts down. Cleanup code is exclusively performed in the UDF related to the *cleanup* event.

The transformed coordination process does not use the extended operator transformations presented in Chapter 5, because timeout is only used in the idiom $STOP \triangleright P$ and external choice is only used to combine processes that cannot perform internal transitions initially. Under these conditions, the extended transformations collapse with the simplified ones presented in Chapter 4.

We use a modified controller to verify that there are never more than two concurrent actions active at a time. The actions in *Protected*, those that are always enclosed by the events *lockDefs* and *unlockDefs* in the coordination process,

$$Protected = \{activateDef, selectDef, deactivateDef, startWf\}$$

are guaranteed to be never concurrent amongst themselves. This is ensured by deadlock-freedom of the process *ConcurrentActions* and the refinement

$$SPEC \sqsubseteq_\mathcal{T} ConcurrentActions\,.$$

Note that the server's administrative control interface is sequential in its coordination process. Replacing the *OfferMenu* process with

$$OfferMenu = ||| \ x : \{PrintStats, DeactivateDef, StartWf\} \bullet x$$

introduces a higher level of concurrency but still ensures exclusive access to the workflow definitions of the actions in *Protected*.

The UDFs of the workflow server are implemented by a few lines of Java code (about five lines on average) that serve a well-defined purpose. Concurrently executed UDFs do not access shared objects. Despite our ultimate goal to create fully verified systems, the UDFs are not formally verified. This remains to be done as further work.

8.3. Modeling Business Process in CSP

Like the Petri Net oriented workflow community, we claim that a rigorous mathematical method should be used for modeling business processes and also for the modeling and implementation of workflow server. CSP is especially well suited for modeling business processes because it offers a mature formalism that incorporates the concept of processes as a first-order citizen, offers a rich set of control constructs, and is supported by a wide range of tools supporting the exploration and verification of processes.

We propose to map basic tasks, activities and events of business processes to CSP events and to define the control constructs in terms of process operators. The ordering of the events in the traces of the resulting process then specifies the ordering amongst the tasks of a business process. According to our simulation of truly concurrent CSP as presented in chapters 4 and 5, simultaneity and conflict of actions can also be effectively modeled in CSP. Hence, causality can be expressed via prefixing or sequential composition, for example. For purposes of intuition, we present two simple workflow patterns [vdADtHW02, vdAtHKB03] in CSP.

8.3 Modeling Business Process in CSP

WP 1 Sequence: An activity in a workflow process is enabled after the completion of another activity in the same process. Example: After the activity order registration the activity customer notification is executed. [vdADtHW02]

Let $x, y \in \Sigma$ model actions of a workflow. Both prefixing and sequential composition yield the desired behavior:

$$P = x \rightarrow y \rightarrow P'$$
$$Q = x \rightarrow SKIP; \; y \rightarrow Q'$$

WP 5 Simple Merge: A merge is a point in the workflow process where two or more alternative branches come together [...]. Example: After the payment is received or the credit is granted the car is delivered to the customer. [vdAtHKB03]

Merging is formalized by process sharing in CSP. Assume that P_0, P_1 are alternatives. No matter, which of them was executed, the path is merged to continue with process Q. Then we have:

$$P_0 \,;\, Q \quad \text{and} \quad P_1 \,;\, Q \,.$$

For example, Q is merged in

$$(P_0 \sqcap P_1) \,;\, Q \quad \text{and} \quad P_0 \,;\, Q \sqcap P_1 \,;\, Q \,.$$

It is noteworthy that the patterns are given in a way that is deeply influenced by Petri Nets. Modeling such control structures in CSP seems rather trivial, because of its higher level of abstraction compared to Petri Nets. For example, as shown above, merging of alternative paths is not an issue and provided by CSP 'for free'.

Furthermore, since process terms describe connected processes by definition, there is no need to define a special class of workflow processes in CSP (as, e.g., Workflow Nets [vdA00]). Any well-formed CSP process term is a well-formed workflow as well. However, we have to address the soundness of workflows. Informally, a sound workflow is a process that is deadlock-free and always able to eventually terminate. This implies that a sound workflow must also be livelock-free. It is therefore obvious that the processes div or $STOP$, for example, should not denote sound workflows. Since successful termination is handled by $SKIP$ in CSP, we define the soundness of workflows with respect to $SKIP$:

Definition 4 (Soundness of Process Definitions) *Every process P satisfying the following equality is a sound workflow:*

$$P \setminus \Sigma_P = SKIP$$

This equality states that $SKIP$ refines $P \setminus \Sigma_P$ in the failures-divergences model and vice versa. We use FDR to check both refinements.

According to the above definition, $SKIP$ is the simplest sound workflow. Process definitions such as

$$P = SKIP \sqcap STOP \sqcap div \quad \text{or} \quad Q = a \to Q$$

are not sound according to definition 4. The reason is that P may not terminate successfully but lead to deadlock or livelock. Q models unguarded recursion and cannot terminate.

Disregarding the common requirement of termination of a workflow, there are cases in which nonterminating or even divergent workflows are reasonable. Running an office should in general be an example of a nonterminating workflow. Divergent processes can be used to model nonterminating server processes that do not require any user interaction as described in the next section, for example. Furthermore, appropriate implementations of the *CspEventExecutor* interface can be used to coordinate diverging processes in a way that allows the processes to eventually escape the sequence of internal transitions (as discussed in Section 7.4). Consider the following process definition:

$$R = \mu R' \bullet ((a \to R') \sqcap SKIP) \setminus \{a\}$$

R is obviously divergent but a coordinated implementation would not necessarily have to be nonterminating as well. The reason is that the code resolving the internal choice could implement some kind of fairness constraint eventually leaving the nonterminating recursion. Thus, R could be regarded as a valid business process definition as well. To allow such definitions, one commonly resorts to strong fairness assumptions [vdA00]. Nevertheless, all these processes are ruled out by definition 4.

To underpin the applicability of our approach, we model the marked Workflow Net, which is shown in Figure 8.2, in CSP. In [vdA05], v. d. Aalst presents that very Workflow Net as a challenge for people who prefer other formalisms to Petri Nets to show how that process can be easily modeled in their formalisms. The workflow spawns two threads of control after its initial task a is

8.3 Modeling Business Process in CSP

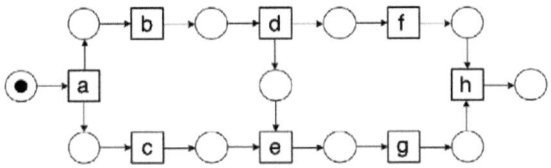

Figure 8.2.: A sound Workflow Net.

performed. One thread performs the tasks b, d and f, while the other performs c, e and g, where e is causally dependent on d. When both threads have completed, the final task h may be performed.

Our CSP model of that process is shown in Figure 8.3. The process terms can be easily derived from the Petri Net system. Process P contains events for each transition: event a models the firing of transition a and so on. An event modeling a transition t with more than one output places ($\#(t \bullet) > 1$) is followed by a parallel composition, the joining of paths is naturally modeled using CSP synchronization.

The Workflow Net shown in Figure 8.2 can produce the following ten firing sequences:

$$abcdefgh, abcdegfh, abcdfegh, abdcefgh, abdcegfh,$$

$$abdcfegh, abdfcegh, acbdefgh, acbdegfh, acbdfegh.$$

Let $SPEC$ be a process that produces exactly these traces (and any of its sub-traces of course) and then terminates successfully. The CSP_M script shown in Appendix B.8 encodes P, its specification $SPEC$ and assertions to prove

$$SPEC \equiv_T P \quad \text{and} \quad P \setminus \Sigma = SKIP.$$

FDR discharges these assertions instantly. Hence, P produces the same traces as the Workflow Net and is a sound workflow process as well.

Note that we do not claim that it is easier to model business processes in CSP than modeling them in any other formalism. Instead, we claim that

```
channel a,b,c,d,e,f,g,h
P   =  a ->              (L0 [| {e,g,h} |] R0)
L0  =  b -> d ->         (L1 [| {h} |] R1)
R0  =  c -> R1
L1  =  f -> h ->         SKIP
R1  =  e -> g -> h ->    SKIP
```

Figure 8.3.: CSP model of the workflow shown in Figure 8.2.

CSP is as suitable for modeling business processes as any other formalism commonly used for this purpose. Nevertheless, the advantage of CSP is its mature verification support.

8.4. Workflow Definitions

The workflow server accepts workflow definitions that are also modeled and implemented using our coordination approach. This means that the workflow is modeled in CSP and that this model is provided as a CSP_M script. Our workflow server accepts workflow definitions bundled as a Jar file. The Jar file must contain the following three components:

1. A properties file defining the names of the *CspEventExecutor* and the *CspSimulator* implementation classes of the workflow.

2. The CSP_M model of the workflow.

3. Its implementation classes, e. g., implementations of a custom *CspSimulator* and an *CspEventExecutor*.

Note that the CSP coordination environment also supports the translation of a CSP_M file into a Java source file. However, our workflow server does not support workflow definitions that are obtained in this way. The reason is that the CSP_M model of the workflow is checked prior to activation of a workflow definition. Consequently, the workflow server creates the instances of the process operators at runtime to ensure that the workflow instance belongs to the model accompanying the workflow's implementation classes. The workflow server could, of course, generate the Java code from the CSP_M script by itself to speedup the creation of workflow instances.

When the *Loader* process detects new Jar files, the definition is loaded. Loading of a workflow definition is performed in three steps:

1. Load the workflow definition Jar into the server.

2. Verify the CSP model of the workflow.

3. Load its *CspSimulator* and *CspEventExecutor* implementation classes.

Only if all these steps succeed is the workflow definition activated.

The first step makes the Jar accessible to the subsequent steps. The second step begins by loading the `wf.properties` configuration resource from the Jar. It is used to locate the other required elements within the Jar. The CSP_M script is then dumped to a temporary file. The necessary assertions for checking the soundness of the script (definition 4) are also added to the file. The script is sound if FDR successfully checks all of its assertions. In the last step, the *CspEventExecutor* and the *CspSimulator* classes referenced in the properties file of the workflow definition are finally loaded. If any of these steps fails, the workflow definition is not activated. Otherwise, the workflow definitions are locked and the workflow definition is activated.

Active workflow definitions are used to create new workflow instances. This is done by the *StartWf* utility process. The code snippet to create a new coordinated system as shown in Figure 7.1 is not only used in the workflow server's main routine, but also in the startup code of workflows, which creates a new workflow instance of a given workflow definition. The UDF implementing the event *startWf*, triggers code the creates a new *CspEnvironment* with the definition's initial process, *CspEventExecutor* and *CspSimulator*. Since process definitions do not interfere with the workflow server's processes, creating new processes affects neither the validity of the assertions proved on the server's specification nor of those proved on the process definition.

8.5. Compensation

Transaction commonly use locks to prevent intermediate changes to interfere with other transaction and perform a complete rollback of intermediate changes in an error occurs. In the context of long running transactions, i. e., a day or a week instead of seconds, it is often more advantageous to publish intermediate values and to compensate effects of such intermediate changes as much as possible if the transaction fails. So the main difference between rollback and compensation is that compensation deals with non-local changes, but its aim is also to undo the effects of the preceding work items that resulted in or were affected by the error. The effectiveness of this recovery strategy is largely governed by the richness of the events captured in the execution log and some events (e. g., resource allocation) cannot be undone. The advantage of compensation is that it provides a more flexible means of remedying the effects of the error. In general, compensation handlers are responsible for well-defined parts of the transaction and are to be executed in reverse order after an error occured. Now, because workflows can be regarded as long running transactions, the error handling concept of compensation is an important subject for our approach to the modeling and management of workflows.

As explained above, every well-formed CSP process is also a *well-formed workflow*, and a workflow P is *sound* if and only if $P \setminus \Sigma = SKIP$. Thus ✓ handles termination of a workflow and a sound workflow is guaranteed to eventually terminate. To assign a workflow-specific meaning to events, Σ is partitioned into the set of activities (workflow tasks) $\Upsilon \subseteq \Sigma$ and the workflow control events $\Gamma \subseteq \Sigma$. The main problem in modeling and implementing compensation is how to stack-up compensation handlers and possible parameters as the long-running transaction progresses. In the presence of parallelism, for example, an exception might cause cancellation and subsequent compensation of multiple processes. The overall soundness condition must not be violated by compensation. So, if P is a divergence-free (but possibly unsound) workflow that either terminates successfully or eventually performs an event indicating an error, and $F(P)$ is its compensable version, then

$$F(P) \setminus \Sigma = SKIP$$

must hold. The requirement of divergence-freedom stems from the fact that divergence cannot (in theory) be cured by any CSP construction.

In the sequel, a compensable sequential process is called a milestone. We require that the first event emitted by a milestone is parameterized such that it determines the compensation handler of that milestone. Let I be a set of milestone identifiers, $l \in I^*$, $m : I$ a milestone channel such that $\{\!|\, m \,|\!\} \subset \Gamma$, $fail \in \Gamma$ an event indicating an error of P, $S_{F(P)} = \Sigma_P \cup \{abort, commit\}$ where *abort* and *commit* are fresh events relative to Σ_P. Compensation of P is modeled using the following compensation process $F(P)$:

$$F(P) = ((P\,;commit \rightarrow SKIP) \triangle abort \rightarrow SKIP) \,|S_{F(P)}|\, C(\langle\rangle)$$
$$C(l) = commit \rightarrow SKIP$$
$$\square\ (x : (\Sigma_P \setminus (\{\!|\, m \,|\!\} \cup \{fail\}))) \rightarrow C(l)$$
$$\square\ m?id \rightarrow C(\langle id \rangle \frown l)$$
$$\square\ fail \rightarrow abort \rightarrow Comp(l)$$
$$Comp(l) = SKIP \triangleleft l = \langle\rangle \triangleright Handler(head(l))\,;Comp(tail(l))$$

Furthermore, we assume that $Handler(id)$ yields a compensation handler H such that $\Sigma_H \cap \Sigma_P = \emptyset$ and $H \setminus \Sigma_H = SKIP$. Due to the synchronization on $S_{F(P)}$, $F(P)$ records all visible events performed by P, in particular the error and milestone events. Since $abort \notin \Sigma_P$, the controller aborts P (including its running subprocesses) by refusing $\Sigma_P \cup \{commit\}$ and accepting *abort* exclusively. It then executes the compensation handlers in reverse order to the occurrences of their respective milestones. If P terminates successfully

$F(P)$ also terminates successfully as shown by the following theorem (using ProB-like LTL syntax where [.] denotes occurrence of an event).

Theorem 7 *Given divergence-free P such that $P \models \Diamond([\checkmark] \vee [\mathit{fail}])$, the following holds:*
$$F(P) \setminus \Sigma = \mathit{SKIP}\,.$$

The proof exploits the $F(P)$ construction and considers the cases of successful termination and failure of the workflow. It is shown in Appendix A.6.

The following properties hold by construction of $F(P)$:

- If P is either a sound workflow or divergence-free and eventually performs an error event then $F(P)$ is a sound workflow;

- The compensation handlers are executed in reverse order to the occurrences of their respective milestones if and only if an error occurs;

- P cannot make any progress while the compensation handlers are running.

Thus, this construction cures any chaotic behavior except divergence.

Note that this approach relies on the fact that events are mapped to user-defined functions by our CSP-based coordination environment. It is further assumed that these functions store the relevant data needed for compensation. The compensation handlers are started only after termination of the actions being performed at the occurrence of an error (maintaining the e-non-refusability property 2).

8.6. Discussion

In this chapter, we have presented a workflow server modeled in CSP and implemented as a coordinated Java program. Prototyping the workflow server has shown that our coordination environment is well suited for developing highly concurrent Java software. The organization of code in small parts that are to be attached to events (the UDFs) was a great help in designing and coding the system. As a result, the implementation of the workflow server consists only of approximately 500 lines of Java code and about 100 lines of CSP_M specification. Developing the workflow server prototype has shown that careful sequential designs allow us to determine sources of data races easily.

The coordination process of the workflow server is verified using FDR and the server uses FDR internally to verify workflows before activation.

The CSP_M encoding of the workflow server's coordination process is shown in Appendix B.9. Its timed variant, used for the verification of livelock-freedom, is shown in Appendix B.10. The transformed processes are shown in Appendix B.11.

The server supports workflows that are modeled in CSP. Workflow definitions are given as coordinated Java programs. The workflow server uses FDR to verify workflow definitions. To support compensation of workflows, we presented an approach to the modeling of compensable workflows in standard CSP. It is based on milestones and a protocol process recording the milestones. The model of compensation presented above is published in [Kle10].

Since this thesis is primarily concerned with the control-flow perspective of systems, other important aspects of a workflow server such as persistency, distribution, fault tolerance, authentication and access control are not yet supported. However, it underpins the applicability of our approach to coordination.

The workflow server described in this chapter is an updated and extended version of the workflow server presented in [KG10]. The version presented in that paper is based on a preliminary version of the coordination environment presented in Chapter 7 which was called *CSP4J*.

9 Related Work

In this chapter, related work is presented. We begin with a presentation of approaches to coordinating concurrent (component) systems in Section 9.1. The presentation includes formal approaches as well as informal ones. Related work also covers the area of interleaving versus non-interleaving (truly concurrent) semantics for CSP being discussed in Section 9.2. In Section 9.3, CSP-like concurrency frameworks are presented. In that section, we focus on Java frameworks because Java is the target language of the implementation accompanying this thesis (as presented in Chapter 7). In Section 9.4, related work concerning the modeling of business processes and the implementation of workflow systems is presented. This also extends to formal approaches to compensation, because this issue arises naturally in the context of workflows.

9.1. Coordination

Approaches to coordination are driven by the idea to reduce the complexity of the development of concurrent systems by abstracting from concurrency primitives necessary for implementing such systems and offering some high-level constructs for this purpose. Such approaches are either motivated by practical needs or theoretical interest. For example, Linda [ACG86] is driven by practical needs and offered the implementation of a coordination language prior to its formal investigation. Circus [WC02] is located at the other end of the spectrum being a combination of CSP and Z [ASM80, Spi92] targeting the formal specification of a concurrent system and offering a refinement calculus for deriving implementations from Circus designs.

In this section, we present a number of approaches that we consider to belong to this spectrum, situated between Linda and Circus. We first present approaches using other formalisms than CSP, then we discuss some of those using CSP.

9.1.1. Non-CSP Approaches

In [CJY95], Ciancarini et al. present a number of formal semantics for Linda. They consider the issue of true concurrency and present operational semantics, multistep operational semantics, and a Petri Net-based (hence truly concurrent) semantics, for example. Although they do not touch the topic of verifying Linda programs, their work enables the use of Petri Net tools for the verification of Linda programs, for example. However, Linda primarily targets the implementation of concurrent systems as opposed to modeling and verifying such systems. Our approach differs in various points from the approaches described above. In contrast to Linda, it builds on ordinary shared memory communication (as built into the underlying language) instead of a special memory model (the so-called *tuplespace*). Moreover, our approach supports verification because it is based on the mature formal method CSP which is supported by a number of industrial-strength tools.

In [CDS00], Cleaveland et al. present the graphical modeling language GCCS which is a graphical front-end to Milner's Calculus of Communicating Systems (CCS) [Mil89] (see e. g., [Hoa06] for a comparison of CCS with CSP). The purpose of GCCS is to enable formal verification of designs using standard CCS tools and to derive implementation stubs from the designs. They understand GCCS as a coordination language because it is supported by code generators for multiple target languages. The generated code then implements the coordination conforming to the GCCS design and is to be extended with user-defined operations implementing the sequential computations of the system. CCS is taken 'as is'. It is not discussed if true concurrency is an issue in that setting. Unlike our approach, internal transitions are not considered.

Another formal approach to the modeling and verification of distributed component based systems is described by Baier et al. [BBKK09]. Their approach is based on the model checker Vereofy which supports multiple input languages capable of modeling concurrent systems. However, their approach does not extend to implementing such systems but remains on the modeling level.

Reference Nets [Kum02] provide an object-oriented High-Level Petri Net formalism where instances of Petri Nets carry references to other instances of Petri Nets instead of tokens. In that model, the firing of a transition moves a reference from one place to another. The concept of synchronous channels allows Petri Net instances to communicate when a transition fires. Reference Nets extend this to the execution of arbitrary (terminating) Java code. Thus, in that model, a Petri Net can be regarded as the coordination process of a system and the code attached to transitions relates to our understanding of actions. Unlike our approach, Reference Nets do not support verification of the coordination process and lack proof obligations relating the ordering of Petri Net transitions (as defined by their firing sequences) to the pre- and postconditions of their associated implementations, for example.

Timed Communicating Object-Z (TCOZ) [MD98] is a formal method based on the Unifying Theories of Programming (UTP) of Hoare and He [HH98]. It combines Timed-CSP [DS95] with Object-Z [DRS95] and enables the concise modeling of concurrent object-oriented real-time systems. Again, the idea is to specify state and operations of components (Object-Z) separately from interaction of components (Timed-CSP). In that sense, it takes Timed-CSP as a coordination language for components modeled in Object-Z. However, it is not supported by verification tools. TCOZ can now be considered a dead language because it is superseded by the Process Analysis Toolkit (PAT) [SLD08]. PAT's input language CSP# implements concepts taken from TCOZ in a simplified manner suitable for automated verification. In contrast to our approach, PAT targets the modeling and verification of CSP based systems instead of implementation.

9.1.2. CSP-based Approaches

In [ST04], Schneider and Treharne present a combination of CSP and B [Abr96] that is now known as CSP ∥ B. The idea of CSP ∥ B is to separate the specification of a component into state related and interaction properties. The B method is used to express requirements on state of the components and their coordination is expressed in CSP. CSP events are associated with operations, hence assuming atomicity of operations.

The main difference between CSP ∥ B and our approach is that CSP ∥ B provides a deep semantic integration of CSP and B whereas our approach provides a rather loose semantical coupling of the coordination model with the coordinated actions (or components). In our approach, a proof obligation relates ordering of events with pre- and postconditions of actions. In CSP ∥ B, the pre- and postconditions of operations (specified in B) are embedded in the CSP semantics. As a consequence, divergence can also be introduced be performing an operation outside its precondition. Another consequence of the deep integration is that hidden events cannot coordinate operations. Note that our approach allows even synchronized events to be hidden. The CSP ∥ B approach enables the verification of coordinated B machines. In [STE05], Schneider et al. show how CSP ∥ B models can be decomposed into so-called *chunks* for subsequent verification with FDR. However, their approach does not support the generation of code implementing the coordination. This remains to be done manually.

In [LB05], Butler and Leuschel also propose an approach combining CSP and B, sometimes referred to as CSP+B. It is closely related to the CSP ∥ B approach but there are some subtle differences on the semantic integration of CSP and B between these two approaches. For example, executing an operation whose precondition is not met yields divergence in CSP ∥ B but simply cannot happen in CSP+B because the latter approach interprets preconditions as guards on the CSP level. Schneider et al. develop a denotational semantics for CSP ∥ B targeting FDR, while Leuschel and Butler present an operational semantics for CSP+B which is natively supported by the ProB tool. ProB is capable of animating and verifying CSP+B specifications. Neither of the two approaches deals with truly concurrent semantics. They assume operations on B machines to be atomic. Again, implementation of the CSP part of a model must be done manually.

The rCOS formalism (standing for refinement of component and object systems) introduced by He et al. [HLL05] is a contract based formalism tailored for the specification and verification of guarded service components. In [CHL06], the rCOS formalism is extended with the notion of processes and coordination. To that end they introduce CSP-like parallel composition and hiding operators and define a semantics based on traces, failures and divergences in a CSP-like manner. The resulting denotational semantics appears to be quite similar to that developed for CSP ∥ B. Again, the CSP-like operators remain to be implemented manually and coordination does not extend to internal actions.

In [Fis97], Fischer introduces CSP-OZ, a formalism combining CSP and Object-Z. In that formalism, Object-Z is used to specify the state space of Java objects and CSP expressions specify the valid order of method calls on them. In [Fis00], Fischer introduces Jass (Java with Assertions), a Java annotation language with a pre-compiler adding the option of design by contract to Java, and presents a translation of CSP-OZ specifications into Jass. To specify sets of valid traces of method calls on Java object, Jass provides *trace assertions* (that are derived from the CSP part of a CSP-OZ class). Trace assertions are CSP expressions enriched with Java fragments that are used to check if the history of the program adheres to its specified traces. In Fischer's approach, events are mapped to method calls. This is very similar to our notion of an action that allows user-coded functions to be attached to events. The advantage of Fischer's approach is that it combines verification of properties relating to concurrency and state and also supports the derivation of executable code. Its drawback is that, unlike in our approach, the traces cannot be statically verified owing to the complexities of the Java programming language. Instead, the assertions are checked at runtime.

Circus [WC02] targets the specification of both data and behavioral aspects of concurrent and reactive systems by combining Z [ASM80, Spi92] and CSP. It supports stepwise development through refinement. The main reason for the selection of Z and CSP as the basis for the design of Circus is their notion of refinement. The semantic model proposed for Circus is based on the Unifying Theories of Programming (UTP) of Hoare and He [HH98]. The semantics allows precise description of different programming paradigms in an incremental fashion, hence leaving room for extension. Circus supports the development of safety-critical concurrent systems and is equipped with verification tools, for example the model checker developed by Freitas [Fre05]. However, compared to approaches based on the B method Circus is a rather academic approach. For example, we are not aware of any code generators for Circus.

By mapping an event to an action, our approach assumes the precondition of the action to hold in the states the process is willing to perform the respective event. This approach is similar to Reference Nets that allow arbitrary Java code to be performed when a transition fires. By contrast, integrations of CSP with state-based formalisms such as CSP ∥ B or CSP-OZ use the predicates specifying pre- and postconditions of operations as pre- and postconditions of the events as well.

From a formal point perspective, the latter approach is much more of an integration than the former one. Our approach is based on the assumption that the CSP part of the specification completely describes the ordering of the system's actions.

9.2. Truly Concurrent Semantics for CSP

Our work relates particularly to other approaches that consider 'non interleaving' or 'truly concurrent' semantics of process algebra. In particular, it is influenced by the work of Kwiatkowska and Phillips [KP95] and Taubner and Vogler [TV89]. In a sense, our approach combines the two by simulating the concurrency relation developed in the former, while maintaining the concurrent events in a structure that generalizes the steps defined in the latter.

In [KP95], Kwiatkowska and Phillips have proposed a (denotational) 'failures with divergence and conflict' semantics for CSP. Furthermore, they distinguish *possible* conflict from *guaranteed* conflict. Analogously, they define a concurrency relation *co*. Our definitions 1 and 2 (and proposition 3 in particular) relate to their notions of possible concurrency and guaranteed conflict-freedom. In contrast to their work, rather than define a new semantics of CSP we have used the standard denotational semantics to simulate 'truly concurrent CSP'. In our approach, concurrency is encountered whenever the controller's bag X grows beyond one element with frequency one. In particular, a single event is concurrent with itself if and only if there is a trace t such that its cardinality in the bag is greater than one after t. By contrast, each trace is by definition concurrent with itself in the semantics given by Kwiatkowska and Phillips.

Another important difference with that work is in refinement of concurrency information. In their semantics, only the refinement

$$a \to b \to STOP \;\square\; b \to a \to STOP \;\sqsubseteq\; a \to STOP \;|_\emptyset|\; b \to STOP$$

holds but not conversely. Using the modified controller $C1$ to incorporate concurrency information in the traces of a process yields the opposite refinement relation, as shown in Section 4.4.1. Thus, in our approach, a process refines another with a higher level of concurrency.

In [TV89], Taubner and Vogler present a non-interleaving semantics of CSP based on the notion of 'step'. In their semantics, a step is a finite bag of events from $\Sigma_{\checkmark}$. Traces and failures are lifted from sequences of events to sequences of steps, and refusals are defined over sets of steps. The empty step is called the null-step, and refusal of the null-step corresponds to divergence. A non-divergent process may never refuse the null-step. Their semantics generalizes the interleaving semantics of CSP in the sense that the special case of singleton steps is exactly the interleaving semantics.

That approach, like ours, realizes possible concurrency in the sense that whenever a step is possible, all of its sub-steps are also possible. One distinguishing feature of their semantics is that it lacks the commonly used τ event to model internal actions. While the authors present this as a theoretical advantage because they succeed in establishing the common CSP laws in their semantics, it might be considered a disadvantage from a practical perspective. For that reason, our approach aims to detect any concurrent events, whether they are visible or hidden. The code related to an externally visible event a is likely to interfere with the code of a hidden a that is executed concurrently. Therefore, our controller registers even externally invisible events. Compared with their semantics, ours appears more verbose because it records not only the steps but also the creation of the steps (filling the bag).

On the level of traces our approach can be regarded as generalizing theirs: the controller can be modified to ensure that it refuses new s events after an e event until its bag is empty; that yields traces such that the state of the bag before the first e after each nonempty sequence of s events are exactly the steps in their semantics. Our approach, like the step-failures semantics, can be used to optimize systems at runtime by predicting maximal parallelism. It also takes into account duration of user-defined functions related to events.

9.3. CSP-like Concurrency Frameworks

The programming language occam [Bar92] implements an early version of Hoare's CSP and provides primitives like guards, sequential composition, alternatives, parallelism, channels and timers. Process operators like internal choice, timeout, interrupt and hiding, are not supported.

CSP++ [Gar05], is a mature framework which realizes CSP concurrency on top of POSIX threads for C++. The framework defines a whole development life-cycle starting with a CSP_M specification that is refined down to a CSP implementation model. The implementation model is finally translated into C++ using the CSP++ framework. This framework implements channels as a communication primitive and allows us to bind user-coded functions to events that are executed when the event is performed. The CSP++ framework implements an occam-style subset of CSP supporting sequential composition, external choice, interleaving and parallel composition. Unlike our coordination environment, Gardner's framework does not allow user-coded functions to be attached to events that are used in synchronization sets between processes. Nevertheless, CSP++ was tailored to be applicable in practice and comes with an IDE that helps in writing CSP_M models and to attach user-coded functions to events [GMOC+09]. The IDE also interfaces with FDR and ProBE to support verification and animation of CSP_M models.

JCSP [WM00, Wel00] is a well-known Java library offering CSP concepts as a foundation for developing concurrent systems in an event-based style. In this framework, processes communicate over channels which are basically buffers. JCSP realizes CSP's synchronous communication between Java threads by blocking the send operation until the value is read by its receiver. This is realized using the Java primitives *synchronize*, *wait* and *notify*. Processes (implemented as Java threads) are not allowed to invoke each other's methods but they may be combined to wait passively on a number of alternative events. The external generation of such an event triggers the processes into action according to the CSP semantics of the process operator combining the events. JCSP implements the channel concept and offers a set of process operators that resemble the occam programming language rather than full CSP.

JCSProB [YP07, YP09] is an implementation strategy for CSP+B targeting the creation of multi-threaded Java programs. Yang and Poppleton motivate their approach as follows:

> The main issue in developing an implementation strategy for ProB is how to implement the concurrency model of the B+CSP specification in a correct and straightforward way. Furthermore, we need an explicit formal definition, or even automatic tool support, to close the gap between the abstract specification and concrete programming languages. [YP07, p.3]

Hence, their ultimate goal is the same as ours. However, they do not support 'full' CSP and do not consider consider concurrently executed operations. Furthermore, noninvasiveness is not an issue. They implement the CSP+B concurrency model as a Java framework inspired by JCSP. Their approach supports multi-threaded Java, implements the channel concept, and supports occam-like process operators.

Hilderink et al. have developed another CSP library for Java, called CTJ [HBB99, HBB00]. Like JCSP, CTJ implements occam-like process operators and channels for Java, and neither supports hiding nor resolution of nondeterminism. Unlike JCSP, it builds up a completely new thread architecture to deal with concurrency. This makes it more flexible but adds the overhead of proprietary concurrency primitives to Java monitors. Link drivers implement internal or external communication means such as shared memory or TCP/IP connectors and can be plugged into channels. This makes processes highly independent of their physical location on the total system. Furthermore, there is a tool to support the channel skeleton code creation. In summary, the CTJ framework focuses on process/thread scheduling and channel link drivers. The idea of link drivers is related to our concept of an event chooser that also allows the implementation of different communication means. In [CS02], Cavalcanti and Sampaio present an approach for the development of concurrent Java programs using the CTJ framework from CSP-OZ specifications. The

9.3 CSP-like Concurrency Frameworks

CTJ framework is also ported to C and C++ (CTC and CTC++). The obvious advantages of CTJ over our approach are that it is apparently widely used and supports distributed systems. The advantage of our approach is that it supports a richer CSP in terms of process operators and allows us to use a CSP process directly as coordination processes of the final system.

The JACK framework presented by Freitas [Fre02] aims to fully implement CSP, but some process operators such as renaming, timeout and interrupt are not yet supported. It thus provides a richer set of process operators than the previously mentioned approaches. Besides JACK, little work has been done on implementing full CSP, such as the one described by Roscoe in [Ros05], which is the version that we focus on. Again, this framework implements the channel concept and has to deal with restrictions on communications. Unlike CTJ, JACK uses a strong type system to define channels, alphabets, types, and communication patterns. JACK provides backtracking facilities to deal with infinite state CSP models. In addition, concepts such as guards are implemented, making the framework quite complex.

CSP software frameworks as the ones mentioned above focus on message passing concurrency. They implement CSP-like channels as inter-thread communication facilities but realize only a limited set of CSP operators. Furthermore, they require the implementation of specific process classes. This makes it harder (compared to our approach) to prove conformance of a system implemented using one of these frameworks to a coordination script.

Unlike the frameworks described above, ours does not incorporate the channel concept. Instead, events are merely symbols used for synchronization, and hence to enforce a specific ordering of the UDFs. The interpretation of events – and whether or not an event is seen as an indivisible symbol rather than a channel with possible input or output parameters – is essential for an implementation strategy for CSP, of course. Even the idea of a channel can be refined further. A channel can be seen either as a remote method invocation or as a communication link. The former is basically a synchronous communication, while the latter relates to asynchronous communication. Channels are commonly implemented as blocking queues to facilitate inter-thread communication (hence using a natively asynchronous mechanism and enforcing synchrony by blocking communication partners until the communication has completed). While an event relates to a method invocation in Jass, the other frameworks mentioned above implement channels. Our approach deliberately does not implement any of these two options but regards the events being the extension of a channel as abstractions of arbitrary actions.

Since sequential processes in CSP are viewed as executions of computational entities exhibiting their specific observable behavior in terms of events, it is natural to map a single sequential process to its own thread. This is the general idea underlying CSP++, JCSP, CTJ and JACK. Our approach does not necessarily map two causally dependent threads to the same thread. It merely maintains the order of UDFs as defined by the events of the CSP script coordinating the system. This is comparable to LINDA's feature of distributing tasks at runtime. Hence it enables us to implement load-balancing by distributing UDFs amongst threads.

9.4. Modeling and Managing Business Processes

In this section, we first present a number of modeling techniques for business processes focusing on their practical relevance and support for formal verification. We then go on to present related work dealing with compensation in Section 9.4.2.

9.4.1. Modeling Techniques

Popular modeling techniques for business processes are the Unified Modeling Language (UML) (as treated in [EW02]), Business Process Modeling Notation (BPMN) (as treated in [WG08]), Workflow Graphs (as defined in [SO96]) and Workflow Nets (see, e.g., [vdA00]). Of these, only the latter two were equipped with a formal semantics when they were first applied to business process modeling.

Petri Nets are widely used for modeling workflows and even for defining semantics of other (semi-formal) workflow modeling techniques. In [EW02], for example, Eshuis and Wieringa present an approach to the verification of workflows modeled as UML Activity Diagrams by transforming them into Petri Nets. As shown in [vdAHV02], Workflow Graphs can also be verified in terms of Petri Nets.

YAWL (Yet Another Workflow Language) [vdAtH02] is designed to ease the modeling of common workflow patterns [vdAtHKB03]. It is semantically founded on Petri Nets. YAWL is supported by a specialized execution engine [vdAADtH04]. It also offers support for standard languages from the area of business processes and web services choreography. It is still actively developed and maintained.

9.4 Modeling and Managing Business Processes 143

Reference Nets have been successfully applied for modeling and managing workflows. For example, the modeling of workflow patterns in Reference Nets is shown by Moldt and Rölke in [MR03]. The Reference Net Workshop [KWD+04] supports graphical editing and animation of Reference Nets. The workflow server that is conceptually the closest to ours is the Renew [KWD+04] workflow plugin described by Jacob et al. in [JKMUN02]. The workflow plugin realizes a workflow server using Reference Nets. Like our system, this plugin is built using the same means which it promotes for building the workflow definitions. Although far more developed in terms of features such as persistency and user management, this workflow server lacks the capability of built-in workflow verification. The reason is that there are so far no verification tools for Reference Nets.

The graphical nature of Petri Nets is often claimed an advantage for the modeling of workflows. However, we think that CSP offers a more elegant way for expressing complex workflows due to its higher level of abstraction.

After the publication of common workflow patterns by v. d. Aalst et al. in [vdAtHKB03], several attempts were made to model these patterns using different formalisms. Examples are the π-calculus by Puhlmann and Weske in [PW05] and Orc by Cook et al. in [CPM06]. In [WG07], Wong and Gibbons show how to model and verify business processes in CSP. In particular, they present CSP models for a number of workflow patterns. They use the CSP refinement calculus to verify implementation models of a workflow with respect to its specification model. They did not, however, attempt to implement and execute the CSP-based workflows. Nor did they transfer the notions of soundness from the theory of workflows to CSP. In [WG08], Wong and Gibbons contributed to the modeling of business processes using CSP by defining the semantics of BPMN in CSP.

Regarding the possibility of using graphical tools to develop the CSP part of workflow definitions, e. g., gCSP [JOLB04], our CSP-based approach to modeling workflows lacks none of the benefits that are claimed for Workflow Graphs or Petri Nets. For example, existing BPMN models of business processes can be translated into CSP and thus ported to our workflow server. This can be realized using the BPMN to CSP translator presented by Wong and Gibbons in [WG08], along with their BPMN semantics defined in CSP, for example.

In [FV08], Friborg et al. use CSP for the modeling of scientific workflows. Their approach is supported by the PyCSP framework [BVA07], a Python concurrency framework in the tradition of JCSP. Unlike the other approaches that build on managed workflows, they use PyCSP for implementing the workflows as standalone systems. Such an approach is also possible with our coordination environment. However, it lacks the benefits provided by a dedicated workflow server.

9.4.2. Compensation

Exception handling patterns for workflows are discussed by Lerner et al. in [LCO+10]. However, their patterns are semi formally defined as UML activity diagrams and in BPMN.

A more general approach to exception handling is known as *compensation*. This approach defines reversibility of long-running transactions without the rigorous protection (locking) of intermediate values. Workflows can be regarded as long-running transactions which possibly publish intermediate values that have to be undone if a certain fault occurs. Since these intermediate values may be used by other transactions, rollback does not work in such a situation. Instead, compensation handlers are used to recover from faults in long-running actions and to undo as many of the changes of the failed transaction as possible. The Structured Activity Compensation (StAC) [BF04] language, for example, explicitly targets the modeling of compensation. [BMM05] presents a general semantic framework for compensation in flow composition language. Semantics of compensable processes are also considered by Butler et al. in [BHF05].

Rabbi et al. define Compensable Workflow Nets in [RWM10] and introduce a graphical modeling language for compensable workflows. Compensable Workflow Nets are defined as a subclass of colored Petri Nets [Jen95]. In particular, they adopt the common definition of Workflow Nets (and their soundness), as defined in [vdA00]. They construct Compensable Workflow Nets by replacing ordinary (non-compensable) workflow tasks with sound (but more complex) Workflow Nets representing compensable tasks. This corresponds to refinement in Petri Net theory. They propose a model checking approach for the verification of Compensable Workflow Nets. In summary, they define compensation on the granularity of tasks, while we define it for milestones.

Compensation is not a native feature of CSP, but extensions of CSP with compensation such as cCSP [BR05] exist. In [ZCW11], Chen et al. present a theory of failures-divergences refinement for cCSP. To that end, they extend the syntax of cCSP with operators representing deterministic and nondeterministic choice, generalized parallel composition and recursion. They also propose to extend FDR to support the semantics of cCSP. However, tool support for their approach is not yet available.

Since one of our goals is the reuse of existing CSP tools (e. g., FDR and ProB), we model compensation in plain CSP. This distinguishes our approach from other approaches (e. g., [BR05, BMM05]) that build compensation into the language. However, it introduces a considerable overhead in modeling the compensable workflow, similar to the approach presented in [RWM10].

9.5. Summary

In this chapter, we have presented other approaches to coordination, truly concurrent CSP, the implementation of CSP, modeling and management of workflows, and compensation. Regarding the practice of coordination, Reference Nets come quite close to our approach. On the theoretical level, CSP $\parallel$ B and CSP+B are those related most closely. We are not aware of other approaches to truly concurrent CSP that are supported by verification tools. In particular, none of them can be used with FDR or ProB. Other implementations of CSP are very different from our coordination environment because it does not build on the channel concept but on the assumption that an event models an arbitrary action of a system not necessarily concerned with communication. We have also presented related work concerning the application of CSP to the theory of workflows. However, implementation support is lagging in comparison to Petri Net-based workflow systems. This is the slot targeted by our workflow server: like the Reference Net-based approach to the modeling and management of workflows, our approach uses coordination processes for the workflow server and for the workflows themselves but offers verification support for the coordinated systems (the implementation of the workflow server and the workflows). Moreover, we have discussed other approaches to compensable workflows.

10 Conclusion

> It is easier to resist at the beginning than at the end.
>
> *(Leonardo da Vinci)*

This chapter summarized and evaluates the most important results of the preceding chapters. We begin with a summary of the thesis in Section 10.1. The main contributions of the thesis are highlighted in Section 10.2. Pointers to future work are given in Section 10.3. In Section 10.4, we relate the contents of this thesis to other publications of ours.

10.1. Summary

In this thesis, we have presented our CSP-based approach for the construction of provably correct concurrent systems. CSP is chosen because it offers an intermediate-level formalism for reasoning about complex concurrent systems. Another reason for choosing CSP is its maturity in terms of theoretical work and tool support that ranges from refinement checking over animation and LTL model checking to theorem proving.

The main idea of our approach is to use CSP to coordinate the operations of the basic components of a system that are implemented in an arbitrary sequential host language. Our approach targets the following goals.

- Support for full CSP.
- Support for true concurrency.
- Coordinations of operations in a noninvasive manner.
- Take advantage of CSP's mature tool support.

The main challenges in using CSP as a coordination language are how to unravel the abstractions built into CSP for the construction of executable concurrent implementations. For example, CSP events are designed to be instantaneous and atomic. Associating events with truly concurrent operations requires theoretical justification. Furthermore, CSP deals with internal transitions that most likely relate to internal operations of a system (operations that are not available for external synchronization). This assumption must also be justified formally.

As a solution, we have developed a syntactical transformation of processes that allows us to simulate truly concurrent processes in the standard interleaving semantics of CSP and to statically compute pairs of possibly concurrent events. The transformation serves as formal foundation of a target language independent coordination environment that allows us to compose sequential terminating actions to a concurrent system. The coordination environment simulates a coordination process at runtime thus ensuring that properties verified on that process are also satisfied by the final system. Data independence of actions is ensured by proof obligations relating concurrency of actions with the frames of their corresponding implementations. Our approach is supported by a Java implementation of the coordination environment and the case study of a workflow server implemented using the Java coordination environment.

The theoretical background of the thesis is developed in chapters 4, 5 and 6. Chapter 4 develops a construction that replaces each process with an equivalent version explicitly realising the possibility of concurrency. The construction transforms a process meanwhile splitting its events and synchronizes the transformed process with a controller C. The controller maintains a bag X whose contents represent the events of the original process that are possibly concurrent after the trace that has lead to the current state. This bag can be used in various ways to query concurrency information of a process. The construction is capable of simulating the traces semantics of its input process. Restricting the syntax of the input processes yields subsets of CSP such that the simulation preserves the failures-divergences semantics of its input process.

In Chapter 5, we extend the transformation to overcome the limitations of its initial version. Chapter 5 lifts the transformation of processes to be failures-divergences preserving even in the general case. Extended transformations are presented for the operators external choice, timeout and interrupt. An interesting result is that the three operators external choice, timeout and interrupt also incorporate internal concurrency. This is, of course, due to the models presented in Chapter 5 but justified by the observation that these op-

10.1 Summary 149

erators combine processes that await some external trigger (constantly offering an event) and may perform internal actions at the same time.

Chapter 6 presents a generic model of a coordination environment based on the transformation T. It unravels the abstractions built into CSP. The coordination environment aims to separate the concurrency structure of a system from the implementations of its basic components and to coordinate these by simulating a CSP process at runtime. Dividing the system into basic actions of components and coordination structure makes a concurrent system easier to understand and amenable to more specialized verification methods. Correctness of coordinated systems can be ensured by proving that concurrent events are not mapped to user-defined functions whose frames overlap and one modifies data being read by the other.

An implementation of such a coordination environment in Java is presented in Chapter 7. It simulates a coordination process at runtime to guide the execution of a concurrent program implemented in Java. Events are associated with user-defined functions which are executed whenever the respective event is performed. Hidden events are dealt with by listeners. The coordination environment assigns UDFs to threads according to some configurable strategy. Our approach is capable of handling infinite state and divergent processes. Compared to other coordination languages, ours has the advantage of its strong integration with formal methods. However, this comes at the cost of the runtime overhead of explicitly managing processes and events caused by simulation of CSP.

In Chapter 8 the theory and practice of workflows being deeply influenced by Petri Nets is transferred to CSP. Soundness of workflows given in CSP is defined. Our approach to the modeling and management of workflows presented in that chapter is based on the observation that CSP is well suited not only for modeling business processes and verifying workflows but also for executing them using our CSP-based coordination environment. The approach is supported by the prototypical implementation of a CSP-based workflow server using the coordination environment both for the server itself and for the execution of workflows. In that chapter, we have also presented a construction that allows compensation of workflows and yields a sound workflow given a workflow that either terminates successfully or signals an error before behaving chaotically (including deadlock but excluding divergence). The construction ensures that the compensation handlers are executed in reverse order to the occurrences of their respective milestones if and only if an error occurs. It also ensures that the workflow is aborted before the compensation handlers are run. The approach supports verification of compensable workflows using the standard CSP tools FDR and ProB. It is also supported by the CSP-based workflow server implementation.

10.2. Contributions

The main contribution of this thesis is a target language independent CSP-based framework for the construction of provably correct concurrent systems. To that end, we have presented a simulation of truly concurrent CSP encoded in standard CSP. It allows processes to be analyzed with respect to their internal concurrency using the standard CSP tools FDR and ProB. Furthermore, this transformation provides the semantical foundation of a coordination environment for the runtime coordination of concurrent components. The transformation is also used within the proof obligation ensuring data independence of the coordinated concurrent operations of components.

True Concurrency True concurrency is realized by a syntactical transformation of processes splitting the events of a process. The simulation is presented in different flavors realizing different levels of concurrency. For example, we identified subsets of CSP such that internal actions are never conflicting with actions that are available for external synchronization. These subsets realize a rather low level of concurrency. Our transformation of full CSP (including the interrupt operator, which is particularly important in practice) realizes a higher level of concurrency. Internal actions that are in conflict with actions awaiting external synchronizations may occur concurrently without resolving the conflict. This complicates the transformation but allows us to reestablish the failures-divergences semantics of original process. Our approach to truly concurrent CSP is tailored for use with the standard CSP tools FDR and ProB.

Coordinating Concurrent Components We have presented a coordination environment based on the simulation of truly concurrent CSP. It starts a user-defined function (UDF) after the start event of a split event and performs its end event after termination of the UDF. The coordination environment builds on ordinary (unprotected) shared memory communication of UDFs. We have presented proof obligations for ensuring data independence of concurrent UDFs and for relating pre- and postconditions of UDFs to traces of the coordination process. Although being transformed into truly concurrent processes, coordination processes can still be verified using standard CSP tools.

10.3. Future Work

Hiding Java Concurrency Primitives As a proof of concept, our coordination environment is implemented in Java. It enables the automated verification of concurrency aspect of the system on the CSP level using state-of-the-art CSP tools such as FDR and ProB, while enabling verification of sequential aspects using state-of-the-art software verification systems such as Krakatoa or KeY. It is noninvasive, i.e., it allows us to compose a concurrent system of purely sequential Java implementations. Hence, it hides Java concurrency from the programmer and makes the development of multi-threaded Java programs less error-prone.

Workflows with CSP We have shown how the soundness of workflows can be expressed and verified in CSP. Workflows can also be executed using our approach to CSP-based coordination as shown by our prototype of a CSP-based workflow server.

Compensation We have also presented a way of encoding compensable workflows in plain CSP. Compensation is based on so-called milestones that identify parts of a workflow that require special care when undoing the effects of that part (the milestone).

10.3. Future Work

The work presented offers many opportunities for further work in different directions. General directions are obviously theoretical extensions as well as practical ones. In this section, we present the most advantageous possible extensions.

The theory can be extended in various ways, supporting further operators and specialized verification techniques. In terms of supported CSP operators, it would be interesting to extend the simulation to support the exception operator [Ros08a]. This operator makes CSP even more expressive and is supported by the latest version of FDR (at the time of writing). Also, there are more useful derived operators that are not yet explicitly supported by our transformation, e.g., *chaining* or *linked parallel* (a generalization of chaining). It is planned to realize *interleaving* according to the 'de-parallelize' operator proposed by Taubner and Vogler in [TV89]:

$$P \;|||\; Q \quad \text{corresponds to} \quad P \bowtie_A Q$$

where $A \subseteq \Sigma$ and $\bowtie_A$ is an operator ensuring

$$\forall x, y : A \cdot (x, y) \notin conc(P \bowtie_A Q).$$

We also propose to extend our coordination environment to the coordination of distributed systems. Coordination environment can either be composed as a tree, where the root environment coordinates its child environments, or as a more general graph, where environments interact cooperatively.

Another interesting issue is the extraction of concurrency information in different ways. The method described here uses FDR to perform this by modifying the controller and checking whether or not the modified version violates the equality or querying fresh non-conflicting events. Unfortunately, FDR does not perform very well on such assertions because the bags grow rapidly and the functional part of CSP_M does not provide the most efficient way to model a process for analysis with FDR. One possible solution is to implement a specialized procedure that works on the original process P, to compute $conc(P)$. This procedure could be an extension of FDR's procedure to compute the traces of P that performs the transformation as well as synchronization with the controller internally before computing the traces. Such a procedure would be of great benefit for discharging the proof obligation for absence of data races, for example. This may be achieved by integration with a verifier for the specifications of UDFs as, e. g., the Boogie verifier [BCD+05], which is designed to support the development of custom static source code verifiers.

It might also be worthwhile to try the approach with the CSP-Prover [IR05], in view of the performance penalty caused by the controller process (see Section 4.4.3) during verification with FDR. Mechanizing the theory presented in chapters 4 and 5 requires extension of the CSP-Prover with respect to supported CSP operators. In addition to overcoming FDR's and ProB's limitations regarding the size (of the state-space) of the coordination processes encountered at verification-time, it would allow us to mechanically check the proofs presented in this thesis.

Another prospective research direction is static compilation. The approach presented here builds on dynamic computation of the LTS that coordinates the system. The ultimate goal of static compilation would be to create a system that by construction conforms to the coordination process without the dynamic overhead due to the simulation of CSP at runtime.

10.4. Related Publications

The formal background of the work presented here is published in [KS10a, KS10b]. The coordination environment based on the simulation of truly concurrent CSP is presented in [Kle11]. A preliminary version of the Java implementation of the coordination environment is presented in [KB10]. [KG10] reports on our CSP-based approach to workflows and our workflow server. Our approach to compensation is presented in [Kle10].

10.5. Acknowledgements

This thesis and the underlying research is a result of the DFG project VATES (Grant JA 379/17-1) and would not have been possible without it. I thank Stefan Jähnichen for supervising this thesis and for giving me the opportunity to work in his research group at Technische Universität Berlin. I am also very grateful to Michael Leuschel for acting as referee and for his invaluable support, especially with FDR and ProB. My heartfelt gratitude to Jeff Sanders for his support and guidance not only during my stay at United Nations University International Institute for Software Technology (UNU-IIST) in Macau.

I am indebted to Björn Bartels, Thomas Göthel, Paula Herber, Christoph Höger, Elke Salecker and Henry Sudhof for reading and commenting on drafts of this thesis. I also thank my former colleagues at Technische Universität Berlin for the friendly and relaxed working atmosphere, where there is always time for inspiring discussions and thrilling foosball matches: Lars Alvincz, Björn Bartels, Thomas Göthel, Steffen Helke (for advice and motivation in many occasions, and exciting squash matches), Paula Herber, Christoph Höger, Florian Lorenzen, Mark-Oliver Reiser, Judith Rohloff, and Henry Sudhof.

I thank my parents, my wife, and my daughter for their love and support.

A Proofs

A.1 Proof of Theorem 1

Proof 6 *The proof proceeds by induction on the construction of P.*

Prefix choice:

$Ext(x\!:\!X \to P(x))$

$= \qquad\qquad\qquad\qquad\qquad\qquad\qquad\qquad\qquad\qquad\qquad\qquad$ *Lemma 1*

$Hr(T(x\!:\!X \to P(x)))$

$= \qquad\qquad\qquad\qquad\qquad\qquad\qquad\qquad\qquad\qquad\qquad T(x\!:\!X \to P(x))$

$Hr(s?x\!:\!X \to e.x \to T(P(x)))$

$= \qquad\qquad\qquad\qquad\qquad\qquad\qquad\qquad\qquad\qquad\qquad\qquad$ *step s.x*

$x\!:\!X \to Hr(e.x \to T(P(x)))$

$= \qquad\qquad\qquad\qquad\qquad\qquad\qquad\qquad\qquad\qquad\qquad\qquad$ *step e.x*

$x\!:\!X \to Hr(T(P(x)))$

$= \qquad\qquad\qquad\qquad\qquad\qquad\qquad\qquad\qquad\qquad\qquad\qquad$ *Lemma 1*

$x\!:\!X \to Ext(P(x))$

$= \qquad\qquad\qquad\qquad\qquad\qquad\qquad\qquad\qquad\qquad$ *induction hypothesis*

$x\!:\!X \to P(x)\,.$

Sequential Composition:

$Ext(P\,;Q)$

$= \qquad\qquad\qquad\qquad\qquad\qquad\qquad\qquad\qquad\qquad\qquad\qquad$ *Lemma 1*

$Hr(T(P\,;Q))$

$= \qquad\qquad\qquad\qquad\qquad\qquad\qquad\qquad\qquad\qquad\qquad\qquad T(P\,;Q)$

$Hr(T(P);T(Q))$

$=$ *distributivity of hiding and renaming over* ;

$Hr(T(P));Hr(T(Q))$

$=$ *Lemma 1*

$Ext(P);Ext(Q)$

$=$ *induction hypothesis*

$P;Q$.

External Choice:

$Ext(P \square Q)$

$=$ *Lemma 1*

$Hr(T(P \square Q))$

$=$ $T(P \square Q)$

$Hr(T(P) \square T(Q))$

$=$ *definition of Hr*

$(T(P) \square T(Q)) \setminus H[s.x \leftarrow x \mid x \in \Sigma_P \cup \Sigma_Q]$

$=_{\mathcal{T}}$ *distributivity of hiding over $\square$ in $\mathcal{T}$*

$(T(P) \setminus H \square T(Q) \setminus H)[s.x \leftarrow x \mid x \in \Sigma_P \cup \Sigma_Q]$

$=$ *distributivity of renaming over $\square$*

$T(P) \setminus H[s.x \leftarrow x \mid x \in \Sigma_P] \square T(Q) \setminus H[s.x \leftarrow x \mid x \in \Sigma_Q]$

$=$ *definition of Hr*

$Hr(T(P)) \square Hr(T(Q))$

$=$ *Lemma 1*

$Ext(P) \square Ext(Q)$

$=$ *induction hypothesis*

$P \square Q$.

Parallel Composition:

$Ext(P \mid_A \mid Q)$

$=$ *Lemma 1*

$Hr(T(P \mid_A \mid Q))$

$=$ $T(P \mid_A \mid Q)$

$Hr(T(P) \mid_{\{s.x, e.x \mid x \in A\}} \mid T(Q))$

$=$ *Lemma 2*

$Hr(T(P) \mid_{\{s.x \mid x \in A\}} \mid T(Q))$

$=$ *distributivity of hiding and renaming over $\mid_{\{s.x \mid x \in A\}} \mid$*

$Hr(T(P)) \mid_A \mid Hr(T(Q))$

$=$ *Lemma 1*

$\quad Ext(P) \mid_A \mid Ext(Q)$

$=$ $\hfill$ *induction hypothesis*

$\quad P \mid_A \mid Q$.

Renaming:

$\quad Ext(P[M])$

$=$ $\hfill$ *Lemma 1*

$\quad Hr(T(P[M]))$

$=$ $\hfill$ $T(P[M])$

$\quad Hr(T(P)[s.x \leftarrow s.y, e.x \leftarrow e.y \mid (x,y) \in M])$

$=$ $\hfill$ *hiding of e events by definition of Hr*

$\quad Hr(T(P)[s.x \leftarrow s.y \mid (x,y) \in M])$

$=$ $\hfill$ *independence of* $[s.x \leftarrow s.y \mid (x,y) \in M]$ *and hiding of H*

$\quad Hr(T(P))[M]$

$=$ $\hfill$ *Lemma 1*

$\quad Ext(P)[M]$

$=$ $\hfill$ *induction hypothesis*

$\quad P[M]$.

Hiding:

$\quad Ext(P \setminus A)$

$=$ $\hfill$ *Lemma 1*

$\quad Hr(T(P \setminus A))$

$=$ $\hfill$ $T(P \setminus A)$

$\quad Hr(T(P)[s.x \leftarrow sh.x, e.x \leftarrow eh.x \mid x \in A])$

$=$ $\hfill$ *definition of Hr*

$\quad T(P)[s.x \leftarrow sh.x, e.x \leftarrow eh.x \mid x \in A] \setminus H[s.x \leftarrow x \mid x \in \Sigma_P]$

$=$ $\hfill$ *commutativity of hiding and renaming*

$\quad T(P) \setminus H \setminus \{s.x \mid x \in A\}[s.x \leftarrow x \mid x \in \Sigma_P]$

$=$ $\hfill$ *commutativity of hiding and renaming*

$\quad T(P) \setminus H[s.x \leftarrow x \mid x \in \Sigma_P] \setminus A$

$=$ $\hfill$ *definition of Hr*

$\quad Hr(T(P)) \setminus A$

$=$ $\hfill$ *Lemma 1*

$\quad Ext(P) \setminus A$

$=$ $\hfill$ *induction hypothesis*

$\quad P \setminus A$.

Internal Choice

$Ext(P \sqcap Q)$

$= \qquad\qquad\qquad\qquad\qquad\qquad\qquad\qquad\qquad\qquad\qquad\qquad$ *Lemma 1*

$Hr(T(P \sqcap Q))$

$= \qquad\qquad\qquad\qquad\qquad\qquad\qquad\qquad\qquad\qquad\qquad\qquad\qquad$ $T(P \sqcap Q)$

$Hr(sh.ic\_i \to eh.ic\_i \to (T(P) \sqcap T(Q)))$

$= \qquad\qquad\qquad\qquad\qquad\qquad\qquad\qquad\qquad\qquad\qquad\qquad$ *step $sh.ic\_i$*

$Hr(eh.ic\_i \to (T(P) \sqcap T(Q)))$

$= \qquad\qquad\qquad\qquad\qquad\qquad\qquad\qquad\qquad\qquad\qquad\qquad$ *step $eh.ic\_i$*

$Hr(T(P) \sqcap T(Q))$

$= \qquad\qquad\qquad\qquad$ *distributivity of hiding and renaming over $\sqcap$*

$Hr(T(P)) \sqcap Hr(T(Q))$

$= \qquad\qquad\qquad\qquad\qquad\qquad\qquad\qquad\qquad\qquad\qquad\qquad\qquad$ *Lemma 1*

$Ext(P) \sqcap Ext(Q)$

$= \qquad\qquad\qquad\qquad\qquad\qquad\qquad\qquad\qquad\qquad\qquad$ *induction hypothesis*

$P \sqcap Q$.

Timeout:

$Ext(P \triangleright Q)$

$= \qquad\qquad\qquad\qquad\qquad\qquad\qquad\qquad\qquad\qquad\qquad\qquad\qquad$ *Lemma 1*

$Hr(T(P \triangleright Q))$

$= \qquad\qquad\qquad\qquad\qquad\qquad\qquad\qquad\qquad\qquad\qquad\qquad\qquad$ $T(P \triangleright Q)$

$Hr((T(P) \square sh.to\_i \to eh.to\_i \to T(Q))$

$= \qquad\qquad\qquad\qquad\qquad\qquad\qquad\qquad\qquad\qquad\qquad$ *definition of Hr*

$(T(P) \square sh.to\_i \to eh.to\_i \to T(Q)) \setminus H[s.x \leftarrow x \mid x \in \Sigma_P \cup \Sigma_Q]$

$= \qquad\qquad\qquad\qquad\qquad\qquad\qquad\qquad\qquad\qquad\qquad$ *hiding $sh.to\_i$*

$((T(P) \square eh.to\_i \to T(Q)) \setminus H \sqcap (eh.to\_i \to T(Q)) \setminus H)[s.x \leftarrow x \mid x \in \Sigma_P \cup \Sigma_Q]$

$= \qquad\qquad\qquad\qquad\qquad\qquad\qquad\qquad\qquad\qquad\qquad$ *hiding $eh.to\_i$*

$(((T(P) \square T(Q)) \setminus H \sqcap T(Q) \setminus H) \sqcap T(Q) \setminus H)[s.x \leftarrow x \mid x \in \Sigma_P \cup \Sigma_Q]$

$= \qquad\qquad\qquad\qquad\qquad\qquad\qquad\qquad$ *associativity and idempotency of $\sqcap$*

$((T(P) \square T(Q)) \setminus H \sqcap T(Q) \setminus H)[s.x \leftarrow x \mid x \in \Sigma_P \cup \Sigma_Q]$

$= \qquad\qquad\qquad\qquad\qquad\qquad\qquad\qquad$ *distributivity of renaming over $\sqcap$*

$(T(P) \square T(Q)) \setminus H[s.x \leftarrow x \mid x \in \Sigma_P \cup \Sigma_Q] \sqcap T(Q) \setminus H[s.x \leftarrow x \mid x \in \Sigma_Q]$

$= \qquad\qquad\qquad\qquad\qquad\qquad\qquad\qquad\qquad\qquad\qquad$ *definition of Hr*

$Hr(T(P) \square T(Q)) \sqcap Hr(T(Q))$

$=_{\mathcal{T}} \qquad\qquad\qquad$ *distributivity of hiding and renaming over $\square$ in $\mathcal{T}$*

$(Hr(T(P)) \square Hr(T(Q))) \sqcap Hr(T(Q))$

$= \qquad\qquad\qquad\qquad\qquad\qquad\qquad\qquad\qquad\qquad\qquad$ *definition of $\triangleright$*

$Hr(T(P)) \triangleright Hr(T(Q))$

$$= \qquad Lemma\ 1$$

$$Ext(P) \triangleright Ext(Q)$$

$$= \qquad induction\ hypothesis$$

$$P \triangleright Q\ .$$

$$\square$$

A.2 Proof of equation (4.5)

Proof 7 *The proof proceeds by algebraic rewriting*

$$Ext((a \to STOP \setminus \{a\}) \,\square\, b \to STOP)$$

$$= \qquad Lemma\ 1$$

$$Hr(T((a \to STOP \setminus \{a\}) \,\square\, b \to STOP))$$

$$= \qquad T(P \,\square\, Q)$$

$$Hr(T(a \to STOP \setminus \{a\}) \,\square\, T(b \to STOP))$$

$$= \qquad T(P \setminus A)$$

$$Hr(T(a \to STOP)[s.x \leftarrow sh.x, e.x \leftarrow eh.x \mid x \in \{a\}] \,\square\, T(b \to STOP))$$

$$= \qquad T(x \to P),\ T(STOP),\ and\ renaming$$

$$Hr(sh.a \to eh.a \to STOP \,\square\, s.b \to e.b \to STOP)$$

$$= \qquad hiding\ of\ initial\ events\ in\ H\ over\ \square$$

$$(b \to STOP) \triangleright STOP$$

$$= \qquad P \triangleright Q = (P \sqcap STOP) \,\square\, Q$$

$$((b \to STOP) \sqcap STOP) \,\square\, STOP$$

$$= \qquad P \,\square\, STOP = P$$

$$(b \to STOP) \sqcap STOP$$

$$\square$$

A.3 Proof of Theorem 2

Proof 8 *The proof proceeds by induction on the construction of P.*

SKIP:

$Hr(T(SKIP))$

$= \qquad \qquad \qquad \qquad \qquad \qquad \qquad \qquad \qquad \qquad \qquad \qquad T(SKIP)$

$Hr(SKIP)$

$= \qquad \qquad \qquad \qquad \qquad \qquad \qquad \qquad \text{neutrality of SKIP w.r.t. hiding and renaming}$

$SKIP$.

Prefix choice:

$Hr(T(x:X \to P(x)))$

$= \qquad \qquad \qquad \qquad \qquad \qquad \qquad \qquad \qquad \qquad \qquad \qquad T(x:X \to P(x))$

$Hr(s?x:X \to e.x \to T(P(x)))$

$= \qquad \qquad \qquad \qquad \qquad \qquad \qquad \qquad \qquad \qquad \qquad \qquad \text{step } s.x$

$x:X \to Hr(e.x \to T(P(x)))$

$= \qquad \qquad \qquad \qquad \qquad \qquad \qquad \qquad \qquad \qquad \qquad \qquad \text{step } e.x$

$x:X \to Hr(T(P(x)))$

$= \qquad \qquad \qquad \qquad \qquad \qquad \qquad \qquad \qquad \qquad \qquad \text{induction hypothesis}$

$x:X \to P(x)$.

Sequential Composition:

$Hr(T(P\,;Q))$

$= \qquad \qquad \qquad \qquad \qquad \qquad \qquad \qquad \qquad \qquad \qquad \qquad T(P\,;Q)$

$Hr(T(P)\,;T(Q))$

$= \qquad \qquad \qquad \qquad \qquad \qquad \qquad \text{distributivity of hiding and renaming over } ;$

$Hr(T(P))\,;Hr(T(Q))$

$= \qquad \qquad \qquad \qquad \qquad \qquad \qquad \qquad \qquad \qquad \qquad \text{induction hypothesis}$

$P\,;Q$.

External Choice:

$Hr(T(P \,\square\, Q))$

$= \qquad \qquad \qquad \qquad \qquad \qquad \qquad \qquad \qquad \qquad \qquad \qquad T(P \,\square\, Q)$

$Hr(T(P) \,\square\, T(Q))$

$=$ *definition of Hr*

$(T(P) \,\square\, T(Q)) \setminus H[s.x \leftarrow x]$

$=$ *distributivity of hiding of non-initial events over external choice*

$(T(P) \setminus H \,\square\, T(Q) \setminus H)[s.x \leftarrow x]$

$=$ *distributivity of renaming over external choice*

$T(P) \setminus H[s.x \leftarrow x] \,\square\, T(Q) \setminus H[s.x \leftarrow x]$

$=$ *definition of Hr*

$Hr(T(P)) \,\square\, Hr(T(Q))$

$=$ *induction hypothesis*

$P \,\square\, Q$.

Parallel Composition:

$Hr(T(P \mid_A \mid Q))$

$=$ $T(P \mid_A \mid Q)$

$Hr(T(P) \mid_{\{s.x, e.x \mid x \in A\}} \mid T(Q))$

$=$ *Lemma 2*

$Hr(T(P) \mid_{\{s.x \mid x \in A\}} \mid T(Q))$

$=$ *distributivity of hiding and renaming over* $\mid_{\{s.x \mid x \in A\}}\mid$

$Hr(T(P)) \mid_A \mid Hr(T(Q))$

$=$ *induction hypothesis*

$P \mid_A \mid Q$.

Renaming:

$Hr(T(P[M]))$

$=$ $T(P[M])$

$Hr(T(P)[s.x \leftarrow s.y, e.x \leftarrow e.y \mid (x,y) \in M])$

$=$ *hiding of e events by definition of Hr*

$Hr(T(P)[s.x \leftarrow s.y \mid (x,y) \in M])$

$=$ *independence of* $[s.x \leftarrow s.y \mid (x,y) \in M]$ *and hiding of H*

$Hr(T(P))[M]$

$=$ *induction hypothesis*

$P[M]$.

                                                                                     $\square$

A.4 Proof of Theorem 4

Proof 9 *The proof uses the lemmas and auxiliary definitions presented in sections 5.1 and 5.2.*

$Hr(T(P \square Q))$

$= \qquad T(P \square Q)$

$Hr((T(P)))) T(Q)) \wr_{\overline{\Sigma}_T \cup H_\wr} \wr C_\square)$

$= \qquad \text{definition of } \wr_A\wr$

$Hr(((T(P)))) T(Q)) |_{\overline{\Sigma}_T \cup H_\wr}| C_\square)[unprime] \setminus H_\wr)$

$= \qquad H \cap H_\wr = \emptyset \text{ and } Hr(X[unprime]) = Hr(X)[unprime]$

$Hr(((T(P)))) T(Q)) |_{\overline{\Sigma}_T \cup H_\wr}| C_\square))[unprime] \setminus H_\wr$

$= \qquad \text{Lemma 4}$

$(Hr(T(P)))) T(Q)) |_{\overline{\Sigma} \cup H_\wr}| (C_0 \square C_1))[unprime] \setminus H_\wr$

$= \qquad \text{distributivity of } Hr \text{ over }))) \text{ because } H \cap \emptyset = \emptyset$

$((Hr(T(P))))) Hr(T(Q))) |_{\overline{\Sigma} \cup H_\wr}| (C_0 \square C_1))[unprime] \setminus H_\wr$

$= \qquad \text{induction hypothesis: } Hr(T(P)) = P \text{ and } Hr(T(P)[prime]) = P[prime]$

$((P))) Q) |_{\overline{\Sigma} \cup H_\wr}| (C_0 \square C_1))[unprime] \setminus H_\wr$

$= \qquad \text{definitions of } \wr_A\wr \text{ and } \overline{\Sigma}$

$(P))) Q) \wr_{\Sigma_P \cup \Sigma'_Q \cup H_\wr} \wr (C_0 \square C_1)$

$= \qquad \text{definition of } \square'$

$P \square' Q$

$= \qquad \text{Lemma 3}$

$P \square Q .$

$\square$

A.5 Proof of Theorem 5

Proof 10 *The proof uses the lemmas and auxiliary definitions presented in sections 5.1 and 5.3.*

$Hr(T(P \triangleright Q))$

$= \qquad\qquad\qquad\qquad\qquad\qquad\qquad\qquad\qquad\qquad\qquad\qquad\qquad T(P \triangleright Q)$

$Hr((T(P) \lll sh.to\_i \rightarrow eh.to\_i \rightarrow T(Q)) \wr_{\overline{\Sigma}_T \cup H_n} \wr C_\triangleright)$

$= \qquad\qquad\qquad\qquad\qquad\qquad\qquad\qquad\qquad\qquad\qquad \text{definition of } \wr_A\wr$

$Hr(((T(P) \lll sh.to\_i \rightarrow eh.to\_i \rightarrow T(Q))|_{\overline{\Sigma}_T \cup H_n}| C_\triangleright)[unprime] \setminus H_n)$

$= \qquad\qquad\qquad\qquad H \cap H_n = \emptyset \text{ and } Hr(X[unprime]) = Hr(X)[unprime]$

$Hr(((T(P) \lll sh.to\_i \rightarrow eh.to\_i \rightarrow T(Q))|_{\overline{\Sigma}_T \cup H_n}| C_\triangleright))[unprime] \setminus H_n$

$= \qquad\qquad\qquad\qquad\qquad\qquad\qquad\qquad\qquad\qquad\qquad\qquad\qquad\qquad \text{Lemma 6}$

$(Hr(T(P) \lll sh.to\_i \rightarrow eh.to\_i \rightarrow T(Q))|_{\overline{\Sigma} \cup H_n}| (C_0 \triangleright C_1))[unprime] \setminus H_n$

$= \qquad\qquad\qquad \text{distributivity of } Hr \text{ over } \lll \text{ because } H \cap \emptyset = \emptyset$

$((Hr(T(P)) \lll Hr(sh.to\_i \rightarrow eh.to\_i \rightarrow T(Q)))|_{\overline{\Sigma} \cup H_n}| (C_0 \triangleright C_1))[unprime] \setminus H_n$

$= \qquad\qquad\qquad\qquad\qquad\qquad\qquad \text{hiding of steps } sh.to\_i \text{ and } eh.to\_i$

$((Hr(T(P)) \lll Hr(T(Q)))|_{\overline{\Sigma} \cup H_n}| (C_0 \triangleright C_1))[unprime] \setminus H_n$

$= \qquad\qquad \text{induction hypothesis: } Hr(T(P)) = P \text{ and } Hr(T(P)[prime]) = P[prime]$

$((P \lll Q)|_{\overline{\Sigma} \cup H_n}| (C_0 \triangleright C_1))[unprime] \setminus H_n$

$= \qquad\qquad\qquad\qquad\qquad\qquad\qquad\qquad \text{definitions of } \wr_A\wr \text{ and } \overline{\Sigma}$

$(P \lll Q) \wr_{\Sigma_P \cup \Sigma'_Q \cup H_n} \wr (C_0 \triangleright C_1)$

$= \qquad\qquad\qquad\qquad\qquad\qquad\qquad\qquad\qquad\qquad\qquad \text{definition of } \triangleright'$

$P \triangleright' Q$

$= \qquad\qquad\qquad\qquad\qquad\qquad\qquad\qquad\qquad\qquad\qquad\qquad\qquad \text{Lemma 5}$

$P \triangleright Q$.

$\square$

A.6 Proof of Theorem 7

Proof 11 *Distributed termination of parallel composition restricts successful termination of $F(P)$ to the following two cases: successful termination or failure. Case 1. Assume that P performs $\sigma \in (\Sigma_P \setminus \{fail\})^*$ and then terminates successfully:*

$$(((P\,;commit \rightarrow SKIP) \triangle\, abort \rightarrow SKIP)\,|_{S_{F(P)}}|\, C(\langle\rangle)) \setminus \Sigma/\sigma$$

= *synchronization on* $\Sigma_P \cup \{abort, commit\}$

$$(((P/\sigma\,;commit \rightarrow SKIP) \triangle\, abort \rightarrow SKIP)\,|_{S_{F(P)}}|\, C(\langle\rangle)/\sigma) \setminus \Sigma$$

= *termination of P and $\exists l : I^* \cdot C(\langle\rangle)/\sigma = C(l)$*

$$(((commit \rightarrow SKIP) \triangle\, abort \rightarrow SKIP)\,|_{S_{F(P)}}|\, C(l)) \setminus \Sigma$$

= *step commit because $C(l)$ cannot refuse commit but refuses abort*

$$((SKIP \triangle\, abort \rightarrow SKIP)\,|_{S_{F(P)}}|\, SKIP) \setminus \Sigma$$

= *distributed termination because left hand side refuses abort*

$SKIP$

Case 2. Assume that P performs $\sigma \frown \langle fail \rangle \in \Sigma_P^*$ such that fail in σ:

$$(((P\,;commit \rightarrow SKIP) \triangle\, abort \rightarrow SKIP)\,|_{S_{F(P)}}|\, C(\langle\rangle)) \setminus \Sigma/\sigma \frown \langle fail \rangle$$

= *synchronization on all elements in σ and $\exists l : I^* \cdot C(\langle\rangle)/\sigma = C(l)$*

$$(((P/\sigma\,;commit \rightarrow SKIP) \triangle\, abort \rightarrow SKIP)\,|_{S_{F(P)}}|\, C(l)) \setminus \Sigma/\langle fail \rangle$$

= *synchronization on fail*

$$(((P/\sigma \frown \langle fail \rangle\,;commit \rightarrow SKIP) \triangle\, abort \rightarrow SKIP)$$
$$|_{S_{F(P)}}|\, abort \rightarrow Comp(l)) \setminus \Sigma$$

= *step abort because $abort \rightarrow Comp(l)$ refuses Σ_P and $\Sigma_P \subseteq S_{F(P)}$*

$$(SKIP\,|_{S_{F(P)}}|\, Comp(l)) \setminus \Sigma$$

= *by assumption $\Sigma_{Comp(l)} \cap S_{F(P)} = \emptyset$*

$Comp(l) \setminus \Sigma$

= $\forall i$ *in* $l : Handler(i) \setminus \Sigma = SKIP$ *by assumption*

$SKIP$

□

B Examples

B.1 Choice versus Concurrency

CSP_M encoding of the example presented in Section 4.4.1:

```
-- The original system
channel a, b
P = a -> b -> STOP [] b -> a -> STOP
Q = a -> STOP [|{}|] b -> STOP

assert P [FD= Q
assert Q [FD= P

-- Transformed Version
-- CSPm replacement for bags
add(bag, element) = bag ^ <element>
remove(bag, element) =
  if null(bag) then bag else
    if head(bag) == element then tail(bag) else
      <head(bag)> ^ remove(tail(bag),element)

-- The following datatype represents the renamed original events
datatype RENAMED = r_a | r_b
channel s, e, sh, eh : RENAMED
channel co : Seq(RENAMED)
channel term
```

```
-- The controller process with limited bag size
C(bag) = #bag < 3 & (s?x -> C(add(bag,x))
   [] sh?x -> C(add(bag,x))
   [] e?x -> C(remove(bag,x))
   [] eh?x -> C(remove(bag,x))
   [] term -> SKIP)

-- Modified controller process with limited bag size
C1(bag) = #bag < 3 & (co.bag -> (s?x -> C1(add(bag,x)))
   [] sh?x -> C1(add(bag,x))
   [] e?x -> C1(remove(bag,x))
   [] eh?x -> C1(remove(bag,x))
   [] term -> SKIP))

-- Hiding, renaming and the extension Ext
Hr(P) = R(H(P))
H(P) = P \{|sh, e, eh, term|}
R(P) = P [[s.r_a <- a, s.r_b <- b]]
Ext(P) = Hr((P; term -> SKIP) [|{|s, sh, e, eh, term|}|] C(<>))
Ext1(P) = Hr((P; term -> SKIP) [|{|s, sh, e, eh, term|}|] C1(<>))

-- The transformed processes (T_P = T(P))
T_P = s.r_a -> e.r_a -> s.r_b -> e.r_b -> STOP
   [] s.r_b -> e.r_b -> s.r_a -> e.r_a -> STOP
T_Q = s.r_a -> e.r_a -> STOP [|{}|] s.r_b -> e.r_b -> STOP

assert P [FD= Ext(T_P)
assert Ext(T_P) [FD= P

assert Q [FD= Ext(T_Q)
assert Ext(T_Q) [FD= Q

-- Never have a and b concurrently
SPEC = []x:{<r_a>,<r_b>,<>}@co.x -> SPEC

assert SPEC [T= Ext1(T_P) \{a,b}
assert SPEC [T= Ext1(T_Q) \{a,b}

assert Ext1(T_P) [FD= Ext1(T_Q)
assert Ext1(T_Q) [FD= Ext1(T_P)

channel conc_a_b
```

```
F(P) = P [[co.<r_a,r_b> <- conc_a_b, co.<r_b,r_a> <- conc_a_b]]
MAIN_P = F(Ext1(T_P))
MAIN_Q = F(Ext1(T_Q))

-- G not [conc_a_b]
MAIN = MAIN_Q -- or alternatively MAIN_P
```

B.2 One-place Buffer

CSP_M encoding of the example presented in Section 4.4.2:

```
-- Simple demonstration of FDR2
-- A single place buffer implemented over two channels
-- Original by D.Jackson 22 September 1992
-- Modified for FDR2 by M. Goldsmith 6 December 1995

-- First, the set of values to be communicated
datatype FRUIT = apples | oranges

-- Channel declarations
channel left,right,mid : FRUIT
channel ack

-- The specification is simply a single place buffer
COPY = left ? x -> right ! x -> COPY

-- The implementation consists of two processes communicating over
-- mid and ack
SEND = left ? x -> mid ! x -> ack -> SEND
REC = mid ? x -> right ! x -> ack -> REC

-- These components are composed in parallel
SYSTEM = (SEND [| {| mid, ack |} |] REC) \ {| mid, ack |}
assert COPY [FD= SYSTEM
assert SYSTEM [FD= COPY


-- Transformed Version
-- CSPm replacement for bags
```

```
add(bag, element) = bag ^ <element>
remove(bag, element) =
  if null(bag) then bag else
    if head(bag) == element then tail(bag) else
      <head(bag)> ^ remove(tail(bag),element)

-- The following datatype represents the renamed original events
datatype RENAMED = r_ack | r_left_a | r_left_o | r_right_a |
    r_right_o | r_mid_a | r_mid_o
channel s, e, sh, eh : RENAMED
channel term

-- The controller process with limited bag size
C(bag) = #bag < 2 & (s?x -> C(add(bag,x))
  [] sh?x -> C(add(bag,x))
  [] e?x -> C(remove(bag,x))
  [] eh?x -> C(remove(bag,x))
  [] term -> SKIP)

-- Hiding, renaming and the extension Ext
Hr(P) = R(H(P))
H(P) = P \{|sh, e, eh, term|}
R(P) = P [[s.r_ack <- ack, s.r_left_a <- left.apples,
          s.r_left_o <- left.oranges, s.r_mid_a <- mid.apples,
          s.r_mid_o <- mid.oranges, s.r_right_a <- right.apples,
          s.r_right_o <- right.oranges]]
Ext(P) = Hr((P;term -> SKIP) [|{|s, sh, e, eh, term|}|] C(<>))

-- The transformed processes
-- hiding of {| mid, ack |}
T_SYSTEM = T_SYSTEM' [[s.x <- sh.x, e.x <- eh.x |
                      x <- {r_mid_a, r_mid_o, r_ack}]]

-- parallel: SYSTEM' = SEND [| {| mid, ack |} |] REC
T_SYSTEM' = T_SEND [|{s.x, e.x |
                    x <- {r_mid_a, r_mid_o, r_ack} }|] T_REC

--prefix: SEND = left ? x -> mid ! x -> ack -> SEND
T_SEND = s.r_left_a -> e.r_left_a -> s.r_mid_a -> e.r_mid_a ->
  s.r_ack -> e.r_ack -> T_SEND
    [] s.r_left_o -> e.r_left_o -> s.r_mid_o -> e.r_mid_o ->
  s.r_ack -> e.r_ack -> T_SEND
```

```
--prefix: REC = mid ? x -> right ! x -> ack -> REC
T_REC = s.r_mid_a -> e.r_mid_a -> s.r_right_a -> e.r_right_a ->
   s.r_ack -> e.r_ack -> T_REC
     [] s.r_mid_o -> e.r_mid_o -> s.r_right_o -> e.r_right_o ->
   s.r_ack -> e.r_ack -> T_REC

assert Ext(T_SYSTEM) [FD= COPY
assert COPY [FD= Ext(T_SYSTEM)

MAIN = Ext(T_SYSTEM)
```

B.3 Dining Philosophers

CSP_M encoding of the example presented in Section 4.4.3:

```
-- The five dining philosophers for FDR: FDR2 version
-- The Theory and Practice of Concurrency, Bill Roscoe, Chapter 2
N = 3
PHILNAMES= {0..N-1}
FORKNAMES = {0..N-1}

channel sits, eats, getsup:PHILNAMES
channel picks, putsdown:PHILNAMES.FORKNAMES

-- A philosopher sits down, picks up two forks, eats, puts down the
-- forks and gets up, in an unending cycle.
PHIL(i) = sits!i -> picks!i!i -> picks!i!((i+1)%N) -> eats!i ->
   putsdown!i!((i+1)%N) -> putsdown!i!i -> getsup!i -> PHIL(i)

-- A fork can only be picked up by one neighbour at once!
FORK(i) = picks!i!i -> putsdown!i!i -> FORK(i)
     []  picks!((i-1)%N)!i -> putsdown!((i-1)%N)!i -> FORK(i)

PHILS = [|{}|] i:PHILNAMES@ PHIL(i)
FORKS = [|{}|] i:FORKNAMES@ FORK(i)

SYSTEM = PHILS[|{|picks, putsdown|}|]FORKS
```

```
assert not SYSTEM :[deadlock free]

-- Transformed Version
-- CSPm replacement for bags
add(bag, element) = bag ^ <element>
remove(bag, element) =
  if null(bag) then bag else
    if head(bag) == element then tail(bag) else
      <head(bag)> ^ remove(tail(bag),element)

-- The following datatype represents the renamed original events
datatype RENAMED = c_sits . PHILNAMES | c_eats . PHILNAMES |
  c_getsup . PHILNAMES | c_picks . PHILNAMES . FORKNAMES |
  c_putsdown . PHILNAMES . FORKNAMES

channel s, e, sh, eh : RENAMED
channel co : Seq(RENAMED)
channel term

-- The controller process with limited bag size
C(bag) = #bag < 4 & (s?x -> C(add(bag,x))
    [] sh?x -> C(add(bag,x))
    [] e?x -> C(remove(bag,x))
    [] eh?x -> C(remove(bag,x))
    [] term -> SKIP)

-- Modified controller process with limited bag size
C1(bag) = #bag < 4 & (co.bag ->(s?x -> C1(add(bag,x))
    [] sh?x -> C1(add(bag,x))
    [] e?x -> C1(remove(bag,x))
    [] eh?x -> C1(remove(bag,x))
    [] term -> SKIP))

-- Hiding, renaming and the extension Ext
Hr(P) = R(H(P))
H(P) = P \{|sh, e, eh, term|}
R(P) = P [[s.c_picks <- picks, s.c_putsdown <- putsdown,
    s.c_sits <- sits, s.c_eats <- eats,
    s.c_getsup <- getsup]]
Ext(P) = Hr((P;term -> SKIP) [|{|s, sh, e, eh, term|}|] C(<>))
Ext1(P) = Hr((P;term -> SKIP) [|{|s, sh, e, eh, term|}|] C1(<>))

-- The transformed processes
```

```
--parallel: SYSTEM = PHILS[|{|picks, putsdown|}|]FORKS
T_SYSTEM = T_PHILS
   [|{|s.c_picks, s.c_putsdown, e.c_putsdown, e.c_picks|}|] T_FORKS

T_PHILS = [|{}|] i:PHILNAMES@ T_PHIL(i)
T_FORKS = [|{}|] i:FORKNAMES@ T_FORK(i)

T_PHIL(i) = s.c_sits!i -> e.c_sits.i -> s.c_picks!i!i ->
   e.c_picks!i!i -> s.c_picks!i!((i+1)%N) -> e.c_picks!i!((i+1)%N) ->
   s.c_eats!i -> e.c_eats!i -> s.c_putsdown!i!((i+1)%N) ->
   e.c_putsdown!i!((i+1)%N) -> s.c_putsdown!i!i -> e.c_putsdown!i!i ->
   s.c_getsup!i -> e.c_getsup!i -> T_PHIL(i)

T_FORK(i) = s.c_picks!i!i -> e.c_picks!i!i -> s.c_putsdown!i!i ->
   e.c_putsdown!i!i-> T_FORK(i)
   [] s.c_picks!((i-1)%N)!i -> e.c_picks!((i-1)%N)!i ->
   s.c_putsdown!((i-1)%N)!i -> e.c_putsdown!((i-1)%N)!i -> T_FORK(i)

Ext_T_SYSTEM = Ext(T_SYSTEM)
Ext1_T_SYSTEM = Ext1(T_SYSTEM)

assert SYSTEM [FD= Ext_T_SYSTEM
assert Ext_T_SYSTEM [FD=SYSTEM

-- Check if the multiplicity of all elements 'elems' is at most
-- 'num' in 'bag'
at_most(bag, elems, num) = null(bag) or
    if member(head(bag), elems) then
        num > 0 and at_most(tail(bag), elems, num -1 ) else
        at_most(tail(bag), elems, num)

Seq0 = {<>}
Seq1 = {<x>|x <- RENAMED}
Seq2 = {x^y | x <- Seq1, y <- Seq1}
Seq3 = {x^y | x <- Seq2, y <- Seq1}
SeqRenamed =
  {x | x <- Union({Seq0,Seq1,Seq2,Seq3}), at_most(x,{|eats|},1)}

-- At most one philosopher is eating at a time
SPEC = [] x : SeqRenamed @ co.x -> SPEC

assert SPEC [T= Ext1_T_SYSTEM\{|sits,putsdown,eats,getsup,picks|}
```

B.4 Van Glabbeek's Owl

CSP_M encoding of the example presented in Section 4.4.4:

```
channel a,b,c,d,e
channel ev : {0..11}

OWL = let
  sync = {ev.1, ev.2, ev.3, ev.4, ev.7, ev.8, ev.9,ev.10}
  P0  = ev.0 -> ((P2 ||| P4) [] (P5 ||| P1))
  P1  = ev.1 -> STOP
  P2  = ev.2-> P3
  P3  = ev.3 -> STOP
  P4  = ev.4 -> STOP
  P5  = ev.5 -> (P10 [] (P9 ||| P7))
  P6  = ev.6 -> ((P2 ||| P4) [] P1)
  P7  = ev.7 -> STOP
  P8  = ev.8 -> STOP
  P9  = ev.9 -> P8
  P10 = ev.10 -> STOP
  P11 = ev.11 -> ((P6 ||| P10) [] (P9 ||| P7))
within P0 [|sync|] P11

-- Renaming to create OWL E
RE(P) = P [[ev.0 <- a, ev.1 <- e, ev.2 <- c, ev.3 <- e,
   ev.4 <- d, ev.5 <- c, ev.6 <- c, ev.7 <- e,
      ev.8 <- d, ev.9 <- c, ev.10 <- d, ev.11 <-b]]
OWL_E = RE(OWL)


-- Renaming to create OWL F
RF(P) = P [[ev.0 <- a, ev.1 <- d, ev.2 <- c, ev.3 <- d,
   ev.4 <- e, ev.5 <- c, ev.6 <- c, ev.7 <- d,
      ev.8 <- e, ev.9 <- c, ev.10 <- e, ev.11 <-b]]
OWL_F = RF(OWL)
assert OWL_E [T= OWL_F
assert OWL_F [F= OWL_E


-- start (se), end (ee), middle (me) events
channel se,ee,me : {0..11}
```

```
-- splitting the events of the owl into two events
T_OWL = let
  sync = {x.y | x <- {se,ee}, y <- {1,2,3,4,7,8,9,10}}
  P0  = se.0 -> ee.0 -> ((P2 ||| P4) [] (P5 ||| P1))
  P1  = se.1 -> ee.1 -> STOP
  P2  = se.2 -> ee.2 -> P3
  P3  = se.3 -> ee.3 -> STOP
  P4  = se.4 -> ee.4 -> STOP
  P5  = se.5 -> ee.5 -> (P10 [] (P9 ||| P7))
  P6  = se.6 -> ee.6 -> ((P2 ||| P4) [] P1)
  P7  = se.7 -> ee.7 -> STOP
  P8  = se.8 -> ee.8 -> STOP
  P9  = se.9 -> ee.9 -> P8
  P10 = se.10 -> ee.10 -> STOP
  P11 = se.11 -> ee.11 -> ((P6 ||| P10) [] (P9 ||| P7))
  within P0 [|sync|] P11

-- Hide middle and end evens to reestablish the OWL
-- R - OWL specific renaming scheme
-- P - OWL process
HR(R,P) = R(P [[se.x <- ev.x| x <- {0 .. 11}]] \{|ee,me|})


-- Hiding and renaming reestablishes the original owls.
assert OWL_E [FD= HR(RE,T_OWL)
assert HR(RE,T_OWL) [FD= OWL_E

assert OWL_F [FD= HR(RF,T_OWL)
assert HR(RF,T_OWL) [FD= OWL_F


-- splitting the events of the owl into three events
T3_OWL = let
  sync = {se.x,me.x,ee.x | x <- {1,2,3,4,7,8,9,10}}
  P0 = se.0 -> me.0 -> ee.0 -> ((P2 ||| P4) [] (P5 ||| P1))
  P1 = se.1 -> me.1 -> ee.1 -> STOP
  P2 = se.2 -> me.2 -> ee.2 -> P3
  P3 = se.3 -> me.3 -> ee.3 -> STOP
  P4 = se.4 -> me.4 -> ee.4 -> STOP
  P5 = se.5 -> me.5 -> ee.5 -> (P10 [] (P9 ||| P7))
  P6 = se.6 -> me.6 -> ee.6 -> ((P2 ||| P4) [] P1)
  P7 = se.7 -> me.7 -> ee.7 -> STOP
  P8 = se.8 -> me.8 -> ee.8 -> STOP
  P9 = se.9 -> me.9 -> ee.9 -> P8
```

```
    P10 = se.10 -> me.10 -> ee.10 -> STOP
    P11 = se.11 -> me.11 -> ee.11 -> ((P6 ||| P10) [] (P9 ||| P7))
    within P0 [|sync|] P11


 -- Hiding and renaming reestablishes the original OLW
 -- => hidden and renamed 3-split owls are equivalent
 assert OWL_E [FD= HR(RE,T3_OWL)
 assert HR(RE,T3_OWL) [FD= OWL_E


 assert OWL_F [FD= HR(RF,T3_OWL)
 assert HR(RF,T3_OWL) [FD= OWL_F


 channel a1,a2,a3,b1,b2,b3,c1,c2,c3,d1,d2,d3,e1,e2,e3
 -- rename the split events according to van Glabbeek and
 -- Vaandrager's renaming scheme
 RSE(P) = P [[se.0 <- a1, se.1 <- e1, se.2 <- c1, se.3 <- e1,
         se.4 <- d1, se.5 <- c1, se.6 <- c1, se.7 <- e1,
           se.8 <- d1, se.9 <- c1, se.10 <- d1, se.11 <-b1,
           me.0 <- a2, me.1 <- e2, me.2 <- c2, me.3 <- e2,
         me.4 <- d2, me.5 <- c2, me.6 <- c2, me.7 <- e2,
           me.8 <- d2, me.9 <- c2, me.10 <- d2, me.11 <-b2,
           ee.0 <- a3, ee.1 <- e3, ee.2 <- c3, ee.3 <- e3,
         ee.4 <- d3, ee.5 <- c3, ee.6 <- c3, ee.7 <- e3,
           ee.8 <- d3, ee.9 <- c3, ee.10 <- d3, ee.11 <-b3]]

 RSF(P) = P [[se.0 <- a1, se.1 <- d1, se.2 <- c1, se.3 <- d1,
         se.4 <- e1, se.5 <- c1, se.6 <- c1, se.7 <- d1,
           se.8 <- e1, se.9 <- c1, se.10 <- e1, se.11 <-b1,
           me.0 <- a2, me.1 <- d2, me.2 <- c2, me.3 <- d2,
         me.4 <- e2, me.5 <- c2, me.6 <- c2, me.7 <- d2,
           me.8 <- e2, me.9 <- c2, me.10 <- e2, me.11 <-b2,
           ee.0 <- a3, ee.1 <- d3, ee.2 <- c3, ee.3 <- d3,
         ee.4 <- e3, ee.5 <- c3, ee.6 <- c3, ee.7 <- d3,
           ee.8 <- e3, ee.9 <- c3, ee.10 <- e3, ee.11 <-b3]]

 T3_OWL_E = RSE(T3_OWL)
 T3_OWL_F = RSF(T3_OWL)


 -- However, the two 3-split owls are different
 -- as shown by the following counterexample given by
 -- Glabbeek and Vaandrager
 --   a c1 c2 b c1 c3 d c2 c3 e
 COUNTEREX = a1 -> a2 -> a3 -> c1 -> c2 -> b1 -> b2 -> b3 ->
```

```
    c1 -> c3 -> d1 -> d2 -> d3 -> c2 -> c3 -> e1 -> STOP

assert T3_OWL_E [T= COUNTEREX
assert not T3_OWL_F [T= COUNTEREX


-- more generally, the two 3-split owls are quite different
assert not T3_OWL_E [T= T3_OWL_F
assert not T3_OWL_F [T= T3_OWL_E

-- however, the 2-split owls are equivalent
assert RSE(T_OWL) [FD= RSF(T_OWL)
assert RSF(T_OWL) [FD= RSE(T_OWL)
```

B.5 Timeout

CSP_M encoding of the example processes P and Q shown in Section 5.5 and their extended transformed versions.

```
add(bag, element) = bag ^ <element>
remove(bag, element) =
  if null(bag) then bag else
    if head(bag) == element then tail(bag) else
      <head(bag)> ^ remove(tail(bag),element)

channel a,b,c
datatype EV = A | A' | B | B' | C | C' | TO_0 | TO_0'
channel s,e,sh,eh : EV
channel t0, t1, i0,i1
H = {t0,t1,i0,i1}

prime(A) = A'
prime(B) = B'
prime(C) = C'
prime(TO_0) = TO_0'
unprime(A') = A
unprime(B') = B
unprime(C') = C
unprime(TO_0') = TO_0
```

```
Par(P,Q) = (((P;t0 -> SKIP) /\ i0 -> SKIP)
       |||
       ((Q;t1 -> SKIP) /\ i1 -> SKIP)
       [[x.y <- x.prime(y) | x <- {s,e,sh,eh}, y <- {A,B,C,TO_0}]])

HR(P) = (P \{|e,sh,eh|}) [[s.A <- a, s.B <- b, s.C <- c]]

P = ((a -> SKIP) ||| (b -> SKIP)) [> c -> SKIP
TP = (s.A -> e.A -> SKIP ||| s.B -> e.B -> SKIP)
       [] (sh.TO_0 -> eh.TO_0 -> s.C -> e.C -> SKIP)

EXTP = HR(TP)
assert EXTP [FD= P
assert P [FD= EXTP

Q = ((a -> SKIP) ||| (b -> SKIP)) \{a,b} [> c -> SKIP
TQ = ((Par((sh.A -> eh.A -> SKIP ||| sh.B -> eh.B -> SKIP),
       (sh.TO_0 -> eh.TO_0 -> s.C -> e.C -> SKIP))
       [|Events|] C_to(<>))
       [[x.y <- x.unprime(y)
       | x <- {s,e,sh,eh}, y <- {A',B',C',TO_0'}]]) \ H

C_to(l) = #l < 3 & (s?x -> C_to'(add(l,x))
       [] sh?TO_0' -> C_to''(l)
       [] t0 -> C_term(l,i1)
       [] sh?x:{A,B,C} -> C_to(add(l,x))
       [] eh?x -> C_to(remove(l,x)))
C_to'(l) = #l < 3 & (s?x -> C_to'(add(l,x))
       [] t0 -> C_term(l,i1)
       [] sh?x:{A,B,C} -> C_to'(add(l,x))
       [] e?x -> C_to'(remove(l,x))
       [] eh?x -> C_to'(remove(l,x)))
C_to''(l) = #l <3 & (eh?x:{A,B,C} -> C_to''(remove(l,x))
       [] null(l) & eh?TO_0' -> C_to'''(l))
C_to'''(l) = #l <3 & (s?x:{A',B',C'} -> C_to'''(add(l,x))
       [] t1 -> C_term(l,i0)
       [] sh?x:{A',B',C'} -> C_to'''(add(l,x))
       [] e?x:{A',B',C'} -> C_to'''(remove(l,x))
       [] eh?x:{A',B',C'} -> C_to'''(remove(l,x)))
C_term(l,ev) = #l < 3 & (eh?x -> C_term(remove(l,x),ev)
       [] null(l) & ev -> SKIP)
```

```
EXTQ = HR(TQ)
assert EXTQ [FD= Q
-- this one should hold but doesn't because
-- FDR still doesn't support the Omega semantics.
assert not Q [FD= EXTQ

-- however, these assertions simulate Omega semantics
assert EXTQ;SKIP [FD= Q;SKIP
assert Q;SKIP [FD= EXTQ;SKIP

Split = {A,B,C,TO_O}
channel co : Set(Split)
CON(bag) = #bag < 4 & co.set(bag) -> (
        s?x:Split -> CON(add(bag,x))
        [] sh?x:Split -> CON(add(bag,x))
        [] e?x:Split -> CON(remove(bag,x))
        [] eh?x:Split -> CON(remove(bag,x)))

EXTP' = HR(TP [|{|s,e,sh,eh|}|] CON(<>))
EXTQ' = HR(TQ [|{|s,e,sh,eh|}|] CON(<>))

SPEC = |~| x : Set({A,B,C,TO_O}) @ card(x) < 3 & co.x -> SPEC

assert SPEC [F= EXTP' \{a,b,c}
assert not SPEC [F= EXTQ' \{a,b,c}
```

B.6 Unfolded Coordination Process

Unfolded CSP_M version of process IMPL from Figure 7.5.

```
ID = {0 .. 1}
channel lock, release, read, write : ID

P0      = lock.0 -> P0'
P0'     = read.0 -> P0''
P0''    = write.0 -> P0'''
P0'''   = release.0 -> P0
P1      = lock.1 -> P1'
```

```
P1'    = read.1 -> P1''
P1''   = write.1 -> P1'''
P1'''  = release.1 -> P1


LOCK   = |~| x : {LOCK0,LOCK1} @ x
LOCK0  = lock.0 -> LOCK0'
LOCK0' = release.0 -> LOCK0
LOCK1  = lock.1 -> LOCK1'
LOCK1' = release.1 -> LOCK1


IMPL   = IMPL' \ {lock.0,lock.1,release.0,release.1}
IMPL'  = IMPL'' [|{lock.0,lock.1,release.0,release.1}|] LOCK
IMPL'' = ||| x : {P0,P1} @ x)
```

B.7 Java Representation of a Coordination Process

The Java code shown below turns the CSP_M script shown in Appendix B.6 into a coordinated concurrent program.

```
final CspProcessStore store = new CspProcessStore();
store.createPrefix("P0","lock.0","P0'");
store.createPrefix("P0'","read.0","P0''");
store.createPrefix("P0''","write.0","P0'''");
store.createPrefix("P0'''","release.0","P0");
store.createPrefix("P1","lock.1","P1'");
store.createPrefix("P1'","read.1","P1''");
store.createPrefix("P1''","write.1","P1'''");
store.createPrefix("P1'''","release.1","P1");
store.createInternalChoice("LOCK","LOCK0,LOCK1");
store.createPrefix("LOCK0","lock.0","LOCK0'");
store.createPrefix("LOCK0'","release.0","LOCK0");
store.createPrefix("LOCK1","lock.1","LOCK1'");
store.createPrefix("LOCK1'","release.1","LOCK1");
store.createHiding("IMPL","IMPL'",
                  "lock.0,lock.1,release.0,release.1");
store.createParallel("IMPL'","IMPL''",LOCK",
                     "lock.0,lock.1,release.0,release.1");
store.createParallel("IMPL''","P0,P1",
```

```
                    "lock.0,lock.1,release.0,release.1");
final CspEnvironment env =
        new CspEnvironment(store, new MyCspEventExecutor());
new SwingCspSimulator("example",env).run();
```

B.8 Workflow Challenge

The following CSP_M script shows the encoding of the Workflow Net presented in Figure 8.2.

```
channel a,b,c,d,e,f,g,h
P = a -> (L0 [|{e,g,h}|] R0)
L0 = b -> d -> (L1 [|{h}|]R1)
R0 = c -> R1
L1 = f -> h -> SKIP
R1 = e -> g -> h -> SKIP

T1 = a -> b -> c -> d -> e -> f -> g -> h -> SKIP
T2 = a -> b -> c -> d -> e -> g -> f -> h -> SKIP
T3 = a -> b -> c -> d -> f -> e -> g -> h -> SKIP
T4 = a -> b -> d -> c -> e -> f -> g -> h -> SKIP
T5 = a -> b -> d -> c -> e -> g -> f -> h -> SKIP
T6 = a -> b -> d -> c -> f -> e -> g -> h -> SKIP
T7 = a -> b -> d -> f -> c -> e -> g -> h -> SKIP
T8 = a -> c -> b -> d -> e -> f -> g -> h -> SKIP
T9 = a -> c -> b -> d -> e -> g -> f -> h -> SKIP
T10 = a -> c -> b -> d -> f -> e -> g -> h -> SKIP

SPEC= T1 [] T2 [] T3 [] T4 [] T5 [] T6 [] T7 [] T8 [] T9 [] T10

assert SPEC [T= P
assert P [T= SPEC
assert P\Events [FD= SKIP
assert SKIP [FD= P\Events
```

B.9 Workflow Server Coordination Process

CSP_M encoding of the workflow server's coordination process as described in Section 8.1.

```
channel lockDefs, unlockDefs, poll, loadCSP, startCheck, checkResult,
  activateDef, loadClasses, reportError, printStatsCmd,
  deactivateDefCmd, selectDef, deactivateDef, startWfCmd, startWf,
  init, shutdown, reportWfError

-- This lock process protects the definitions
DefLock = lockDefs -> DefLock'
  DefLock' = unlockDefs -> DefLock


-- The loader process polls new process definitions from a directory
-- and loads them if they are not yet loaded.
Loader = STOP [> Poll
  Poll = poll -> NewDefs
  NewDefs = NewDef |~| Loader
  NewDef = loadCSP -> NewDef'
  NewDef' = ReportError |~| CheckDef
  CheckDef = startCheck -> CheckDef'
  CheckDef' = checkResult -> CheckDef''
  CheckDef'' = CheckDef''' |~| CheckedDef
  CheckDef''' = STOP [> CheckDef'
  CheckedDef = ReportError |~| LoadClasses
  LoadClasses = loadClasses -> LoadClasses'
  LoadClasses' = ReportError |~| DefLoaded
  ReportError = reportError -> Loader
  DefLoaded = lockDefs -> DefLoaded'
  DefLoaded' = activateDef -> DefLoaded''
  DefLoaded'' = unlockDefs -> NewDefs


LoaderEntry = Poll\{poll, loadCSP, startCheck, checkResult,
  loadClasses, reportError, activateDef}


-- The PrintStats utility process allows to print internal statistics
-- of the Wf Server
PrintStats = printStatsCmd -> SKIP


-- The DeactivateDef utility process allows to deactivate
```

```
-- workflow definitions.
DeactivateDef = deactivateDefCmd -> Available
Available = SKIP |~| DeactivateDef'
DeactivateDef' = lockDefs -> DeactivateDef''
DeactivateDef'' = selectDef -> DeactivateDef'''
DeactivateDef''' = deactivateDef -> DeactivateDef''''
DeactivateDef'''' = unlockDefs -> SKIP

-- The StartWf utility process allows to start a new workflow
StartWf = startWfCmd -> Available'
Available' = SKIP |~| StartWf'
StartWf' = lockDefs -> StartWf''
StartWf'' = selectDef -> StartWf'''
StartWf''' = startWf -> StartWf''''
StartWf'''' = unlockDefs -> StartWf'''''
StartWf''''' = StartWf''''''|~|SKIP
StartWf'''''' = reportWfError -> SKIP

-- The server control interface offers commands to the server admin
-- and executes them.
OfferMenu = []x:{PrintStats,DeactivateDef,StartWf}@x
ServerControl = OfferMenu;ServerControl

-- When the server is running, its server processes are running
-- in parallel
Running = Running'\{lockDefs,unlockDefs}
Running' = DefLock [|{lockDefs,unlockDefs}|] Running''
Running'' = ServerControl ||| LoaderEntry

-- This is the main sever process:
Shutdown = shutdown -> SKIP
Run = Running /\ Shutdown
WfServer = init -> Run \{init}

controlEvents = {poll, loadCSP, startCheck,checkResult, activateDef,
   loadClasses, reportError, printStatsCmd, deactivateDefCmd,
   selectDef, deactivateDef, startWfCmd, startWf,reportWfError}

assert DefLock [F= Running'\diff(Events,{lockDefs,unlockDefs})
assert Running'\diff(Events,{lockDefs,unlockDefs}) [F= DefLock

assert Running :[deadlock free [F]]
assert shutdown -> SKIP [F= WfServer\diff(Events,{shutdown})
```

```
assert WfServer :[livelock free]
```

B.10 Timed Workflow Server Coordination Process

Tock-CSP variant of the workflow server's coordination script (shown in Appendix B.9).

```
include ''wfserver.csp'' -- include the coordination script
channel tock -- signal discrete time steps

Timed = tock -> Timed'
Timed' = []x:{Timed'',Timed'''}@x
Timed'' = poll -> Timed
Timed''' = checkResult -> Timed

TimedPoll = Poll [|{poll, checkResult}|] Timed
TimedLoaderEntry = TimedPoll\{poll, loadCSP, startCheck,
   checkResult, loadClasses, reportError, activateDef}

TimedRunning = TimedRunning'\{lockDefs,unlockDefs}
TimedRunning' = DefLock [|{lockDefs,unlockDefs}|] TimedRunning''
TimedRunning'' = TimedServerControl ||| TimedLoaderEntry

TimedServerControl = tock -> OfferMenu;TimedServerControl

TimedRun = TimedRunning /\ Shutdown
TimedWfServer = init -> TimedRun\{init}

assert TimedWfServer :[livelock free[F]]

TimedSpec = SKIP |~| tock -> TimedSpec
TimedImpl = SKIP [] tock -> TimedImpl
assert TimedSpec [FD= TimedWfServer\diff(Events,{tock})
assert TimedWfServer\diff(Events,{tock}) [FD= TimedImpl
```

B.11 Transformed Workflow Server Coordination Process

Transformed version of the processes shown in Appendix B.9.

```
datatype EVNAME = lockDefs | unlockDefs | poll | loadCSP | startCheck
  | checkResult | activateDef | loadClasses | reportError
  | printStatsCmd | deactivateDefCmd| selectDef | deactivateDef
  | startWfCmd | startWf | reportWfError | to_0 | to_1
  | ic_0 | ic_1 | ic_2 | ic_3 | ic_4 | ic_5 | ic_6 | ic_7

channel s,sh,e,eh : EVNAME
channel co : Set(EVNAME)

add(bag, element) = bag ^ <element>
remove(bag, element) =
  if null(bag) then bag else
    if head(bag) == element then tail(bag) else
      <head(bag)> ^ remove(tail(bag),element)

-- deadlock if there are more than two concurrent actions
C(bag) = #bag < 3 & (
        s?x -> C(add(bag,x))
     [] sh?x -> C(add(bag,x))
     [] e?x -> C(remove(bag,x))
     [] eh?x -> C(remove(bag,x)))

-- make concurrent actions explicit
C1(bag) = #bag < 3 & (co.set(bag) ->(
        s?x -> C1(add(bag,x))
     [] sh?x -> C1(add(bag,x))
     [] e?x -> C1(remove(bag,x))
     [] eh?x -> C1(remove(bag,x))))

Ext(P) = P [|{|s, sh, e, eh|}|] C(<>)
Ext1(P) = P [|{|s, sh, e, eh|}|] C1(<>)

-- transformed workflow server processes
DefLock = s.lockDefs -> e.lockDefs ->
  s.unlockDefs -> e.unlockDefs -> DefLock
```

```
Loader = STOP [] (sh.to_0 -> eh.to_0 -> Poll)
  Poll = s.poll -> e.poll -> NewDefs
  NewDefs = sh.ic_0 -> eh.ic_0 -> (NewDef |~| Loader)
  NewDef = s.loadCSP -> e.loadCSP -> sh.ic_1 -> eh.ic_1 ->
    (ReportError |~| CheckDef)
  CheckDef = s.startCheck -> e.startCheck -> CheckDef'
  CheckDef' = s.checkResult -> e.checkResult -> sh.ic_2 -> eh.ic_2 ->
    (CheckDef''' |~| CheckedDef)
  CheckDef''' = STOP [] (sh.to_1 -> eh.to_1 -> CheckDef')
  CheckedDef = sh.ic_3 -> eh.ic_3 -> (ReportError |~| LoadClasses)
  LoadClasses = s.loadClasses -> e.loadClasses -> sh.ic_4 ->
    eh.ic_4 -> (ReportError |~| DefLoaded)
  DefLoaded = s.lockDefs -> e.lockDefs -> s.activateDef ->
    e.activateDef -> s.unlockDefs -> e.unlockDefs -> NewDefs
  ReportError = s.reportError -> e.reportError -> Loader

hideLoader = {poll, loadCSP, startCheck, checkResult, loadClasses,
  reportError, activateDef}
LoaderEntry = Poll [[s.x <- sh.x, e.x <- eh.x | x <- hideLoader]]


PrintStats = s.printStatsCmd -> e.printStatsCmd -> SKIP

DeactivateDef = s.deactivateDefCmd -> e.deactivateDefCmd ->
  sh.ic_5 -> eh.ic_5 -> (SKIP |~| DeactivateDef')
DeactivateDef' = s.lockDefs -> e.lockDefs -> s.selectDef ->
  e.selectDef -> s.deactivateDef -> e.deactivateDef ->
  s.unlockDefs -> e.unlockDefs -> SKIP

StartWf = s.startWfCmd -> e.startWfCmd -> sh.ic_6 -> eh.ic_6 ->
  (SKIP |~| StartWf')
StartWf' = s.lockDefs -> e.lockDefs -> s.selectDef -> e.selectDef ->
  s.startWf -> e.startWf -> s.unlockDefs -> e.unlockDefs ->
  sh.ic_7 -> eh.ic_7 -> (StartWf'''''|~|SKIP)
StartWf''''' = s.reportWfError -> e.reportWfError -> SKIP

OfferMenu = []x:{PrintStats,DeactivateDef,StartWf}@x
ServerControl = OfferMenu;ServerControl

Running =
  Running' [[s.x <- sh.x, e.x <- eh.x | x <- {lockDefs,unlockDefs}]]
Running' =
  DefLock [|{s.x, e.x | x <- {lockDefs,unlockDefs}}|] Running''
Running'' = ServerControl ||| LoaderEntry
```

```
-- there is no need to split the events in WfServer
-- WfServer = init -> Running\{init} /\ shutdown -> SKIP

DeadlockFree = Ext(Running)
ConcurrentActions = Ext1(Running)\{|s,sh,e,eh|}

assert DeadlockFree :[deadlock free]

Sigma = {x | x <- EVNAME}
Protected = {activateDef,selectDef,deactivateDef,startWf}
Unprotected = diff(Sigma,Protected)
SPEC0 = co.{} -> SPEC0
SPEC1 = |~|x:Sigma,y:Sigma@
    if member(x,Protected) and member(y,Protected) then
      co.{x} -> SPEC1 else co.{x,y} -> SPEC1
SPEC = SPEC0 ||| SPEC1
assert SPEC [T= ConcurrentActions
```

Bibliography

[ABB+05] W. Ahrendt, T. Baar, B. Beckert, R. Bubel, M. Giese, R. Hähnle, W. Menzel, W. Mostowski, A. Roth, S. Schlager, and P. H. Schmitt. The KeY Tool. *Software and System Modeling*, 4:32–54, 2005.

[Abr96] J. Abrial. *The B Book - Assigning Programs to Meanings*. Cambridge University Press, 1996.

[ACG86] S. Ahuja, N. Carriero, and D. Gelernter. Linda and Friends. *Computer*, 19(8):26–34, August 1986.

[ASM80] J. Abrial, S. A. Schuman, and B. Meyer. A Specification Language. In A. M. Macnaghten and R. M. McKeag, editors, *On the Construction of Programs*, pages 343–410. Cambridge University Press, 1980.

[Bar92] G. Barrett. *occam 3 Reference Manual*, March 1992.

[BBKK09] C. Baier, T. Blechmann, J. Klein, and S. Klüppelholz. A Uniform Framework for Modeling and Verifying Components and Connectors. In J. Field and V. Vasconcelos, editors, *Coordination Models and Languages*, volume 5521 of *LNCS*, pages 247–267. Springer, 2009.

[BCC+05] L. Burdy, Y. Cheon, C. R. Cok, M. D. Ernst, J. R. Kiniry, G. T. Leavens, K. R. M. Leino, and E. Poll. An overview of JML tools and applications. *Int. J. Softw. Tools Technol. Transf.*, 7(3):212–232, 2005.

[BCD+05] M. Barnett, B. E. Chang, R. DeLine, B. Jacobs, and K. R. M. Leino. Boogie: A Modular Reusable Verifier for Object-Oriented Programs. In *FMCO*, pages 364–387, 2005.

[BF04]   M. J. Butler and C. Ferreira. An Operational Semantics for StAC, a Language for Modelling Long-running Business Transactions. In R. De Nicola, G. Ferrari, and G. Meredith, editors, *Coordination 2004*, volume 2949. Springer, 2004.

[BHF05] M. Butler, T. Hoare, and C. Ferreira. A Trace Semantics for Long-Running Transactions. In A. E. Abdallah, C. B. Jones, and J. W. Sanders, editors, *CSP25*, volume 3525 of *LNCS*, pages 133–150. Springer, 2005.

[BK11]   B. Bartels and M. Kleine. A CSP-based Framework for the Specification, Verification and Implemenation of Adaptive Systems. In *6th International Symposium on Software Engineering for Adaptive and Self-Managing Systems (SEAMS 2011)*. ACM, 2011.

[BMM05] R. Bruni, H. Melgratti, and U. Montanari. Theoretical foundations for compensations in flow composition languages. In *Symposium on Principles of Programming Languages*, pages 209–220. ACM, 2005.

[BR05]   M. J. Butler and S. Ripon. Executable Semantics for Compensating CSP. In *EPEW/WS-FM*, pages 243–256. Springer, 2005.

[BVA07] J. M. Bjørndalen, B. Vinter, and O. J. Anshus. PyCSP - Communicating Sequential Processes for Python. In *CPA*, pages 229–248, 2007.

[CDS00] R. Cleaveland, X. Du, and S. Smolka. GCCS: A Graphical Coordination Language for System Specification. In A. Porto and G. Roman, editors, *Coordination Languages and Models*, volume 1906 of *LNCS*, pages 207–212. Springer, 2000.

[CGP99] E. M. Clarke, O. Grumberg, and D. A. Peled. *Model Checking*. The MIT Press, 1999.

[CHL06] X. Chen, J. He, and Z. Liu. Component Coordination in rCOS. Technical Report 335, UNU-IIST, P.O.Box 3058, Macau, May 2006.

[CJY95] P. Ciancarini, K. Jensen, and D. Yankelevich. On the operational semantics of a coordination language. In P. Ciancarini, O. Nierstrasz, and A. Yonezawa, editors, *Object-Based Models and Languages for Concurrent Systems*, volume 924 of *LNCS*, pages 77–106. Springer, 1995.

[Coa99] Workflow Management Coalition. Terminology & Glossary, Document Number WFMC-TC-1011, Issue 3.0, 1999.

[CPM06] W. R. Cook, S. Patwardhan, and J. Misra. Workflow patterns in orc. In *In Proceedings of Coordination 06, volume 4038 of LNCS*, pages 82–96. Springer, 2006.

[CS02] A. Cavalcanti and A. Sampaio. From CSP-OZ to Java with Processes. *Parallel and Distributed Processing Symposium, International*, 2:0208, 2002.

[dB07] F. de Boer. A Sound and Complete Shared-Variable Concurrency Model for Multi-threaded Java Programs. In M. Bonsangue and E. Johnsen, editors, *Formal Methods for Open Object-Based Distributed Systems*, volume 4468 of *LNCS*, pages 252–268. Springer, 2007.

[DRS95] R. Duke, G. Rose, and G. Smith. Object-Z: A Specification Language Advocated for the Description of Standards. *Computer Standards and Interfaces*, 17, 1995.

[DS95] J. Davies and S. Schneider. A Brief History of Timed CSP. *Theoretical Computer Science*, 138(2):243–271, 1995.

[EW02] R. Eshuis and R. Wieringa. Verification support for workflow design with UML activity graphs. In *ICSE '02: Proceedings of the 24th International Conference on Software Engineering*, pages 166–176. ACM, 2002.

[Fis97] C. Fischer. CSP-OZ: A combination of Object-Z and CSP. In *FMOODS '97: International Workshop on Formal Methods for Open Object-Based Distributed Systems*, pages 423–438. Chapman & Hall, 1997.

[Fis00] C. Fischer. *Combination and Implementation of Processes and Data: from CSP-OZ to Java*. PhD thesis, University of Oldenburg, January 2000.

[FM07] J. Filliâtre and C. Marché. The Why/Krakatoa/Caduceus Platform for Deductive Program Verification. In *CAV*, pages 173–177, 2007.

[Fon10] M. Fontaine. Towards Reusable Formal Method Tools. In *AVoCS 2010*. Universität Düsseldorf, 2010.

BIBLIOGRAPHY

[Fre02]   L. Freitas. JACK: A process algebra implementation in Java. Master's thesis, Centro de Informatica, Universidade Federal de Pernambuco, April 2002.

[Fre05]   L. Freitas. *Model Checking Circus*. PhD thesis, Department of Computer Science, University of York, October 2005.

[FV08]   R. M. Friborg and B. Vinter. CSPBuilder - CSP based Scientific Workflow Modelling. In *CPA*, pages 347–363, 2008.

[Gar03]   W. B. Gardner. Bridging CSP and C++ with Selective Formalism and Executable Specifications. In *MEMOCODE 03: International Conference on Formal Methods and Models for Co-Design*, pages 237–245. IEEE Computer Society, 2003.

[Gar05]   W. B. Gardner. Converging CSP specifications and C++ programming via selective formalism. *ACM Trans. Embed. Comput. Syst.*, 4(2):302–330, 2005.

[GBGK10]   S. Glesner, B. Bartels, T. Göthel, and M. Kleine. The VATES-Diamond as a Verifier's Best Friend. In S. Siegler and N. Wasser, editors, *Verification, Induction, Termination Analysis*, volume 6463 of *LNCS*, pages 81–101. Springer, 2010.

[GC92]   D. Gelernter and N. Carriero. Coordination languages and their significance. *Commun. ACM*, 35:97–107, 1992.

[GMOC+09] W. B. Gardner, J. Moore-Oliva, J. Carter, A. Gumtie, and Y. Solovyov. CSP++: An Open Source Tool for Building Concurrent Applications from CSP Specifications. Technical report, University of Guelph, 2009.

[GRA05]   M. Goldsmith, B. Roscoe, and P. Armstrong. Failures-Divergence Refinement - FDR2 User Manual. http://www.fsel.com/fdr2_manual.html, 2005.

[GV03]   C. Girault and R. Valk. *Petri Nets for Systems Engineering - A Guide to Modeling, Verification, and Applications*. Springer, 2003.

[HBB99]   G. Hilderink, J. Broenink, and A. Bakkers. Communicating Threads for Java. In B. M. Cook, editor, *Architectures, Languages and Techniques*, pages 243 – 261. IOS Press, 1999.

[HBB00]   G. H. Hilderink, A. W. P. Bakkers, and J. F. Broenink. A Distributed Real-Time Java System Based on CSP. In *ISORC '00:*

BIBLIOGRAPHY 191

Proceedings of the Third IEEE International Symposium on Object-Oriented Real-Time Distributed Computing, page 400. IEEE Computer Society, 2000.

[HH98] J. He and C. A. R. Hoare. Unifying theories of programming. In *RelMiCS*, pages 97–99, 1998.

[HLL05] J. He, Z. Liu, and X. Li. A Theory of Contracts. Technical Report 327, UNU-IIST, P.O.Box 3058, Macau, July 2005. Published in *Electronic Notes of Theoretical Computer Science*, Volume 160 , pp. 173-195 2006.

[Hoa81] C. A. R. Hoare. The Emperor's Old Clothes. *Commun. ACM*, 24(2):75–83, 1981.

[Hoa85] C. A. R. Hoare. *Communicating Sequential Processes*. Prentice Hall, 1985.

[Hoa04] C. A. R. Hoare. *Communicating Sequential Processes*. Prentice Hall, 2004.

[Hoa06] C. A. R. Hoare. Why ever CSP? *Electronic Notes in Theoretical Computer Science*, 162:209 – 215, 2006. Proceedings of the Workshop Essays on Algebraic Process Calculi (APC 25).

[IR05] Y. Isobe and M. Roggenbach. A Generic Theorem Prover of CSP Refinement. In *Tools and Algorithms for the Construction and Analysis of Systems*, pages 108–123. Springer, 2005.

[Jen95] K. Jensen. *Coloured Petri Nets: Basic Concepts, Analysis Methods and Practical Use*, volume 2. Springer, 1995.

[JKMUN02] T. Jacob, O. Kummer, D. Moldt, and U. Ultes-Nitsche. Implementation of Workflow Systems using Reference Nets – Security and Operability Aspects. In K. Jensen, editor, *Fourth Workshop and Tutorial on Practical Use of Coloured Petri Nets and the CPN Tools*. University of Aarhus, 2002.

[JOLB04] D. S. Jovanovic, B. Orlic, G. K. Liet, and J. F. Broenink. gCSP: A Graphical Tool for Designing CSP systems. In *Communicating Process Architectures 2004*, Concurrent Systems Engineering Series 62, pages 233–251. IOS Press, 2004.

[KB10] M. Kleine and B. Bartels. On Using CSP for the Construction of Concurrent Programs. In *International Conference on Software Engineering Theory and Practice (SETP-10)*, 2010.

[KBG+11] M. Kleine, B. Bartels, T. Göthel, S. Helke, and D. Prenzel. LLVM2CSP: Extracting CSP Models from Concurrent Programs. In M. Bobaru, K. Havelund, G. Holzmann, and R. Joshi, editors, *3rd NASA Formal Methods Symposium*, number 6617, pages 500 – 505. Springer, 2011.

[KBGG09] M. Kleine, B. Bartels, T. Göthel, and S. Glesner. Verifying the Implementation of an Operating System Scheduler. In *3rd IEEE International Symposium on Theoretical Aspects of Software Engineering (TASE '09)*, pages 285–286. IEEE Computer Society, 2009.

[KG10] M. Kleine and T. Göthel. Specification, Verification and Implementation of Business Processes using CSP. In *4th IEEE International Symposium on Theoretical Aspects of Software Engineering*, pages 145–154. IEEE Computer Society, 2010.

[KH09] M. Kleine and S. Helke. Low Level Code Verification Based on CSP Models. In M. Oliveira and J. Woodcock, editors, *Brazilian Symposium on Formal Methods (SBMF 2009)*, pages 266–281. Springer, 2009.

[Kle09] M. Kleine. Using CSP for Software Verification. In M. R. Mousavi and E. Sekerinski, editors, *Proceedings of Formal Methods 2009 Doctoral Symposium*, pages 8–13. Eindhoven University of Technology, 2009.

[Kle10] M. Kleine. Compensable Workflows in CSP. In *AVoCS 2010*. Universität Düsseldorf, 2010.

[Kle11] M. Kleine. CSP as a Coordination Language. In W. De Meuter and C. Roman, editors, *Proceedings of the 13th International Conference on Coordination Models and Languages (Coordination 2011)*, volume 6721 of *LNCS*. Springer, 2011.

[KP95] M. Kwiatkowska and I. Phillips. Possible and Guaranteed Concurrency in CSP. In *Structures in Concurrency Theory, Workshops in Computing*, pages 220–235. Springer, 1995.

[KS10a] M. Kleine and J. W. Sanders. Simulating truly concurrent CSP. In *Brazilian Symposium on Formal Methods (SBMF 2010)*. Springer, 2010.

[KS10b] M. Kleine and J. W. Sanders. Simulating truly concurrent CSP. Technical Report 434, UNU-IIST, P.O. Box 3058, Macau,

June 2010.

[Kum02]   O. Kummer. *Referenznetze*. Logos Verlag, Berlin, 2002.

[KWD+04]   O. Kummer, F. Wienberg, M. Duvigneau, J. Schumacher, M. Köhler, D. Moldt, H. Rölke, and R. Valk. An Extensible Editor and Simulation Engine for Petri Nets: Renew. In J. Cortadella and W. Reisig, editors, *ICATPN 2004: Proceedings of the 25th International Conference on Applications and Theory of Petri Nets*, volume 3099 of *LNCS*, pages 484–493. Springer, 2004.

[LB05]   M. Leuschel and M. Butler. Combining CSP and B for Specification and Property Verification. In A. Tarlecki J. Fitzgerald, I. Hayes, editor, *FM 2005: International Symposium of Formal Methods Europe*, volume 3582 of *LNCS*, pages 221–236. Springer, 2005.

[LBR06]   G. T. Leavens, A. L. Baker, and C. Ruby. Preliminary Design of JML: a Behavioral Interface Specification Language for Java. *ACM SIGSOFT Software Engineering Notes*, 31(3):1–38, 2006.

[LCO+10]   B. Staudt Lerner, S. Christov, L. J. Osterweil, R. Bendraou, U. Kannengiesser, and A. Wise. Exception Handling Patterns for Process Modeling. *IEEE Transactions on Software Engineering*, 99(RapidPosts):162–183, 2010.

[Lea02]   D. Lea. JSR 166: Concurrency Utilities. http://www.jcp.org/jsr/detail/166.jsp, 2002.

[LF08]   M. Leuschel and M. Fontaine. Probing the Depths of CSP-M: A new FDR-compliant Validation Tool. In *International Conference on Formal Engineering Methods*, pages 278–297. Springer, 2008.

[LMC01]   M. Leuschel, T. Massart, and A. Currie. How to make FDR Spin: LTL model checking of CSP using Refinement. In P. Zave J. N. Oliviera, editor, *FME 2001: Formal Methods for Increasing Software Productivity*. Springer, March 2001.

[Loc08]   A. Lochbihler. Type Safe Nondeterminism - A Formal Semantics of Java Threads. In *International Workshop on Foundations of Object-Oriented Languages (FOOL 2008)*, January 2008.

[Low08]   G. Lowe. Specification of communicating processes: temporal logic versus refusals-based refinement. *Form. Asp. Comput.*, 20(3):277–294, 2008.

[MD98] B. Mahony and J. S. Dong. Blending Object-Z and Timed CSP: an introduction to TCOZ. In *Proc. (20th) International Conference on Software Engineering*, pages 95–104, 19–25 April 1998.

[Mil89] R. Milner. *Communication and Concurrency*. Prentice Hall, 1989.

[MR03] D. Moldt and H. Rölke. Pattern Based Workflow Design Using Reference Nets. In W. van der Aalst, A. ter Hofstede, and M Weske, editors, *Proceedings of International Conference on Business Process Management, Eindhoven, NL*, volume 2678 of *LNCS*, pages 246–260. Springer, 2003.

[Mül02] P. Müller. *Modular specification and verification of object-oriented programs*. Springer, 2002.

[NPW02] T. Nipkow, L. C. Paulson, and M. Wenzel. *Isabelle/HOL — A Proof Assistant for Higher-Order Logic*, volume 2283 of *LNCS*. Springer, 2002.

[PL08] D. Plagge and M. Leuschel. Seven at one stroke: LTL model checking for High-level Specifications in B, Z, CSP, and more. *STTT*, 2008.

[PW05] F. Puhlmann and M. Weske. Using the π-Calculus for Formalizing Workflow Patterns. In *Business Process Management*, pages 153–168, 2005.

[PY96] A. N. Parashkevov and J. Yantchev. ARC - A Tool for Efficient Refinement and Equivalence Checking for CSP. In *In IEEE Int. Conf. on Algorithms and Architectures for Parallel Processing ICA3PP '96*, pages 68–75, 1996.

[Rey02] J. Reynolds. Separation logic: a logic for shared mutable data structures, 2002.

[Ros94] A. W. Roscoe. *Model-checking CSP*, pages 353–378. Prentice Hall, 1994.

[Ros05] A. W. Roscoe. *The Theory and Practice of Concurrency*. Prentice Hall, 2005.

[Ros08a] A. W. Roscoe. On the expressiveness of CSP. Draft, October

2008.

[Ros08b] A. W. Roscoe. The Three Platonic Models of Divergence-Strict CSP. In *ICTAC*, pages 23–49, 2008.

[RWM10] F. Rabbi, H. Wang, and W. MacCaull. Compensable Work-Flow Nets. In J. Dong and H. Zhu, editors, *Formal Methods and Software Engineering*, volume 6447 of *LNCS*, pages 122–137. Springer, 2010.

[SLD08] J. Sun, Y. Liu, and J. S. Dong. Model Checking CSP Revisited: Introducing a Process Analysis Toolkit. In *International Symposium on Leveraging Applications of Formal Methods, Verification and Validation*, pages 307–322. Springer, 2008.

[SLDP09] J. Sun, Y. Liu, J. S. Dong, and J. Pang. PAT: Towards Flexible Verification under Fairness. *Proceedings of the 21th International Conference on Computer Aided Verification (CAV'09)*, 5643:709–714, 2009.

[SO96] W. Sadiq and M. E. Orlowska. Modeling and Verification of Workflow Graphs, 1996.

[Spi92] J. M. Spivey. *The Z notation: a reference manual*. Prentice Hall, 1992.

[ST04] S. Schneider and H. Treharne. Verifying Controlled Components. In *IFM*, pages 87–107, 2004.

[STE05] S. Schneider, H. Treharne, and N. Evans. Chunks: Component Verification in CSP∥B. In *IFM*, pages 89–108, 2005.

[Sun] Sun. Java 5 concurrency guide. http://java.sun.com/j2se/1.5.0/docs/guide/concurrency/.

[TV89] D. Taubner and W. Vogler. Step failures semantics and a complete proof system. *Acta Inf.*, 27(2):125–156, 1989.

[vdA00] W. M. P. v. d. Aalst. Workflow Verification: Finding Control-Flow Errors Using Petri-Net-Based Techniques. In *Business Process Management*, pages 161–183, 2000.

[vdA05] W. M. P. van der Aalst. Pi calculus versus Petri nets: Let us eat 'humble pie' rather than further inflate the 'Pi hype'. BPTrends, 3(5):1-11, May 2005.

[vdAADtH04] W. M. P. van der Aalst, L. Aldred, M. Dumas, and A. H. M. ter

Hofstede. Design and Implementation of the YAWL System. In *CAiSE*, pages 142–159, 2004.

[vdADtHW02] W. M. P. van der Aalst, M. Dumas, A. H. M ter Hofstede, and P. Wohed. Pattern Based Analysis of BPML (and WSCI). Technical Report FIT-TR-2002-05, Queensland University of Technology, Brisbane, 2002.

[vdAHV02] W. M. P. van der Aalst, A. Hirnschall, and H. M. W. Verbeek. An Alternative Way to Analyze Workflow Graphs. In A. Banks-Pidduck, J. Mylopoulos, C. Woo, and M. Ozsu, editors, *Proceedings of the 14th International Conference on Advanced Information Systems Engineering*, volume 2348 of *LNCS*, pages 535–552. Springer, 2002.

[vdAtH02] W. M. P. van der Aalst and A. H. M. ter Hofstede. YAWL: Yet Another Workflow Language. Technical Report FIT-TR-2002-06, Queensland University of Technology, Brisbane, 2002.

[vdAtHKB03] W. M. P. van der Aalst, A. H. M. ter Hofstede, B. Kiepuszewski, and A. P. Barros. Workflow Patterns. *Distrib. Parallel Databases*, 14(1):5–51, 2003.

[vGV97] R. J. van Glabbeek and F. W. Vaandrager. The Difference between Splitting in n and n+1. *Inf. Comput.*, 136(2):109–142, 1997.

[WC02] J. Woodcock and A. Cavalcanti. The Semantics of Circus. In *ZB*, pages 184–203, 2002.

[Wel00] P. H. Welch. Process Oriented Design for Java: Concurrency for All. In H.R.Arabnia, editor, *Proceedings of the International Conference on Parallel and Distributed Processing Techniques and Applications (PDPTA'2000)*, volume 1, pages 51–57. CSREA, CSREA Press, June 2000.

[WG07] P. Y. H. Wong and J. Gibbons. A Process-Algebraic Approach to Workflow Specification and Refinement. In *Software Composition*, pages 51–65, 2007.

[WG08] P. Y. H. Wong and J. Gibbons. A Process Semantics for BPMN. In *ICFEM '08: Proceedings of the 10th International Conference on Formal Methods and Software Engineering*, pages 355–374. Springer, 2008.

[Win86] G. Winskel. Event Structures. In *Advances in Petri Nets*, pages

325–392, 1986.

[WM00]   P. H. Welch and J. M. R. Martin. A CSP Model for Java Multithreading. In P. Nixon and I. Ritchie, editors, *Software Engineering for Parallel and Distributed Systems*, pages 114–122. IEEE Computer Society, 2000.

[WPM+09]   T. Wrigstad, F. Pizlo, F. Meawad, L. Zhao, and J. Vitek. Loci: Simple Thread-Locality for Java. In *ECOOP*, pages 445–469, 2009.

[YP07]   L. Yang and M. Poppleton. JCSProB: Implementing Integrated Formal Specifications in Concurrent Java. In A. A. McEwan, S. Schneider, W. Ifill, and P. H. Welch, editors, *Communicating Process Architectures*, pages 67–88. IOS Press, 2007.

[YP09]   L. Yang and M. Poppleton. Java implementation platform for the integrated state- and event-based specification in PROB. *Concurrency and Computation: Practice and Experience*, 22(8):1007–1022, October 2009.

[ZCW11]   Z. Liu Z. Chen and J. Wang. A theory of failure-divergence refinement for long running transactions. Technical Report 447, UNU-IIST, P.O. Box 3058, Macau, Jan 2011.

Die VDM Verlagsservicegesellschaft sucht für wissenschaftliche Verlage abgeschlossene und herausragende

Dissertationen, Habilitationen, Diplomarbeiten, Master Theses, Magisterarbeiten usw.

für die kostenlose Publikation als Fachbuch.

Sie verfügen über eine Arbeit, die hohen inhaltlichen und formalen Ansprüchen genügt, und haben Interesse an einer honorarvergüteten Publikation?

Dann senden Sie bitte erste Informationen über sich und Ihre Arbeit per Email an *info@vdm-vsg.de*.

Sie erhalten kurzfristig unser Feedback!

VDM Verlagsservicegesellschaft mbH
Dudweiler Landstr. 99
D - 66123 Saarbrücken

Telefon +49 681 3720 174
Fax +49 681 3720 1749

www.vdm-vsg.de

Die VDM Verlagsservicegesellschaft mbH vertritt

Printed by Books on Demand GmbH, Norderstedt / Germany